W9-CAG-836

Rick Steves®

SNAPSHOT

Norway

Bjorvika
Apartment

CONTENTS

INTRODUCTION

This Snapshot guide, excerpted from my guidebook *Rick Steves Scandinavia*, introduces you to a land with immigrant roots, modern European values, and the great outdoors like nowhere else—Norway.

Start in Oslo, Norway's sharp capital city, with its historic and walkable core, mural-slathered City Hall, and inspiring Nobel Peace Center. Oslo's excellent museums are dedicated to Norwegian art, the paintings of Edvard Munch, Viking ships, traditional folk life, Norway's WWII resistance, and more. Ogle the celebration-of-humanity statues at Vigeland Park, and relive Olympic memories at Holmenkollen Ski Jump.

Then head for Norway's countryside for a dose of natural wonder. The famous "Norway in a Nutshell" ride—by train, ferry, and bus—showcases the scenic splendor of the country, from snowcapped mountains to the striking Sognefjord. Choose a cozy fjordside hamlet (such as Balestrand, Solvorn, or Aurland) as your home base for touring mighty glaciers and evocative stave churches. Explore the Gudbrandsdal Valley, Lillehammer's excellent open-air folk museum, and the impressive Jotunheimen Mountains.

Dip into Bergen, Norway's salty port town, with its lively fish market, colorful Hanseatic quarter, and a funicular to the top of Mount Fløyen. You can round out your Norwegian experience in the lively city of Stavanger, the time-passed Setesdal Valley, and resorty Kristiansand.

To help you have the best trip possible, I've included the following topics in this book:

• **Planning Your Time,** with advice on how to make the most of your limited time

- **Orientation,** including tourist information (abbreviated as TI), tips on public transportation, local tour options, and helpful hints
- **Sights** with ratings:
  - ▲▲▲—Don't miss
  - ▲▲—Try hard to see
  - ▲—Worthwhile if you can make it
  - **No rating**—Worth knowing about
- **Sleeping** and **Eating,** with good-value recommendations in every price range
- **Connections,** with tips on trains, buses, boats, and driving

Practicalities, near the end of this book, has information on money, staying connected, hotel reservations, transportation, and more.

To travel smartly, read this little book in its entirety before you go. It's my hope that this guide will make your trip more meaningful and rewarding. Traveling like a temporary local, you'll get the absolute most out of every mile, minute, and dollar.

Ha en god tur!

Rick Steves

NORWAY

NORWAY

Norge

Norway is stacked with superlatives—it's the most mountainous, most scenic, and most prosperous of all the Scandinavian countries. Perhaps above all, Norway is a land of intense natural beauty, its famously steep mountains and deep fjords carved out and shaped by an ancient ice age.

Norway is also a land of rich harvests—timber, oil, and fish. In fact, its wealth of resources is a major reason why Norwegians have voted *"nei"* to membership in the European Union. They don't want to be forced to share fishing rights with EU countries.

The country's relatively recent independence (in 1905, from Sweden) makes Norwegians notably patriotic and proud of their traditions and history. They have a reputation for insularity, and controversially have tightened immigration laws over the past several years.

Norway's Viking past (c. A.D. 800-1050) can still be seen today in the country's 28 remaining stave churches—with their decorative nods to Viking ship prows—and the artifacts housed in Oslo's Viking Ship Museum.

The Vikings, who also lived in present-day Denmark and Sweden, were great traders, shipbuilders, and explorers. However, they are probably best known for their infamous invasions, which terrorized much of Europe. The sight of their dragon-prowed ships on the horizon struck fear into the hearts of people from Ireland to the Black Sea.

Named for the Norse word *vik,* which means "fjord" or "inlet," the Vikings sailed their sleek, seaworthy ships on extensive voyages, laden with amber and furs for trading—and weapons for fighting. They traveled up the Seine and deep into Russia, through the Mediterranean east to Constantinople, and across the Atlantic to Greenland and even "Vinland" (Canada). In fact, they touched the soil of the Americas centuries before Columbus, causing proud "ya sure ya betcha" Scandinavian immigrants in the US to display bumper stickers that boast, "Columbus used a Viking map!"

History and Hollywood have painted a picture of the Vikings

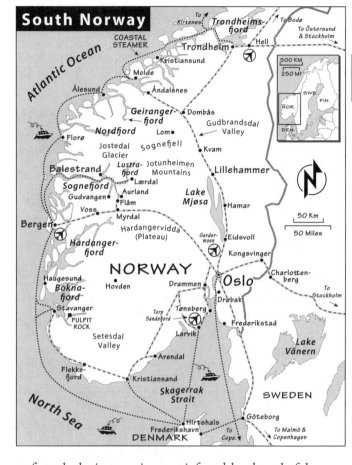

South Norway

To Kirkenes
Trondheims-fjord
To Bodø
To Östersund & Stockholm
COASTAL STEAMER
Trondheim
Hell
Atlantic Ocean
Kristiansund
Molde
500 KM
250 MI
SWE.
FIN.
NOR.
DEN.
Ålesund
Åndalsnes
Geiranger-fjord
Dombås
Nordfjord
Lom
Gudbrandsdal Valley
Florø
Jostedal Glacier
Sognefjell
Kvam
Lustra-fjord
Jotunheimen Mountains
Balestrand
Lillehammer
Lærdal
Sognefjord
Aurland
Lake Mjøsa
Gudvangen
Flåm
Voss
Hamar
Bergen
Myrdal
Hardangervidda (Plateau)
Garder-moen
Eidsvoll
Hardanger-fjord
Kongsvinger
NORWAY
Charlotten-berg
Haugesund
Bokna-fjord
Hovden
Drammen
Oslo
To Stockholm
Stavanger
PULPIT ROCK
Torp Sandefjord
Tønsberg
Drøbak
Setesdal Valley
Larvik
Frederikstad
Flekke-fjord
Arendal
Lake Vänern
Kristiansand
Skagerrak Strait
SWEDEN
North Sea
Frederikshavn
Hirtshals
Göteborg
To Malmö & Copenhagen
DENMARK
To Cope.
50 Km
50 Miles

as fierce barbarians, an image reinforced by the colorful names of leaders like Sven Forkbeard, Erik Bloodaxe, and Harald Bluetooth.

Unless you're handy with an ax, these don't sound like the kind of men you want to hoist a tankard of mead with. They kept slaves and were all-around cruel (though there is no evidence that they forced their subjects to eat lutefisk). But the Vikings also had a gentle side. Many were farmers, fishermen, and craftsmen who created delicate works with wood and metal. Faced with a growing population constrained by a lack of arable land, they traveled south not just to rape, pillage,

Norway Almanac

Official Name: Kongeriket Norge—"The Kingdom of Norway"—or simply Norge (Norway).

Population: Norway's 5.3 million people (about 35 per square mile) are mainly of Nordic and Germanic heritage, with a small population of indigenous Sami people in the north. The growing immigrant population is primarily from Sweden, Poland, Lithuania, Pakistan, and Somalia, with a recent wave from Syria. Most native Norwegians speak one of two official forms of Norwegian (Bokmål and Nynorsk), and the majority speak English as a second language. While church attendance is way down, the vast majority of Norwegian Christians consider themselves Lutheran.

Latitude and Longitude: 62°N and 10°E, similar latitude to Canada's Northwest Territories.

Area: 148,700 square miles, slightly larger than Montana.

Geography: Sharing the Scandinavian Peninsula with Sweden, Norway also has short northern borders with Finland and Russia. Its 51,575-mile coastline extends from the Barents Sea in the Arctic Ocean to the Norwegian Sea and North Sea in the North Atlantic. Shaped by glaciers, Norway has a rugged landscape of mountains, plateaus, and deep fjords. In the part of Norway that extends north of the Arctic Circle, the sun never sets at the height of summer, and never comes up in the deep of winter.

Biggest Cities: Norway's capital city, Oslo, has a population of 660,000; almost a million live in its metropolitan area. Bergen, Norway's second-largest city, has a population of about 275,000.

Economy: The Norwegian economy grows around 2 percent each year, contributing to a healthy $370 billion gross domestic prod-

and plunder, but in search of greener pastures. Sometimes they stayed and colonized, as in northeast England, which was called the "Danelaw," or in northwest France, which became known as Normandy ("Land of the North-men").

The Vikings worshipped many gods and had a rich tradition of mythology. Epic sagas were verbally passed down through generations or written in angular runic writing. The sagas told the heroic tales of the gods, who lived in Valhalla, the Viking heaven, presided over by Odin, the god of both wisdom and war. Like the Egyptians, the Vikings believed in life after death, and chieftains were often buried in their ships within burial mounds, along with prized possessions such as jewelry, cooking pots, food, and Hagar the Horrible cartoons.

Like the Greeks and Etruscans before them, the Vikings never organized on a large national scale and eventually faded away due to bigger, better-organized enemies and the powerful influence of uct and a per capita GDP of $69,200. Its primary export is oil—Norway is the world's seventh-largest oil exporter, making it one of the world's richest countries. By law, the country must save a portion of the oil revenue; the fund is currently worth almost $1 trillion.

Currency: 8 Norwegian kroner (NOK) = about $1.

Government: As the leader of Norway's constitutional monarchy, King Harald V has largely ceremonial powers. In September 2017, Norwegian voters reelected a center-right coalition government, which has been led by Prime Minister Erna Solberg since 2013. Leader of the Conservative Party, Solberg is Norway's second woman prime minister (after the Labor Party's Gro Harlem Brundtland). Solberg's party shares power with the far-right

Progress Party, which wants to restrict immigration and cut taxes. Norway's legislative body is the Stortinget (Parliament), with 169 members elected for four-year terms.

Flag: Red with a blue Scandinavian cross outlined in white.

The Average Norwegian: He or she is 39 years old, has 1.85 children, and will live to be 82. The average Norwegian feels very safe compared to other Europeans—only Iceland has a lower murder rate.

Christianity. By 1150, the Vikings had become Christianized and assimilated into European society. But their memory lives on in Norway.

Beginning in the 14th century, Norway came under Danish rule for more than 400 years, until the Danes took the wrong side in the Napoleonic Wars. The Treaty of Kiel forced Denmark to cede Norway to Sweden in 1814. Sweden's rule of Norway lasted until 1905, when Norway voted to dissolve the union. Like many European countries, Norway was taken over by Germany during World War II. April 9, 1940, marked the start of five years of Nazi occupation, during which a strong resistance movement developed, hindering some of the Nazi war efforts.

Each year on May 17, Norwegians celebrate their idealistic 1814 constitution with fervor and plenty of flag-waving. Men and women wear folk costumes *(bunads)*, each specific to a region of Norway. Parades are held throughout the country. The parade

NORWAY

in Oslo marches past the Royal Palace, where the royal family waves to the populace from their balcony. While the king holds almost zero political power (Norway has a parliament chaired by a prime minister), the royal family is still highly revered and respected.

Several holidays in spring and early summer disrupt transportation schedules: the aforementioned Constitution Day (May 17), Ascension Day (in May or June, 39 days after Easter), and Whitsunday and Whitmonday (a.k.a. Pentecost and the following day, in May or June, 50 days after Easter).

High taxes contribute to Norway's high standard of living. Norwegians receive cradle-to-grave social care: university education, health care, nearly yearlong paternity leave, and an annual six weeks of vacation. Norwegians feel there is no better place than home. Norway regularly shows up in first place on the annual UN Human Development Index.

Visitors enjoy the agreeable demeanor of the Norwegian people—friendly but not overbearing, organized but not uptight, and with a lust for adventure befitting their gorgeous landscape. Known for their ability to suffer any misfortune with an accepting (if a bit pessimistic) attitude, Norwegians are easy to get along with.

Despite being looked down upon as less sophisticated by their Scandinavian neighbors, Norwegians are proud of their rich folk

traditions—from handmade sweaters and folk costumes to the small farms that produce a sweet cheese called *geitost*. Less than 7 percent of the country's land is arable, resulting in numerous small farms. The government recognizes the value of farming, especially in the remote reaches of the country, and provides rich subsidies to keep this tradition alive. These subsidies would not be allowed if Norway joined the European Union—yet another reason the country remains an EU holdout.

Appropriate for a land with countless fjords and waterfalls, Norway is known for its pristine water. Norwegian-bottled artisanal water has an international reputation for its crisp, clean taste. Although the designer Voss water—the H2O of choice for Hollywood celebrities—comes with a high price tag, the blue-collar

Olden is just as good. (The tap water is actually wonderful, too—and much cheaper.)

While the Norwegian people speak a collection of mutually understandable dialects, the Norwegian language has two official forms: *bokmål* (book language) and *nynorsk* (New Norse). During the centuries of Danish rule, people in Norway's cities and upper classes adopted a Danish-influenced style of speech and writing (called Dano-Norwegian), while rural language remained closer to Old Norse. After independence, Dano-Norwegian was renamed *bokmål*, and the rural dialects were formalized as *nynorsk*, as part of a nationalistic drive for a more purely Norwegian language. Despite later efforts to combine the two forms, *bokmål* remains the most commonly used, especially in urban areas, books, newspapers, and government agencies. Students learn both.

The majority of the population under 70 years of age also speaks English, but a few words in Norwegian will serve you well. For starters, see the Norwegian survival phrases at the end of this chapter. If you visit a Norwegian home, be sure to leave your shoes at the door; indoors is usually meant for stocking-feet only. At the end of a meal, it's polite to say "Thanks for the food"—*"Takk for maten"* (tahk for MAH-ten). Norwegians rarely feel their guests have eaten enough food, so be prepared to say *"Nei, takk"* (nay tahk; "No, thanks"). You can always try *"Jeg er mett"* (yay ehr met; "I am full"), but be careful not to say *"Jeg er full"*—"I am drunk."

STAVE CHURCHES

Norway's most distinctive architecture is the stave church. These medieval houses of worship—tall, skinny, wooden pagodas with

dragon's-head gargoyles—are distinctly Norwegian and palpably historic, transporting you right back to the Viking days. On your visit, make it a point to visit at least one stave church.

Stave churches are the finest architecture to come out of medieval Norway. Wood was

plentiful and cheap, and locals had an expertise with woodworking (from all that boat-building). In 1300, there were as many as 1,000 stave churches in Norway. After a 14th-century plague, Norway's population dropped, and many churches fell into disuse or burned down. By the 19th century, only a few dozen stave churches survived. Fortunately, they became recognized as part of the national heritage and were protected. Virtually all of Norway's surviving stave churches have been rebuilt or renovated, with painstaking attention to the original details.

NORWAY

A distinguishing feature of the "stave" design is its frame of tall, stout vertical staves (Norwegian *stav,* or "staff"). The churches typically sit on stone foundations, to keep the wooden structure away from the damp ground (otherwise it would rot). Most stave churches were made of specially grown pine, carefully prepared before being felled for construction. As the trees grew, the tips and most of the branches were cut off, leaving the trunks just barely alive to stand in the woods for about a decade. This allowed the sap to penetrate the wood and lock in the resin, strengthening the wood while keeping it elastic. Once built, a stave church was slathered with black tar to protect it from the elements.

Stave churches are notable for their resilience and flexibility. Just as old houses creak and settle over the years, wooden stave churches can flex to withstand fierce winds and the march of time. When the wind shifts with the seasons, stave churches groan and moan for a couple of weeks...until they've adjusted to the new influences, and settle in.

Even after the Vikings stopped raiding, they ornamented the exteriors of their churches with warlike, evil spirit-fighting drag-

ons reminiscent of their ships. Inside, a stave church's structure makes you feel like you're huddled under an overturned ship. The churches are dark, with almost no windows (aside from a few small "portholes" high up). Typical decorations include carved, X-shaped crossbeams; these symbolize the cross of St. Andrew (who was crucified on such a cross). Round, Romanesque arches near the tops of the staves were made from the "knees" of a tree, where the roots bend to meet the trunk (typically the hardest wood in a tree). Overall, these churches are extremely vertical: the beams inside and the roofline outside both lead the eye up, up, up to the heavens.

Most surviving stave churches were renovated during the Reformation (16th and 17th centuries), when they acquired more horizontal elements such as pews, balconies, pulpits, altars, and other decorations to draw attention to the front of the church. In some (such as the churches in Lom and Urnes), the additions make the church feel almost cluttered. But the most authentic (including Hopperstad near Vik) feel truly medieval. These time-machine churches take visitors back to early Christian days: no pews (worshippers stood through the service), no pulpit, and a barrier between the congregation and the priest, to symbolically separate the physical world from the spiritual one. Incense filled the church, and the priest and congregation chanted the service back and forth to each other, creating an otherworldly atmosphere that likely made worshippers feel close to God. (If you've traveled in Greece, Russia, or the Balkans, Norway's stave churches might remind you of Orthodox churches, which reflect the way all Christians once worshipped.)

When traveling through Norway, you'll be encouraged to see stave church after stave church. Sure, they're interesting, but there's no point in spending time seeing more than a few of them. Of Norway's 28 remaining stave churches, seven are described in this book. The easiest to see are the ones that have been moved to open-air museums in Oslo and Lillehammer. But I prefer to appreciate a stave church in its original fjords-and-rolling-hills setting. My two favorites are both near Sognefjord: Borgund

and Hopperstad. They are each delightfully situated, uncluttered by more recent additions, and evocative as can be. Borgund is in a pristine wooded valley, while Hopperstad is situated on a fjord. Borgund comes with the only good adjacent stave church museum. (Most stave churches on the Sognefjord are operated by the same preservation society; for more details, see www.stavechurch.com.)

Other noteworthy stave churches include the one in Lom, near the Jotunheimen Mountains, which is one of Norway's biggest, and is indeed quite impressive. The Urnes church, across from Solvorn, is technically the oldest of them all—but it's been thoroughly renovated in later ages (it is still worth considering, however, if only for its exquisite carvings and the fun excursion to get to it; see the More on the Sognefjord chapter). The Fantoft church, just outside Bergen, burned down in 1992, and the replica built to replace it has none of the original's magic. The stave church in Undredal (see the Norway in a Nutshell chapter) advertises itself as the smallest. I think it's also the dullest.

NORWAY

Norwegian Survival Phrases

Norwegian can be pronounced quite differently from region to region. These phrases and phonetics match the mainstream Oslo dialect, but you'll notice variations. Vowels can be tricky: å sounds like "oh," æ sounds like a bright "ah" (as in "apple"), and u sounds like the German ü (purse your lips and say u). Certain vowels at the ends of words (such as d and t) are sometimes barely pronounced (or not at all). In some dialects, the letters sk are pronounced "sh." In the phonetics, ī sounds like the long i in "light," and bolded syllables are stressed.

English	Norwegian	Pronunciation
Hello. (formal)	God dag.	goo dahg
Hi. / Bye. (informal)	Hei. / Ha det.	hī / hah deh
Do you speak English?	Snakker du engelsk?	**snahk**-kehr dew **eng**-ehlsk
Yes. / No.	Ja. / Nei.	yah / nī
Please.	Vær så snill.	vayr soh sneel
Thank you (very much).	(Tusen) takk.	(**tew**-sehn) tahk
You're welcome.	Vær så god.	vayr soh goo
Can I help you?	Kan jeg hjelpe deg?	kahn yī **yehl**-peh dī
Excuse me.	Unnskyld.	**ewn**-shuld
(Very) good.	(Veldig) fint.	(**vehl**-dee) feent
Goodbye.	Farvel.	fahr-**vehl**
zero / one / two	null / en / to	newl / ayn / toh
three / four	tre / fire	treh / **fee**-reh
five / six	fem / seks	fehm / sehks
seven / eight	syv / åtte	seev / **oh**-teh
nine / ten	ni / ti	nee / tee
hundred	hundre	**hewn**-dreh
thousand	tusen	**tew**-sehn
How much?	Hvor mye?	voor **mee**-yeh
local currency: (Norwegian) crown	(Norske) kroner	(**norsh**-keh) **kroh**-nehr
Where is...?	Hvor er...?	voor ehr
...the toilet	...toalettet	toh-ah-**leh**-teh
men	menn / herrer	mehn / **hehr**-rehr
women	damer	**dah**-mehr
water / coffee	vann / kaffe	vahn / **kah**-feh
beer / wine	øl / vin	uhl / veen
Cheers!	Skål!	skohl
The bill, please.	Regningen, takk.	**rī**-ning-ehn tahk

OSLO

While Oslo is the smallest of the Scandinavian capitals, this brisk little city offers more sightseeing thrills than you might expect. As an added bonus, you'll be inspired by a city that simply has its act together.

Sights of the Viking spirit—past and present—tell an exciting story. Prowl through the remains of ancient Viking ships, and marvel at more peaceful but equally gutsy modern boats (the *Kon-Tiki, Ra II, Fram,* and *Gjøa*). Dive into the traditional folk culture at the Norwegian open-air folk museum, and get stirred up by the country's heroic spirit at the Norwegian Resistance Museum. For a look at modern Oslo, tour the striking City Hall, peek at sculptor Gustav Vigeland's people-pillars, ascend the exhilarating Holmenkollen Ski Jump, wander futuristic promenades, walk all over the Opera House, and celebrate the world's greatest peacemakers at the Nobel Peace Center.

Situated at the head of a 60-mile-long fjord, surrounded by forests, and populated by more than a half-million people, Oslo is Norway's cultural hub. For 300 years (1624-1924), the city was called Christiania, after Danish King Christian IV. With independence, it reverted to the Old Norse name of Oslo. As an important port facing the Continent, Oslo has been one of Norway's main cities for a thousand years and the de facto capital since around 1300. Still, Oslo has always been small by European standards; in 1800, Oslo had just 10,000 people—one-fiftieth the size of Paris or London.

But Oslo experienced a growth spurt with the Industrial Age, and in 50 years (from 1850 to 1900) its population exploded from about 10,000 to about 250,000. Most of "old Oslo" dates from this period, when the city's many churches and grand buildings were built of stone in the Historicism styles (neo-Gothic and neo-Romanesque) of the late 19th century. Oslo's onetime industrial zone—along the Akers River—has now been reclaimed as a cutting-edge park, with a lush river valley filled with spiffed-up brick warehouses and (on a sunny day) hundreds of sunbathing Norwegian hipsters.

Today the city sprawls out from its historic core to encompass nearly a million people in its metropolitan area, about one in five Norwegians. Oslo's port hums with international shipping and a sizeable cruise industry. Its waterfront, once traffic-congested and slummy, has undergone an extreme urban makeover—with ultramodern yet people-friendly residential zones replacing gritty shipyards. A nearly completed 5.5-mile pedestrian promenade stretches the length of its harbor.

And Oslo just continues to grow: Near the Opera House sprouts a development called the "Barcode Project"; its sleek and distinctive collection of high-rise office buildings resemble the bars in a UPC code. The metropolis feels as if it's rushing to prepare for an Olympics-like deadline. But it isn't—it just wants to be the best city it can be.

And yet, it's delightfully easy to escape the futuristic downtown and harbor area to a sprawling, green, and pastoral countryside—dotted with parks and lakes, and surrounded by hills and forests. For the visitor, Oslo is an all-you-can-see *smörgåsbord* of historic sights, trees, art, and Nordic fun.

PLANNING YOUR TIME

Oslo offers an exciting slate of sightseeing thrills. Ideally, spend two days, and leave on the night boat to Copenhagen, or on the scenic "Norway in a Nutshell" train to Bergen the third morning. Keep in mind that the National Gallery and the Vigeland Museum (at Vigeland Park) are closed on Monday. Spend the two days like this:

Day 1: Take my self-guided "Oslo Walk." Tour the Akershus Fortress and the Norwegian Resistance Museum, and catch the City Hall tour (offered June-Aug; off-season, tour it on your own). Spend the afternoon at the National Gallery (for Norwegian artists) or at the Holmenkollen Ski Jump and museum (to enjoy some wilderness).

Day 2: Ferry across the harbor to Bygdøy and tour the *Fram*, *Kon-Tiki*, and Viking Ship museums. Spend the afternoon at the

Norwegian Folk Museum. Finish the day at Vigeland Park, enjoying Gustav Vigeland's statues.

With More Time: You could easily fill a third day: Slow things down, go for a lazy hike up the Akers River (and eat at the trendy Mathallen Oslo food hall), and/or head out to the islands in the Oslofjord.

In the evening, you could enjoy a pricey dinner by the harbor or near Karl Johans Gate. Or venture to the more appealing, more affordable, and less touristy dining zones around Youngstorget, Mathallen, and Olaf Ryes Plass.

OSLO

Orientation to Oslo

Oslo (pop. 660,000) is easy to manage. Most sights are contained within the monumental, homogenous city center. Much of what you'll want to see clusters in three easy-to-connect zones: **downtown,** around the harbor and the main boulevard, Karl Johans Gate (with the Royal Palace at one end and the train station at the other); in the **Bygdøy** (big-duhy) district, a 10-minute ferry ride across the harbor; and **Vigeland Park** (with Gustav Vigeland's statues), about a mile behind the palace.

With more time, head out of the core to see the more colorful neighborhoods: Majorstuen and Frogner feel "uptown," with chic boutiques, elegant homes, and lots of parks. Grünerløkka—and the adjacent Akers River park—is hipster central, with the foodie-paradise Mathallen and plenty of bohemian cafés. Youngstorget, a quick walk north of Karl Johans Gate, is local-feeling, mostly residential, and packed with tempting restaurants. And Grønland, behind the train station, is the multiethnic immigrants' zone.

TOURIST INFORMATION

The big, high-tech Visit Oslo office is in the Østbanehallen—the traditional-looking building next to the central train station. Standing in the square (Jernbanetorget) by the tiger statue and facing the train station, you'll find the TI's entrance in the red-painted section between the station and Østbanehallen. You can also enter the TI from inside the train station (July-Aug Mon-Sat 8:00-19:00, Sun 9:00-18:00; May-June and Sept daily 9:00-18:00; slightly shorter hours Oct-April; tel. 81 53 05 55, www.visitoslo.com).

At the TI, pick up these freebies: an Oslo map (with a helpful public-transit map on the back); the annual *Oslo Guide* (a handy overview of museums, eating, and nightlife); *U.F.O.* (the exhibition guide, listing current museum events); and the *What's On Oslo* monthly (with updated museum prices and hours, and an extensive events listing). If you're traveling on, pick up the *Bergen Guide* and

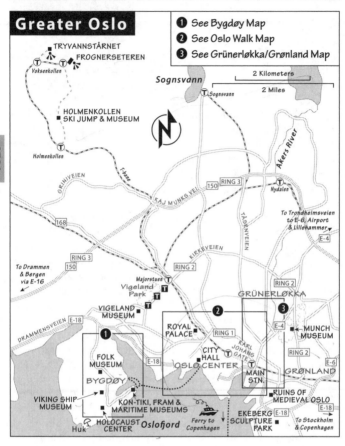

OSLO

Greater Oslo

❶ See Bygdøy Map
❷ See Oslo Walk Map
❸ See Grünerløkka/Grønland Map

information for the rest of Norway, including the useful, annual *Fjord Norway Travel Guide.*

Oslo Pass: Sold at the TI, this pass covers the city's public transit, ferry boats, and entry to nearly every major sight—all described in a useful handbook (395 NOK/24 hours, 595 NOK/48 hours, 745 NOK/72 hours; big discounts for kids ages 4-15 and seniors age 67 and over). Do the math before buying: Add up the individual costs of the sights you want to see and compare to the cost of an Oslo Pass. Students with an ISIC card may be better off without the pass.

ARRIVAL IN OSLO
By Train
The central train station (Oslo Sentralstasjon, or "Oslo S" for short) is slick and helpful. You'll find free Wi-Fi, ATMs, two Forex exchange desks, and luggage storage. The station is plugged into a

lively modern shopping mall called Byporten (Mon-Fri 10:00-21:00, Sat until 20:00, closed Sun), where just inside the entrance you'll find a cheap Bit sandwich shop with seating. Inside the station is a well-stocked Co-op Prix grocery store (long hours Mon-Sat, closed Sun), a small Joker supermarket (long hours daily), and a Vinmonopolet liquor store (Oslo's most central place to buy wine or liquor—which is sold only at Vinmonopolet stores, Mon-Thu 10:00-18:00, Fri from 9:00, Sat 9:00-15:00, closed Sun). The TI is in the Østbanehallen, right next to the train station.

For tickets and train info, you can go to the station's ticket office located between tracks 8 and 9 (Mon-Fri 7:30-20:00, Sat-Sun 10:00-18:00—opens at 7:45 on summer weekends). At this ticket office, you can buy domestic and Norway in a Nutshell tickets, and pick up leaflets on the Flåm and Bergen Railway (Bergensbanen). Only the station office sells international tickets. Domestic tickets can also be bought from the TI (same price) and at the red ticket machines (marked *NSB*); the blue machines (marked *SJ*) are for tickets to Sweden.

By Plane or Boat

For details on arriving in Oslo by plane or cruise ship, see the end of this chapter.

HELPFUL HINTS

Theft Alert: Pickpockets are a problem in Oslo, particularly in crowds on the street and on subways and buses. Oslo's street population loiters around the train station; you may see aggressive panhandlers there and along Karl Johans Gate. While a bit unnerving to some travelers, locals consider this rough-looking bunch harmless (but keep an eye on your wallet). To call the police, dial 112.

Money: Banks in Norway don't change money. Use ATMs or the Forex exchange office at the train station.

Post Office: It's in the train station.

Pharmacy: Jernbanetorgets Vitus Apotek is open 24 hours daily (across from train station on Jernbanetorget, tel. 23 35 81 00).

Laundry: Billig Vask & Rens ("Cheap Wash & Clean") is near Vår Frelsers Cemetery, a half-mile north of the train station (self-serve open daily 8:00-21:00; full-serve Mon-Fri 9:00-18:00, Sat 10:00-15:00, closed Sun; on the corner of Wessels Gate and Ullevålsveien, Ullevålsveien 15, catch bus #37 from station, tel. 41 64 08 33).

Bike Rental: Oslo isn't the best city for cycling. It's quite hilly, downtown streets are congested with buses and trams, and the city lags behind other Scandinavian capitals in bike lanes. But if you'd like wheels, the best spot is **Viking Biking,**

OSLO

run by American Curtis (160 NOK/8 hours, 200 NOK/24 hours, includes helmet and lock, daily 9:30-18:00, Nedre Slottsgate 4, tel. 41 26 64 96, www.vikingbikingoslo.com; see "Tours in Oslo," later, for their guided bike tours). The city also has a public bike-rental system  that lets you grab basic **city bikes** out of locked racks at various points around town (works with a smartphone, details at www.oslobysykkel.no/en).

Movies: The domed **Colosseum Kino** in Majorstuen, one of northern Europe's largest movie houses with 1,500 seats, is a fun place to catch a big-time spectacle. Originally built in 1928, this now high-tech, four-screen theater shows first-run films in their original language (Fridtjof Nansens Vei 6, a short walk west from Marjorstuen T-bane station, www.oslokino.no).

GETTING AROUND OSLO
By Public Transit

Oslo is a big city, and taxi fares are exorbitant. Commit yourself to taking advantage of the excellent transit system, made up of buses, trams, ferries, and a subway (*Tunnelbane*, or T-bane for short; see the "Sightseeing by Public Transit" sidebar). The system is run by Ruter, which has a transit-information center below the tall, skinny, glass tower in front of the central train station (Mon-Fri 7:00-20:00, Sat-Sun 8:00-18:00, tel. 177 or 81 50 01 76, www.ruter.no).

Schedules: To navigate, use the public transit map on the back of the free TI city map, or download the RuterReise app. The system runs like clockwork, with schedules clearly posted and followed. Most stops have handy electronic reader boards showing the time remaining before the next tram arrives (usually less than 10 minutes).

Tickets: A different app—called RuterBillett—lets you buy tickets on your phone (with your credit card) rather than having to buy paper tickets; however, it may not work with American cards, and requires Wi-Fi or data to work. **Individual tickets** work on buses, trams, ferries, and the T-bane for one hour (33 NOK at machines, transit office, Narvesen kiosks, convenience stores such as 7-Eleven or Deli de Luca, or with the RuterBillett app—or a hefty 55 NOK from the driver). Other options include the **24-hour ticket** (90 NOK; buy at machines, transit office, or on RuterBillett app; good for unlimited rides in 24-hour period) and the **Oslo Pass**

Sightseeing by Public Transit

With a transit pass or an Oslo Pass, take full advantage of the T-bane and the trams. Just spend five minutes to get a grip on the system, and you'll become amazingly empowered. Here are the T-bane stations you're likely to use:

Jernbanetorget (central station, bus and tram hub, express train to airport)

Stortinget (top of Karl Johans Gate, near Akershus Fortress)

Nationaltheatret (National Theater, also a train station, express train to airport, near City Hall, Aker Brygge, Royal Palace)

Majorstuen (walk to Vigeland Sculpture Park, trendy shops on Bogstadveien, Colosseum cinema)

Grønland (colorful immigrant neighborhood, cheap and fun restaurant zone, bottom of Grünerløkka district; the underground mall in the station is a virtual trip to Istanbul)

Holmenkollen (famous ski jump, city view)

Frognerseteren (highest point in town, jumping-off point for forest walks and bike rides)

Sognsvann (idyllic lake in forest outside of town)

Trams and buses that matter:

Trams #11 and #12 ring the city (stops at central station, fortress, harborfront, City Hall, Aker Brygge, Vigeland Park, Bogstadveien, National Gallery, and Stortorvet)

Trams #11, #12, and #13 to Olaf Ryes Plass (center of Grünerløkka district)

Trams #13 and #19, and bus #31 (south and parallel to Karl Johans Gate to central station)

Bus #30 (Olaf Ryes Plass in Grünerløkka, train station, near Karl Johans Gate, National Theater, and Bygdøy, with stops at each Bygdøy museum)

(gives free run of entire system; described earlier). Validate your ticket by holding it next to the card reader when you board.

By Taxi

Taxis come with a 150-NOK drop charge (yes, that's nearly $20 just to get in the car) that covers you for three or four kilometers—about two miles (more on evenings and weekends). Taxis are a good value only if you're with a group. If you use a minibus taxi, you are welcome to negotiate an hourly rate. To get a taxi, wave one down, find a taxi stand, or call 02323.

Tours in Oslo

Oslofjord Cruises

A fascinating world of idyllic islands sprinkled with charming vacation cabins is minutes away from the Oslo harborfront. For locals, the fjord is a handy vacation getaway. Tourists can get a glimpse of this island world by public ferry or tour boat. Cheap ferries regularly connect the nearby islands with downtown (free with Oslo Pass).

Several tour boats leave regularly from pier 3 in front of City Hall. **Båtservice** has a relaxing and scenic 1.5-hour hop-on, hop-off service, with recorded multilingual commentary. It departs from the City Hall dock (215 NOK, daily at 9:45, 11:15, 12:45, and 14:15; departs 30 minutes earlier from the Opera House and 30 minutes later from Bygdøy; tel. 23 35 68 90, www.boatsightseeing. com). They won't scream if you bring something to munch. They also offer two-hour fjord tours with lame live commentary (299 NOK, 3/day late March-mid-Oct, may run on winter weekends), a "Summer Evening on the Fjord" dinner cruise on a sailing ship (420 NOK, no narration; "shrimp buffet" is just shrimp, bread, and butter; daily mid-June-Aug 19:00-22:00), and jazz and blues-themed cruises.

Guided Walking Tour

Oslo Guideservice offers 1.5-hour historic "Oslo Promenade" walks from mid-May through August (200 NOK, free with Oslo Pass; Mon, Wed, and Fri at 17:30; leaves from harbor side of City Hall, confirm departures at TI, tel. 22 42 70 20, www.guideservice. no).

Local Guides

You can hire a private guide for around 2,000 NOK for a two- to three-hour tour. I had a good experience with **Oslo Guideservice** (2,000 NOK/2 hours, tel. 22 42 70 20, www.guideservice.no); my guide, Aksel, had a passion for both history and his home-town of Oslo. Or try **Oslo Guidebureau** (tel. 22 42 28 18, www. osloguidebureau.no, info@osloguide.no).

Bike Tours

Viking Biking gives several different guided tours in English, in-cluding a three-hour Oslo Highlights Tour that includes Bygdøy beaches and a ride up the Akers River (350 NOK, May-Sept daily at 14:00, Nedre Slottsgate 4, tel. 41 26 64 96, www.vikingbikingoslo. com). They also rent bikes; see "Helpful Hints," earlier. If you'd rather walk, check out their "Viking Hiking" forest-to-fjord and island hikes.

Bus Tours

While a bus tour can help you get your bearings, most of Oslo's sightseeing is concentrated in a few discrete zones that are well-connected by the public transportation—making pricey bus tours a lesser value. Consider my self-guided tram tour (later) instead.

Båtservice, which runs the harbor cruises, offers four-hour **bus tours** of Oslo, with stops at the ski jump, Bygdøy museums, and Vigeland Park (410 NOK, daily at 10:30, departs from next to City Hall, longer tours available, tel. 23 35 68 90, www.boatsightseeing. com). **HMK** also does daily city bus tours (330 NOK/2.5 hours, 450 NOK/4.5 hours, departs from next to City Hall, tel. 22 78 94 00, www.hmk.no).

Open Top Sightseeing runs **hop-on, hop-off bus tours** (300 NOK/all day, 18 stops, www.city-sightseeing.com; every 30 minutes from City Hall, English headphone commentary, buy ticket from driver). Be aware that you may wait up to an hour at popular stops (such as Vigeland Park) for a chance to hop back on.

Oslo Tram Tour

Tram #12, which becomes tram #11 halfway through its loop (at Majorstuen), circles the city from the train station, lacing together many of Oslo's main sights. Apart from the practical value of being able to hop on and off as you sightsee your way around town (trams come by at least every 10 minutes), this 40-minute trip gives you a fine look at parts of the city you wouldn't otherwise see.

This tour starts at the main train station, at the traffic-island tram stop located immediately in front of the Ruter transit office tower. The route makes almost a complete circle and finishes at Stortorvet (the cathedral square), dropping you off a three-minute walk from where you began the tour.

Starting out, you want tram #12 as it leaves from the second set of tracks, going toward Majorstuen. Confirm with your driver that the particular tram #12 you're boarding becomes tram #11 and finishes at Stortorvet; some turn into tram #19 instead, which takes a different route. If yours becomes #19, simply hop out at Majorstuen and wait for the next #11. (If #11 is canceled due to construction, leave #12 at Majorstuen and catch #19 through the center back to the train station, or hop on the T-bane, which zips every few minutes from Majorstuen to the National Theater—closest to the harbor and City Hall—and then to the station).

Here's what you'll see and places where you might want to hop out:

From the **station,** you'll go through the old grid streets of 16th-century Christiania, King Christian IV's planned Renaissance town. After the city's 17th fire, in 1624, the king finally got fed up. He decreed that only brick and stone buildings would be permitted in the city center, with wide streets to serve as fire breaks.

You'll turn a corner at the **fortress** (Christiana Torv stop; get off here for the fortress and Norwegian Resistance Museum), then head for **City Hall** (Rådhus stop). Next comes the harbor and upscale **Aker Brygge** waterfront neighborhood (jump off at the Aker Brygge stop for the harbor and restaurant row). Passing the harbor, you'll see on the left a few old shipyard buildings that still survive. Then the tram goes uphill, past the **House of Oslo** (a mall of 20 shops highlighting Scandinavian interior design; Vikatorvet stop) and into a district of ugly 1960s buildings (when elegance was replaced by "functionality"). The tram then heads onto the street Norwegians renamed **Henrik Ibsens Gate** in 2006 to commemorate the centenary of Ibsen's death, honoring the man they claim is the greatest playwright since Shakespeare.

After Henrik Ibsens Gate, the tram follows Frognerveien through the chic **Frogner neighborhood.** Behind the fine old facades are fancy shops and spendy condos. Here and there you'll see 19th-century mansions built by aristocratic families who wanted to live near the Royal Palace; today, many of these house foreign embassies. Turning the corner, you roll along the edge of **Frogner Park** (which includes **Vigeland Park,** featuring Gustav Vigeland's sculptures), stopping at its grand gate (hop out at the Vigeland-sparken stop).

Ahead on the left, a statue of 1930s ice queen Sonja Henie marks the arena where she learned to skate. Turning onto Bogstadveien, the tram usually becomes #11 at the Majorstuen stop. **Bogstadveien** is lined with trendy shops, restaurants, and cafés— it's a fun place to stroll and window-shop. (You could get out here and walk along this street all the way to the Royal Palace park and the top of Karl Johans Gate.) The tram veers left before the palace, passing the **National Historical Museum** and stopping at the **National Gallery** (Tullinløkka stop). As you trundle along, you may notice that lots of roads are ripped up for construction. It's too cold to fix the streets in winter, so, when possible, the work is done in summer. Jump out at **Stortorvet** (a big square filled with flower stalls and fronted by the cathedral and the big GlasMagasinet department store). From here, you're a three-minute walk from the station, where this tour began.

Oslo Walk

This self-guided stroll, worth ▲▲, covers the heart of Oslo—the zone where most tourists find themselves walking—from the train station, up the main drag, and past City Hall to the harborfront. Allow a brisk 45 minutes without stops.

OSLO

Train Station: Start at the plaza just outside the main entrance of Oslo's central train station (Oslo Sentralstasjon), near the statue of the **tiger** prowling around out front. This alludes to the town's nickname of Tigerstaden ("Tiger Town"), and commemorates the 1,000th birthday of Oslo's founding, celebrated in the year 2000. In the 1800s, Oslo was considered an urban tiger, leaving its mark on the soul of simple country folk who ventured into the wild and crazy New York City of Norway.

In the middle of the plaza, look for the tall, skinny, glass ❶ **Ruter tower** that marks the public transit office. From here, trams zip to City Hall (harbor, boat to Bygdøy), and the underground subway (T-bane, or *Tunnelbane*—look for the *T* sign to your right) goes to Vigeland Park (statues) and Holmenkollen. Tram #12—featured in the self-guided tram tour described earlier—leaves from directly across the street.

The green building behind the Ruter tower is a shopping mall called **Byporten** (literally, "City Gate," see big sign on rooftop), built to greet those arriving from the airport on the shuttle train. Oslo's 37-floor pointed-glass **skyscraper,** the Radisson Blu Plaza Hotel, pokes up behind that. The hotel's 34th-floor SkyBar welcomes the public with air-conditioned views and pricey drinks. The tower was built with reflective glass so that, from a distance, it almost disappears. The area behind the Radisson—the lively and colorful "Little Karachi," centered along a street called Grønland—is where many of Oslo's immigrants settled. It's become a vibrant nightspot, offering a fun contrast to the predictable Norwegian cuisine and culture.

Oslo allows hard-drug addicts and prostitutes to mix and mingle in the station area. (While it's illegal to buy sex in Norway, those who sell it are not breaking the law.) Troubled young people come here from small towns in the countryside for anonymity and community. The two cameras near the top of the Ruter tower monitor drug deals. Signs warn that this is a "monitored area," but victimless crimes proceed while violence is minimized. (Watch your valuables here.)

• *Note that you are near the Opera House if you'd like to side-trip there now (through the park to the right of the station). Otherwise, turn your back to the station. You're now looking (across the street) up Norway's main drag, called...*

Karl Johans Gate: This grand boulevard leads directly from the train station to the Royal Palace. The street is named for the

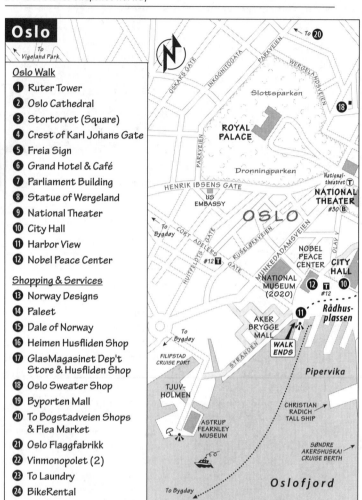

Oslo

To Vigeland Park

Oslo Walk
1. Ruter Tower
2. Oslo Cathedral
3. Stortorvet (Square)
4. Crest of Karl Johans Gate
5. Freia Sign
6. Grand Hotel & Café
7. Parliament Building
8. Statue of Wergeland
9. National Theater
10. City Hall
11. Harbor View
12. Nobel Peace Center

Shopping & Services
13. Norway Designs
14. Paleet
15. Dale of Norway
16. Heimen Husfliden Shop
17. GlasMagasinet Dep't Store & Husfliden Shop
18. Oslo Sweater Shop
19. Byporten Mall
20. To Bogstadveien Shops & Flea Market
21. Oslo Flaggfabrikk
22. Vinmonopolet (2)
23. To Laundry
24. BikeRental

OSLO

Slottsparken
ROYAL PALACE
Dronningparken
Nationaltheatret T
NATIONAL THEATER #30 B
OSLO
US EMBASSY
HENRIK IBSENS GATE
OSKARS GATE · INKOGNITOGATA · PARKVEIEN · WERGELANDSVEIEN
PARKVEIEN
To Bygdøy
CORT ADELERS GATE
RUSELØKKVEIEN
HUITFELDTS GATE
MUNKEDAMSVEIEN
NOBEL PEACE CENTER
CITY HALL
NATIONAL MUSEUM (2020)
#12 T
12 T #12
11 10
Rådhusplassen
AKER BRYGGE MALL
WALK ENDS
To Bygdøy
FILIPSTAD CRUISE PORT
STRANDEN
TJUVHOLMEN
ASTRUP FEARNLEY MUSEUM
Pipervika
CHRISTIAN RADICH TALL SHIP
SØNDRE AKERSHUSKAI CRUISE BERTH
Oslofjord
To Bygdøy

French general Jean Baptiste Bernadotte, who was given a Swedish name, established the current Swedish dynasty, and ruled as a popular king (1818-1844) during the period after Sweden took Norway from Denmark.

Walk three blocks up Karl Johans Gate. This stretch is sometimes called **"Desolation Row"** by locals because it has no soul—just shops greedily devouring tourists' money. If you visit in the snowy winter, you'll walk on bare concrete: Most of downtown Oslo's pedestrian streets are heated.

• Hook right around the curved old brick structure of an old market and walk to the...

❷ **Oslo Cathedral** (Domkirke): This Lutheran church is the third cathedral Oslo has had, built in 1697 after the second one

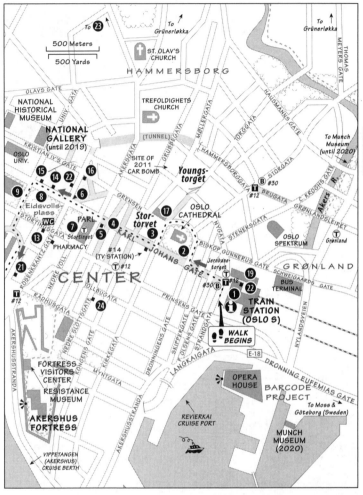

burned down. It's where Norway commemorates its royal marriages and deaths. Seventy-seven deaths were mourned here following a tragic bombing and mass shooting in July 2011 (see the "In Cold Blood" sidebar, later). In the grass in front of the cathedral, you may see a plastic heart on a pole—a semipermanent memorial to the victims.

Look for the cathedral's cornerstone (near the base of the steeple), a thousand-year-old carving from Oslo's first and long-gone cathedral showing how the forces of good and evil tug at each of us. Look high up on the tower. The tiny square windows midway up the copper cupola were once the lookout quarters of the fire watchman.

Step inside (daily 10:00-16:00, open overnight on Fri) beneath the red, blue, and gold seal of Oslo and under an equally colorful ceiling (late Art Deco from the 1930s). The box above on the right is for the royal family. The fine Baroque pulpit and altarpiece date from 1700. The chandeliers are from the previous cathedral (which burned in the 17th century). The colorful windows in the choir (leading up to the altar) were made in 1910 by Emanuel Vigeland (Gustav's less famous brother). Leaving the church, stroll around to the right, behind the church. The **courtyard** is lined by a circa-1850 circular row of stalls from an old market. Rusty meat hooks now decorate the lamps of a peaceful café, which has

quaint tables around a fountain. The atmospheric **$$$$ Café Bacchus,** at the far left end of the arcade, serves food outside and in a classy café downstairs (sandwiches, salads, full meals, good cakes, coffee, Mon-Sat 11:30-22:30, closed Sun, tel. 22 33 34 30).

• *The square that faces the cathedral is called...*

❸ **Stortorvet:** In the 17th century, when Oslo's city wall was located about here, this "Big Square" was the point where farm-

ers were allowed to enter and sell their goods. Today it's still lively as a flower and produce market (Mon-Fri). The statue shows Christian IV, the Danish king who ruled Norway around 1600, dramatically gesturing at some geraniums. He named the city, rather immodestly, Christiania. (Oslo took back its old Norse name only in 1925.) Christian was serious about Norway. During his 60-year reign, he visited it 30 times (more than all other royal visits combined during 300 years of Danish rule). The big GlasMagasinet department store is a landmark on this square.

• *Return to Karl Johans Gate, and continue up the boulevard past street performers, cafés, shops, and hordes of people. At the next corner, Kongens Gate leads left, past the 17th-century grid-plan town to **Akershus Fortress** (described in "Sights in Oslo," later). But we'll continue hiking straight up to the crest of the hill, enjoying some of the buskers along the way.*

Pause at the wide spot in the street just before Akersgata (near the T-bane stop) to appreciate the...

❹ **Crest of Karl Johans Gate** (Egertorget): Look back at the train station. A thousand years ago, the original (pre-1624) Oslo was located at the foot of the wooded hill behind the station (described later). Now look ahead to the **Royal Palace** in the distance, which was built in the 1830s "with nature and God behind it and the people at its feet." If the flag flies atop the palace, the king is in the country. For details on visiting the palace, see the listing later, under "Sights in Oslo."

Karl Johans Gate, a parade ground laid out in about 1850 from here to the palace, is now the axis of modern Oslo. Each May 17, Norway's Constitution Day, an annual children's parade turns this street into a sea of marching student bands and costumed young flag-wavers, while the royal family watches from the palace balcony. Since 1814, Norway has preferred peace. Rather than celebrating its military on the national holiday, it celebrates its children.

In the middle of the small square, the *T* sign marks a stop of the T-bane (Oslo's subway). W. B. Samson's bakery is a good place for a quick, affordable lunch, with a handy cafeteria line (WC in back)—duck inside and be tempted by the pastries. Two traditional favorites are *kanelboller* (cinnamon rolls) and *skolebrød* ("school bread," with an egg-and-cream filling).

High overhead, the big neon ❺ **Freia sign** (dating from 1911) trumpets another sweet Norwegian treat. Norway's answer to Cadbury, the Norwegian chocolatier Freia is beloved...or it was, until it was bought by an American company. Still, the local factory is partly operational, and nostalgic Norwegians will always think of Freia as "a little piece of Norway."

From here, the street called **Akersgata** (on the right) kicks off a worthwhile stroll past the site of the July 2011 bombing, the national cemetery, and through a parklike river gorge to the Mathallen food hall and the trendy Grünerløkka quarter (an hour-long walk, described later, under "Sights in Oslo").

Continuing down Karl Johans Gate: People-watching is great along Karl Johans Gate, but remember that if it's summer, half of the city's regular population is gone—vacationing in their cabins or farther away—and the city center is filled mostly with visitors.

Hike two blocks farther down Karl Johans Gate, passing the big brick Parliament building (on the left). On your right, seated in the square, is a bearded, tubby statue of the 19th-century painter Christian Krohg.

If you'd like to get a city view (and perhaps some pricey refreshment), enter the glass doors facing the street at #27 (not the bank entrance at the corner) and take the elevator to the eighth-floor rooftop bar, aptly named Eight (cocktails-150 NOK, beers-90 NOK).

A few doors farther down Karl Johans Gate, just past the Freia

Browsing

Oslo's pulse is best felt by strolling. Three good areas are along and near the central Karl Johans Gate, which runs from the train station to the palace (follow my self-guided "Oslo Walk"); in the trendy harborside Aker Brygge mall, a glass-and-chrome collection of sharp cafés, fine condos, and polished produce stalls (really lively at night, tram #12 from train station); and along Bogstadveien, a bustling shopping street with no-nonsense modern commerce, lots of locals, and no tourists (T-bane to Majorstuen and follow this street back toward the palace and tourist zone). While most tourists never get out of the harbor/Karl Johans Gate district, the real, down-to-earth Oslo is better seen elsewhere, in places such as Bogstadveien. The bohemian, artsy Grünerløkka district, described on page 66, is good for a daytime wander.

shop (selling that favorite Norwegian chocolate at only slightly inflated prices), the venerable **Grand Hotel** (Oslo's celebrity hotel—Nobel Peace Prize winners sleep here) overlooks the boulevard.

• *Politely ask the waiter at the Grand Café—part of the Grand Hotel—if you can pop inside for a little sightseeing (he'll generally let you).*

❻ Grand Café: This historic café was for many years the meeting place of Oslo's intellectual and creative elite (playwright Henrik Ibsen was a regular here). While it's been renovated, it still has some beautiful old artwork—including (at the far back) a wall-length **mural** showing Norway's literary and artistic clientele—from a century ago—enjoying this fine hangout. On the far left, find Ibsen, coming in as he did every day at 13:00. Edvard Munch is on the right, leaning against the window behind the waiter, looking pretty drugged. Names are on the sill beneath the mural.

• *For a cheap bite with prime boulevard seating, continue past the corner to Deli de Luca, a convenience store with a super selection of takeaway food and a great people-watching perch. Across the street, a little park faces Norway's...*

❼ Parliament Building (Stortinget): Norway's parliament meets here (along with anyone participating in a peaceful protest outside). *Stortinget*—from an old Viking word—basically means "Big Gathering." Built in 1866, the building seems to counter the Royal Palace at the other end of Karl Johans Gate. If the flag's flying, parliament's in session. Today the king is a figurehead, and Norway is run by a unicameral parliament and a prime minister. Guided tours of the Stortinget are offered for those interested in Norwegian government (free, 1 hour, typically Sat mornings, may be more frequent in summer—check schedule at www.stortinget. no, enter on Akersgata—on the back side of the building).

• *Cross over into the long median park. On your left, notice the red, white, and blue coin-op public WCs. (Free WCs are inside the Paleet shopping mall, on the right side of the boulevard).*

Enjoying the park, stroll toward the palace, past the fountain. Pause at the...

❽ **Statue of Wergeland:** The poet Henrik Wergeland helped inspire the national resurgence of Norway during the 19th century. Norway won its independence from Denmark in 1814, but within a year it lost its freedom to Sweden. For nearly a century, until Norway won independence in 1905, Norwegian culture and national spirit was stoked by artistic and literary patriots like Wergeland. In the winter, the pool here is frozen and covered with children happily ice-skating.

Across the street behind Wergeland stands the ❾ **National Theater** and statues of Norway's favorite playwrights: Ibsen and Bjørnstjerne Bjørnson. Across Karl Johans Gate, the pale yellow building is the first university building in Norway, dating from 1854. A block behind that is the National Gallery, with Norway's best collection of paintings (self-guided tour on page 43).

Take a moment here to do a 360-degree spin to notice how quiet and orderly everything is. People seem content—and, according to most surveys, Norwegians are among the happiest people on earth. If you ask them why, their hunch is that it's because they live collectively. The Vikings would famously share one large bowl of mead, passing it around the circle. Nobody—no matter how big, angry, hairy, or smelly—gulped more than his share. They all made sure that everyone got some.

In modern times, Norwegians at the dinner table are still mindful when helping themselves not to take too much: They mentally ration enough for the people who come after them. It's a very considerate—and a very Norwegian—way of thinking. (Similarly, upper-Midwesterners in the US are familiar with the "Minnesota Slice": The Scandinavian-American tendency to carve off a little sliver of the last slice of pie, rather than take the entire thing for themselves.)

• *Facing the theater, turn left and follow Roald Amundsens Gate to the towering brick...*

❿ **City Hall** (Rådhuset): Built mostly in the 1930s with contributions from Norway's leading artists, City Hall is full

OSLO

Oslo at a Glance

▲▲▲**City Hall** Oslo's artsy 20th-century government building, lined with huge, vibrant, municipal-themed murals, best visited with included tour. **Hours:** Daily 9:00-16:00, until 18:00 June-Aug; 3 tours/day June-Aug. See page 33.

▲▲▲**National Gallery** Norway's cultural and natural essence, captured on canvas. **Hours:** Tue-Fri 10:00-18:00, Thu until 19:00, Sat-Sun 11:00-17:00, closed Mon. See page 42.

▲▲▲**Vigeland Park** Set in sprawling Frogner Park, with tons of statuary by Norway's greatest sculptor, Gustav Vigeland, and the studio where he worked (now a museum). **Hours:** Park—always open; Vigeland Museum—Tue-Sun 10:00-17:00, Sept-April 12:00-16:00, closed Mon year-round. See page 50.

▲▲▲**Fram Museum** Captivating exhibit on the Arctic exploration ships *Fram* and *Gjøa*. **Hours:** Daily June-Aug 9:00-18:00, May and Sept 10:00-17:00, Oct and March-April until 16:00; Nov-Feb Mon-Fri 10:00-15:00, Sat-Sun until 16:00. See page 60.

▲▲**Norwegian Folk Museum** Norway condensed into 150 historic buildings in a large open-air museum. **Hours:** Daily 10:00-18:00—grounds open until 20:00; mid-Sept-mid-May Mon-Fri 11:00-15:00, Sat-Sun until 16:00, but most historical buildings closed. See page 58.

▲▲**Norwegian Resistance Museum** Gripping look at Norway's tumultuous WWII experience. **Hours:** Mon-Sat 10:00-17:00, Sun from 11:00; Sept-May Mon-Fri until 16:00, Sat-Sun from 11:00. See page 38.

▲▲**Viking Ship Museum** An impressive trio of ninth-century Viking ships, with exhibits on the people who built them. **Hours:** Daily 9:00-18:00, Oct-April 10:00-16:00. See page 59.

▲▲***Kon-Tiki* Museum** Adventures of primitive *Kon-Tiki* and *Ra II*

of great art and is worth touring (see listing later, under "Sights in Oslo"). The mayor has his office here (at the base of one of the two 200-foot towers), and every December 10, this building is where the Nobel Peace Prize is presented. The semicircular square facing the building, called Fridtjof Nansens Plass, was designed to evoke Il Campo, the main square in Siena, Tuscany. Just like Oslo, Siena's main building (dominating Il Campo) is its City Hall.

For the City Hall's best exterior art, step up into the U-shaped ships built by Thor Heyerdahl. **Hours:** Daily 9:30-18:00, March-May and Sept-Oct 10:00-17:00, Nov-Feb until 16:00. See page 63.

▲**Oslo Opera House** Stunning performance center that's helping revitalize the harborfront. **Hours:** Foyer and café/restaurant open Mon-Fri 10:00-23:00, Sat from 11:00, Sun 12:00-22:00; Opera House tours—3/day year-round. See page 41.

▲**Akershus Fortress Complex and Tours** Historic military base and fortified old center, with guided tours, a ho-hum castle interior, and the excellent Norwegian Resistance Museum (listed earlier). **Hours:** Park generally open daily 6:00-21:00—until 18:00 in winter; one-hour tour daily July-mid-Aug, weekends-only off-season. See page 37.

▲**Norwegian Maritime Museum** A briny voyage through Norway's rich seafaring heritage. **Hours:** Daily 10:00-17:00; Sept-mid-May Tue-Sun until 16:00, closed Mon. See page 63.

▲**Ekeberg Sculpture Park** Hilly, hikeable 63-acre forest park with striking contemporary art and city views. See page 264.

▲**Edvard Munch Museum** Works of Norway's famous Expressionistic painter. **Hours:** Daily 10:00-17:00, early Oct-early May until 16:00. See page 71.

▲**Grünerløkka** Oslo's trendy former working-class district, with bustling cafés and pubs. See page 66.

▲**Aker Brygge and Tjuvholmen** Oslo's harborfront promenade, and nearby trendy Tjuvholmen neighborhood with Astrup Fearnley Museum, upscale galleries, shops, and cafés. See page 37.

▲**Holmenkollen Ski Jump and Ski Museum** Dizzying vista and a schuss through skiing history, plus a zip line off the top. **Hours:** Daily 9:00-20:00, May and Sept 10:00-17:00, Oct-April until 16:00. See page 73.

OSLO

courtyard and circle it clockwise, savoring the colorful woodcuts in the arcade. Each shows a scene from Norwegian mythology, well-explained in English: Thor with his billy-goat chariot, Ask and Embla (a kind of Norse Adam and Eve), Odin on his eight-legged horse guided by ravens, the swan maidens shedding their swan disguises, and so on.

Facing City Hall, circle around its right side (through a lovely garden) until you reach the front. Like all of the statues adorning the building, the **six figures** facing the waterfront—dating from a period of Labor Party rule in Norway—celebrate the nobility of the working class. Norway, a social democracy, believes in giving respect to the workers who built their society and made it what it is, and these laborers are viewed as heroes.

• *Walk to the...*

❶ **Harbor:** Over a decade ago, you would have dodged several lanes of busy traffic to reach Oslo's harborfront. Today, the traffic passes beneath your feet in tunnels. In addition, the city has made its town center relatively quiet and pedestrian-friendly by levying a 34-NOK toll on every car entering town. (This system, like a similar one in London, subsidizes public transit and the city's infrastructure.)

At the water's edge, find the shiny metal plaque (just left of center) listing the contents of a sealed time capsule planted in 2000 out in the harbor in the little Kavringen lighthouse straight ahead (to be opened in 1,000 years).

Head to the end of the stubby pier (just to the right). This is the ceremonial "enter the city" point for momentous occasions. One such instance was in 1905, when Norway gained its independence from Sweden and a Danish prince sailed in from Copenhagen to become the first modern king of Norway. Another milestone event occurred at the end of World War II, when the king returned to Norway after the country was liberated from the Nazis.

• *Stand on that important pier and give the harbor a sweeping counterclockwise look.*

Harborfront Spin-Tour: Oslofjord is one big playground, with 40 city-owned, parklike islands. Big white cruise ships—a large part of the local tourist economy—dock just under the Akershus Fortress on the left. (The big, boxy building clinging to the top of the fortress—just under the green steeple—is the excellent Norwegian Resistance Museum.) Just this side of the fort's impressive 13th-century ramparts, a **statue of FDR** grabs the shade. He's here in gratitude for the safe refuge the US gave to members of the royal family (including the young prince, Harald, who is now Norway's king) during World War II—while the king and his government-in-exile waged Norway's fight against the Nazis from London.

Panning left, enjoy the grand view of City Hall. The yellow building farther to the left was the old West Train Station; today it houses the ❷ **Nobel Peace Center,** which celebrates the work of Nobel Peace Prize winners. Just to the left and behind that is the construction site for the new home of the National Museum, including the fine art collection of the National Gallery (slated to open in 2020).

The next pier over is the launchpad for harbor boat tours and the shuttle boat to the Bygdøy museums. At the base of this pier, the glassy box is a new fish market, serving a mix of locals and tourists. You may see a fisherman mooring his boat near here, selling shrimp from the back. Also in this area, look for a bright-orange container box—an information point for Oslo's impressive harbor promenade, the nearly complete 5.5-mile walkway that runs the entire length of the city's futuristic harborfront.

Along the right side of the harbor, shipyard buildings (this was the former heart of Norway's once-important shipbuilding industry) have been transformed into
Aker Brygge—Oslo's thriving restaurant/shopping/nightclub zone (see "Eating in Oslo").

Just past the end of Aker Brygge is a new housing development—dubbed Norway's most expensive real estate—called **Tjuvholmen.** It's anchored by the Astrup Fearnley Museum, an international modern art museum complex designed by renowned architect Renzo Piano (most famous for Paris' Pompidou Center).

An ambitious urban renewal project called Fjord City (Fjordbyen)—which kicked off years ago with Aker Brygge, and led to the construction of Oslo's dramatic Opera House—has made remarkable progress in turning the formerly industrial waterfront into a flourishing people zone.

• *From here, you can stroll out Aker Brygge and through Tjuvholmen to a tiny public beach at the far end; tour City Hall; visit the Nobel Peace Center; hike up to Akershus Fortress; take a harbor cruise (see "Tours in Oslo," earlier); or catch a boat across the harbor to the museums at Bygdøy (from pier 3). All of these sights are described in detail in the following section.*

Sights in Oslo

NEAR THE HARBORFRONT
▲▲▲City Hall (Rådhuset)

In 1931, Oslo tore down a slum and began constructing its richly decorated City Hall. It was finally finished—after a WWII delay—in 1950 to celebrate the city's 900th birthday. Norway's leading artists all contributed to the building, which was an avant-garde thrill in its day. City Halls, rather than churches, are the dominant buildings in Scandinavian capitals. The prominence of this building on the harborfront makes sense in this most humanistic, yet least churchgoing, northern end of the Continent. Up here, people pay high taxes, have high expectations, and are generally satisfied with what their governments do with their money.

Cost and Hours: Free, daily 9:00-16:00—until 18:00 June-Aug, free and fine WC in the basement, tel. 23 46 12 00.

Tours: Only in the summer months (June-Aug), the City Hall offers 50-minute guided tours daily at 10:00, 12:00, and 14:00.

◑ Self-Guided Tour: For descriptions of the building's exterior features and symbolism, see the City Hall section of my "Oslo Walk," earlier. On this tour, we'll focus on the interior.

The visitor entrance is on the Karl Johans Gate side (away from the harbor). You'll step into a cavernous **main hall,** which feels like a temple to good government, with its altar-like murals celebrating "work, play, and civic administration." It's decorated with 20,000 square feet of bold and colorful Socialist Realist murals celebrating a classless society, with everyone—town folk, country folk, and people from all walks of life—working harmoniously for a better society. The huge murals take you on a voyage through the collective psyche of Norway, from its simple rural beginnings through the scar tissue of the Nazi occupation and beyond. Filled with significance and symbolism—and well-described in English—the murals become even more meaningful with the excellent guided tours.

First, turn around and face the mural over the door you came in, which celebrates the **traditional industries** of Norway (from left to right): the yellow-clad fisherman (standing in his boat, glancing nervously at a flock of seagulls), the factory worker (with his heavy apron), the blue-clad sailor (he's playing with exotic beads acquired through distant trade), the farmer (in a striped dress, with a bushel under her arm), and the miner (lower right, lifting a heavy rock). Flanking these figures are portraits of two important Norwegians: On the far right is Bjørnstjerne Bjørnson (1832-1910), a prominent poet and novelist whose works pluck the patriotic heartstrings of Norwegians. And on the far left is Fridtjof Nansen (1861-1930), the famous Arctic explorer (you can learn more about him at the Fram Museum on Bygdøy). Here Nansen is seen shedding the heavy coat of his most famous endeavor—polar exploration—as he embarks on his "second act": Once retired from seafaring, he advocated for the dissolution of Norway's union with Sweden—which took place in 1905, making Norway fully independent.

Now turn 180 degrees and face the hall's main mural, which emphasizes **Oslo's youth** participating in community life—and rebuilding the country after Nazi occupation. Across the bottom, the slum that once cluttered up Oslo's harborfront is being cleared out to make way for this building. Above that, scenes show Norway's pride in its innovative health care and education systems. Left of center, near the top, Mother Norway stands next to a church—reminding viewers that the Lutheran Church of Norway (the official state religion) provides a foundation for this society. On the right, four forms represent the arts; they illustrate how creativity springs from children. And in the center, the figure of Charity is surrounded by Culture, Philosophy, and Family.

The **"Mural of the Occupation"** lines the left side of the hall, tucked under the balustrade. Scan it from left to right to see the

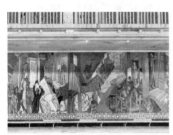

story of Norway's WWII experience: First, the German blitzkrieg overwhelms the country. Men head for the mountains to organize a resistance movement. Women huddle around the water well, traditionally where news is passed, while Quislings (traitors named after the Norwegian fascist who ruled the country as a Nazi puppet) listen in. While Germans bomb and occupy Norway, a family gathers in their living room. As a boy clenches his fist (showing determination) and a child holds the beloved Norwegian flag, the Gestapo steps in. Columns are toppled to the ground, symbolizing how Germans shut down the culture by closing newspapers and the university. Two resistance soldiers stand up against a wall—about to be executed by firing squad. A cell of resistance fighters (wearing masks and using nicknames, so if tortured they can't reveal their compatriots' identities) plan a sabotage mission. Finally, prisoners are freed, the war is over, and Norway celebrates its happiest day: May 17, 1945—the first Constitution Day after five years under Nazi control.

While gazing at these murals, keep in mind that the Nobel Peace Prize is awarded in this central hall each December (though the general Nobel Prize ceremony occurs in Stockholm's City Hall). You'll see photos of this event in the little foyer with the strollers (on the right from where you entered). You can see videos of the ceremony and acceptance speeches in the adjacent Nobel Peace Center (listed next).

At the base of the grand marble staircase is a mural of the 11th-century **St. Hallvard,** the patron saint of Oslo. Above his head, he holds his symbol—three arrows—and he rests a millstone on his knee. As the story goes, Hallvard took pity on a pregnant woman (the naked woman in front of him) who had been wrongly accused of theft by three men. They attempted to escape, but the accusers killed the woman, shot Hallvard with three arrows, tied a millstone around his neck, and tossed him into the fjord. Miraculously, he survived (or perhaps rose from the dead). This story of compassion in the face of injustice swayed Norwegians at a time when Christianity was making its bid to be the country's main religion.

In front of the mural is a **bell** from the ship that brought Norway's royal family back home after World War II—landing at the pier right in front of City Hall.

Now head up the stairs and explore several **ceremonial rooms,** each well-described in English. The wood-paneled Munch Room is dominated by the artist's oil painting *Life.* Circle around the gallery to the City Council Assembly Room, where Oslo's leadership steers the agenda of this impressive city. Notice the "three arrows and millstone" motif, recalling St. Hallvard. The city council acts collectively as a virtual "mayor"—a system, originating here in Oslo in 1986, called "parliamentary metropolitan government." Notice how this room evokes the semicircular shape of the square where you entered. Out in the hall, you'll pass gifts from visiting heads of state (*gave fra* means "gift from").

Nearby: Fans of the explorer Fridtjof Nansen might enjoy taking a break for a bite and a coffee or beer across the street at **Fridtjof,** an atmospheric bar filled with memorabilia from Nansen's Arctic explorations. A model of his ship, the *Fram,* hangs from the ceiling, and 1894 photos and his own drawings are upstairs (Mon-Sat 12:00 until late, Sun 14:00-22:00, Nansens Plass 7, tel. 93 25 22 30).

Nobel Peace Center (Nobels Fredssenter)

This museum, housed in the former West Train Station (Vestbanen), poses the question, "What is the opposite of conflict?" It celebrates the 800-some past and present Nobel Peace Prize winners with touchscreen exhibits (with good English explanations).

Cost and Hours: 100 NOK; daily 10:00-18:00, closed Mon Sept-mid-May; includes English guided tours at 14:00 and 15:00—off-season weekends only at 14:00; Brynjulfs Bulls Plass 1, tel. 48 30 10 00, www.nobelpeacecenter.org.

Visiting the Center: The ground floor is dominated by generally good, thought-provoking temporary exhibits. The permanent collection upstairs is modest: First you'll step into "The Nobel Field," a sea of lights and touchscreens profiling various past prize-winners (from Teddy Roosevelt to Mother Theresa). Next, "The Nobel Chamber" has a big virtual book that invites you to learn more about the life and work of Alfred Nobel, the Swedish inventor of dynamite, who initiated the prizes—perhaps to assuage his conscience. While it's a nice museum, unless the temporary exhibits intrigue you, save your time and money for the better Nobel Prize Museum in Stockholm.

▲Aker Brygge and Tjuvholmen

Oslo's harborfront was dominated by the **Aker Brygge** shipyard until it closed in 1986. In the late 2000s, it became the first finished part of a project (called Fjordbyen, or Fjord City) to convert the central stretch of Oslo's harborfront into a people-friendly park and culture zone. Today's Aker Brygge is a stretch of trendy, if overpriced, yacht-club style restaurants facing a fine promenade—just the place to join in on a Nordic paseo on a balmy summer's eve.

The far end of Aker Brygge is marked by a big black anchor from the wreck of the German warship *Blücher,* sunk by Norwegian forces near Drøbak while heading for Oslo during the Nazi invasion on April 9, 1940. From there a bridge crosses over onto **Tjuvholmen** (where they hung thieves back in the 17th century). This is a planned futuristic community, with the trendiest and costliest apartments in town, private moorings for luxury jet boats, boardwalks with built-in seating to catch the sun, elegant shops and cafés, and the striking, wood-clad, glass-roofed **Astrup Fearnley Museum of Modern Art** (good temporary exhibits of contemporary art, closed Mon, www.afmuseet.no). On the harbor side of the museum, find the grassy little knob of land with an appealing sculpture park. This area is well worth a wander—and don't be afraid to explore the back lanes away from the waterfront. As you stroll through Tjuvholmen, admire how, while the entire complex feels cohesive, each building has its own personality.

Eating: Dining here is appealing, but be prepared to pay royally for the privilege. Choose from many restaurants, or—to eat on a budget—take advantage of the generous public benches, lounge chairs, and picnic tables that allow people who can't afford a fancy restaurant meal to enjoy the best seats of all (grocery stores are a block away from the harborfront views). For recommendations, see "Eating in Oslo," later.

▲AKERSHUS FORTRESS COMPLEX

This parklike complex of sights scattered over Oslo's fortified old center is still a military base. (You'll see uniformed members of the Royal Guard keeping watch, because the castle is a royal mausoleum.) But the public is welcome, and as you dodge patrol guards and vans filled with soldiers, you'll see the castle, war memorials, the Norwegian Resistance Museum, and cannon-strewn ramparts affording fine harbor views and picnic perches. There's an unimpressive changing of the guard—that's singular "guard," as in just one—daily at 13:30 (at the parade ground, deep in the castle complex). The park is generally open daily 6:00-21:00 (until

18:00 in winter), but because the military is in charge here, times can change without warning. Expect bumpy cobblestone lanes and steep hills. To get here from the harbor, follow the stairs (which lead past the FDR statue) to the park.

Getting Oriented: It's a sprawling complex. You can hike up the stairs by the FDR statue on the harbor, or (less steeply) from the grid of streets just east of City Hall. As you hike up toward the ramparts, go through the gate smack in the middle of the complex (rather than hooking up around to the right). You'll pop out into an inner courtyard. The visitors center (described next) is to the left, and the other sights are through the gate on the right. Heading through this gate, you'll curl up along a tree-lined lane, then pass the Norwegian Resistance Museum on your right (capping the ramparts). The entrance to the castle is dead ahead. There are terrific harbor views (often filled with a giant cruise ship) from the rampart alongside the Resistance Museum.

Fortress Visitors Center: Stop here to pick up the fortress trail and site map, quickly browse through a modest exhibit tracing the story of Oslo's fortifications from medieval times, use the free WCs, and consider catching a tour (daily July-mid-Aug 11:00-17:00, until 16:00 in shoulder season, shorter hours off-season, tel. 23 09 39 17, www.akershusfestning.no).

Fortress Tours: The 60-NOK, hour-long English walking tours of the grounds help you make sense of the most historic piece of real estate in Oslo (July-mid-Aug daily in English at 13:00, weekends-only off-season; departs from Fortress Visitors Center, call ahead to confirm tour is running).

▲▲Norwegian Resistance Museum (Norges Hjemmefrontmuseum)

This fascinating museum tells the story of Norway's WWII experience: appeasement, Nazi invasion (they made Akershus one of their headquarters), resistance, liberation, and, finally, the return of the king. With good English descriptions, this is an inspirational look at how the national spirit can endure total occupation by a malevolent force. While the exhibit grows a bit more old-fashioned with each passing year, for those with an appetite for WWII history and the patience to read the displays, it's still both riveting and stirring. Norway had the fiercest resistance movement in Scandinavia, and this museum shows off their (hard-earned) pride.

Cost and Hours: 60 NOK; Mon-Sat 10:00-17:00, Sun from 11:00; Sept-May Mon-Fri 10:00-16:00, Sat-Sun from 11:00; next to castle, overlooking harbor, tel. 23 09 31 38, www.forsvaretsmuseer.no.

Visiting the Museum: It's a one-way, chronological, can't-get-lost route. As you enter the exhibit, you're transported back to 1940, greeted by an angry commotion of rifles aimed at you. A German notice proclaiming "You will submit or die" is bayonetted onto a gun in the middle. A **timeline** on the right wall traces the brief history of skirmishes between Nazi and improvised Norwegian forces following the invasion on April 9, 1940. This ends abruptly on June 10, when the Norwegian government officially capitulates.

On the left, you'll see the German ultimatum to which King Haakon VII gave an emphatic "No." A video screen nearby plays the radio address by Vidkun Quisling, the fascist Nasjonal Samling (National Union Party) politician who declared himself ruler of Norway on the day of the invasion. (Today, Quisling's name remains synonymous with "traitor"—the Norwegian version of Benedict Arnold.)

Head **downstairs** and take some time with the in-depth exhibits. Various displays show secret radios, transmitters, and underground newspapers. The official name for the resistance was Milorg (for "Military Organization")—but Norwegians affectionately referred to the ragtag, guerilla force as simply *gutta på skauen* ("the boys in the forest"). Look for the display case explaining wartime difficulty and austerity in Norway. Red knit caps were worn by civilians to show solidarity with the resistance—until the hats were outlawed by Nazi officials. In the same case, notice the shoes made of fish skin, and the little row of *erstatning* (ersatz, or replacement) products. With the Nazi occupation, Norway lost its trade partners, and had to improvise.

You'll also learn about the military actions against the occupation. British-trained special forces famously blew up a strategic heavy water plant (a key part of the Nazis' atomic bomb program)—still fondly recalled by Norwegians, and immortalized in the not-so-accurate 1965 Kirk Douglas film *The Heroes of Telemark*. Nearby, see the case of crude but effective homemade weapons, and the German machine used to locate clandestine radio stations. Exhibits explain how the country coped with 350,000 occupying troops; how airdrops equipped a home force of 40,000 so they were ready to coordinate with the Allies when liberation was imminent; and the happy day when the resistance army came out of the forest, and peace and freedom returned to Norway. Liberation day was May 8, 1945...but it took a few days to pull together the celebration, which coincided neatly with the 17th of May—Constitution Day. (That's partly why May 17 is still celebrated so fiercely today.)

Back **upstairs,** notice the propaganda posters trying to recruit Norwegians to the Nazi cause and "protect the eastern border" from the Soviets and communism. A more recent addition to the museum (downstairs) considers the many Norwegians who did choose to cooperate with (and profit from) the Nazis.

The museum is particularly poignant because many of the patriots featured inside were executed by the Germans right outside the museum's front door; a **stone memorial** marks the spot. (At war's end, the traitor Vidkun Quisling was also executed at the fortress, but at a different location.)

Akershus Castle

Although it's one of Oslo's oldest buildings, the castle overlooking the harbor is mediocre by Euro-

pean standards; the big, empty rooms recall Norway's medieval poverty. The first fortress here was built by Norwegians in 1299. It was rebuilt much stronger by the Danes in 1640 so the Danish king (Christian IV) would have a suitable and safe place to stay during his many visits. When Oslo was rebuilt in the 17th century, many of the stones from the first Oslo cathedral were reused here, in the fortress walls.

Cost and Hours: 100 NOK, includes audioguide; Mon-Sat 10:00-16:00, Sun from 12:00; Sept-April Sat-Sun 12:00-17:00 only, closed Mon-Fri; tel. 23 09 35 53. Note that renovation work may affect these hours or close the castle; check locally.

Visiting the Castle: From the old kitchen, where the ticket desk and gift shop are located, you'll follow a one-way circuit of rooms open to the public. Descend through a secret passage to the dungeon, crypt, and royal tomb. Emerge behind the altar in the chapel, then walk through echoing rooms including the Daredevil's Tower, Hall of Christian IV (with portraits of Danish kings of Norway on the walls), and Hall of Olav V.

Old Christiania

In the mid-1600s, the ruling Danes had the original Oslo leveled and built a more modern grid-planned city. They built with stone so it wouldn't burn, and located the new city just below the castle so it was easier to control and defend. They named it Christiania, after their king. The checkerboard neighborhood between the castle and the cathedral today—aptly called Kvadraturen—marks that original Christiania town. There's little to see, but curious tourists can wander through this sleepy zone (between the castle and Karl Johans Gate) and look for some 17th-century buildings. Bits of Christiania's original Dutch Renaissance-style buildings survive. (Norwegian builders, accustomed to working with wood, lacked skill with stone, so the Danes imported Dutch builders.) The area's main square, Christiania Torv (near the recommended Café Skansen), is marked by a modern fountain called "The Glove." The sculpture of Christian IV's glove points as if to indicate, "This is where we'll build my city." The old City Hall, now the Gamle Raadhus restaurant, survives.

ON THE WATERFRONT, NEAR THE TRAIN STATION
▲Oslo Opera House (Operahuset Oslo)

Opened in 2008, Oslo's striking Opera House was a huge hit. The building angles up from the water on the city's eastern harbor, across the highway from the train station. Its boxy, low-slung, glass center holds a state-of-the-art 1,400-seat main theater with a 99-piece orchestra "in the pit," which can rise to put the orchestra "on the pedestal." The season is split between opera and ballet.

Cost and Hours: Foyer and café/restaurant open Mon-Fri 10:00-23:00, Sat from 11:00, Sun 12:00-22:00.

Tours: Year-round, you can take a fascinating 50-minute guided tour of the stage, backstage area, and architecture (100 NOK; usually 3 tours/day in English—generally at 11:00, 12:00, and 14:00; reserve online at www.operaen.no, tel. 21 42 21 00).

Daytime Mini-Concerts: For a few weeks in the summer, the Opera House offers sporadic one-hour daytime "Concerts at the Balcony" (70 NOK, many days in late July at 14:00).

Getting There: You'll find it on Bjørvika, the next harbor over from City Hall and Akershus Fortress—just below the train station.

Visiting the Opera House: Information-packed, 50-minute tours explain what makes this one of the greenest buildings in Europe and why Norwegian taxpayers helped foot the half-billion-dollar cost for this project—to make high culture (ballet and opera) accessible to the younger generation and a stratum of society who normally wouldn't care. You'll see a workshop employing 50 people who hand-make costumes, and learn how the foundation of 700 pylons set 40 or 50 meters deep support the jigsaw puzzle of wood, glass, and 36,000 individual pieces of marble. The construction masterfully integrates land and water, inside and outside, nature and culture.

The jutting white marble planes of the Opera House's roof double as a public plaza. You feel a need to walk all over it. The

Opera House is part of a larger harbor-redevelopment plan that includes rerouting traffic into tunnels and turning a once-derelict industrial zone into an urban park. If you hike all the way to the top of the building (watch your footing—it's slippery when wet), you can peek over the back railing to see the high-rise development known as the "Barcode Project." The new Munch Museum (likely opening in 2020) resides in the futuristic Lambda building on the adjacent pier.

DOWNTOWN MUSEUMS
▲▲▲National Gallery (Nasjonalgalleriet)

While there are many schools of painting and sculpture displayed in Norway's National Gallery, focus on what's uniquely Norwegian. Paintings come and go in this museum, but you're sure to see plenty that showcase the harsh beauty of Norway's landscape and people. A thoughtful visit here gives those heading into the mountains and fjord country a chance to pack along a little of Norway's cultural soul. Tuck these images carefully away with your goat cheese—they'll sweeten your explorations.

The gallery also has several Picassos, a noteworthy Impressionist collection, a Van Gogh self-portrait, and some Vigeland statues. Its many raving examples of Edvard Munch's work, including one of his famous *Scream* paintings, make a trip to the Munch Museum unnecessary for most. It has about 50 Munch paintings in its collection, but only about a third are on display. Be prepared for changes, but don't worry—no matter what the curators decide to show, you won't have to scream for Munch's masterpieces.

Cost and Hours: 100 NOK, free on Thu; Tue-Fri 10:00-18:00, Thu until 19:00, Sat-Sun 11:00-17:00, closed Mon; obligatory lockers, Universitets Gata 13, tel. 21 98 20 00, www.nasjonalmuseet. no. Pick up the guidebooklet to help navigate the collection.

Tours: Invest 50 NOK in the thoughtful, evocative audioguide, which supplements my self-guided tour.

Eating: The richly ornamented **$$ French Salon café** offers an elegant break (150-NOK lunches).

Closure and Move: The gallery is scheduled to close in September 2019, when the collection will move to a new purpose-built home in the new National Museum near the harbor, behind the Nobel Peace Center (not far from City Hall, likely opening in 2020). Confirm details locally. As the museum is in flux, you may find even more changes to the collection than usual.

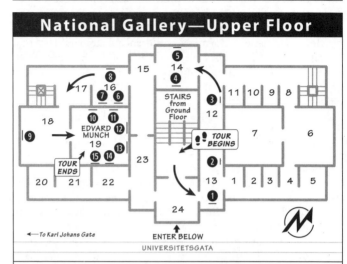

National Gallery—Upper Floor

- ❶ DAHL — View from Stalheim
- ❷ DAHL — Hellefossen near Hokksund
- ❸ FEARNLEY — The Labro Falls at Kongsberg
- ❹ TIDEMAND & GUDE — Bridal Procession on the Hardangerfjord
- ❺ PETERSSEN — Christian II
- ❻ KROHG — Sick Girl
- ❼ KROHG — Albertine to See the Police Surgeon
- ❽ WERENSKIOLD — Peasant Burial
- ❾ SOHLBERG — Winter Night in the Mountains
- ❿ MUNCH — Self Portrait with a Cigarette
- ⓫ MUNCH — Madonna
- ⓬ MUNCH — The Scream
- ⓭ MUNCH — Dance of Life
- ⓮ MUNCH — Puberty
- ⓯ MUNCH — The Sick Child

➲ Self-Guided Tour

This easy-to-handle museum gives an effortless tour back in time and through Norway's most beautiful valleys, mountains, and fjords, with the help of its Romantic painters (especially Johan Christian Dahl).

· *Go up the stairs, pausing at the top of the...*

Stairwell—Norway Past and Present

Two historical paintings by Christian Krohg hang in the stairwell, offering a helpful backstory to the collection we're about to see. Over the stairs is a big, dynamic painting of Viking explorer **Leiv Eirikson** (Leif Eriksson), on rough seas. He was born in Iceland, lived most of his life in Greenland, and was very likely the first European to set foot in the Americas (specifically, today's Newfoundland). At this point, the Vikings rule one of the biggest territories on earth...and it's about to get that much bigger.

Now turn right, as we tumble from Norway's high-water mark

to its lowest: *Struggle for Survival* (1889). Desperately poor, grubby, almost animal-like Norwegian children and mothers clamor for a scrap of food. This is the context of much of the art you're about to see: Norway is part of Denmark for four centuries, then part of Sweden for nearly a century. Norwegians felt like second-class citizens in their own homeland...their cities weren't really theirs. Seeking a sense of national pride, they looked to nature: fjords, mountains, villages.

• *To see some of that, step into Room 24, and turn left into Room 13.*

Landscape Paintings and Romanticism

Landscape painting has always played an important role in Norwegian art, perhaps because Norway provides such an awesome and varied landscape to inspire artists. The style reached its peak during the Romantic period in the mid-1800s, which stressed the beauty of unspoiled nature. (This passion for landscapes sets Norway apart from Denmark and Sweden.) After 400 years of Danish rule, the soul of the country was almost snuffed out. But with semi-independence and a constitution in the early 1800s, there was a national resurgence. Even though the cities and palaces still felt foreign (which is why you'll rarely see those depicted in art), Norwegians could claim their countryside as their own. Romantic paintings featuring the power of Norway's natural wonders and the toughness of its salt-of-the-earth folk came into vogue.

• *On the right wall as you enter is...*

❶ **Johan Christian Dahl**, *View from Stalheim*, **1842:** This painting epitomizes the Norwegian closeness to nature. It shows a view very similar to the one that 21st-century travelers enjoy on their Norway in a Nutshell excursion (see that chapter): mountains, rivers, and farms clinging to hillsides. Painted in 1842, it's quintessential Romantic style. Nature rules—the background is as detailed as the foreground, and you are sucked in.

Johan Christian Dahl (1788-1857) is considered the father of Norwegian Romanticism. Romantics such as Dahl (and Turner, Beethoven, and Lord Byron) put emotion over rationality. They reveled in the power of nature—death and pessimism ripple through their work, though in this scene a double rainbow and a splash of sunlight give hope of a better day. The birch tree—standing boldly front and center—is a standard symbol for the politically downtrodden Norwegian people: hardy, weathered, but defiantly sprouting new branches. In the mid-19th century, Norwegians were awakening to their national identity. Throughout Europe, nationalism and Romanticism went hand in hand.

Find the farm buildings huddled near the cliff's edge, smoke rising from chimneys, and the woman in traditional dress tending her herd of goats, pausing for a moment to revel in the glory of nature. It reminds us that these farmers are hardworking, independent, small landowners. There was no feudalism in medieval Norway. People were poor...but they owned their own land. You can almost taste goat cheese.

• *Look at the other works in Rooms 13 and 12. Dahl's paintings and those by his Norwegian contemporaries, showing heavy clouds and glaciers, repeat these same themes—drama over rationalism, nature pounding humanity. Human figures are melancholy. Norwegians, so close to nature, are fascinated by those plush, magic hours of dawn and twilight. The dusk makes us wonder: What will the future bring?*

In particular, focus on the painting to the right of the door marked 13.

❷ **Dahl, *Hellefossen near Hokksund*, 1838:** Another typical Dahl setting: romantic nature and an idealized scene. A fisherman checks on wooden baskets designed to catch salmon migrating up the river. In the background, a water-powered sawmill slices trees into lumber. Note another Dahl birch tree at the left, a subtle celebration of the Norwegian people and their labor.

• *Now continue into Room 12. On the right is...*

❸ **Thomas Fearnley, *The Labro Falls at Kongsberg*, 1837:** Man cannot control nature or his destiny. The landscape in this painting is devoid of people—the only sign of humanity is the jumble of sawn logs in the foreground. A wary eagle perched on one log seems to be saying, "While you can cut these trees, they'll always be mine."

• *Continue to the end of Room 12, and turn left into Room 14. On the left is...*

❹ **Adolph Tidemand and Hans Gude, *Bridal Procession on the Hardangerfjord*, 1848:** This famous painting shows the ultimate Norwegian scene: a wedding party with everyone decked out in traditional garb, heading for the stave church on the quintessential fjord (Hardanger). It's a studio work and a collaboration: Hans Gude painted the landscape, and Adolph Tidemand painted the people. Study their wedding  finery. This work trumpets the greatness of both the landscape and Norwegian culture.

• *Also in Room 14, on the opposite wall, is an example of...*

The Photographic Eye

At the end of the 19th century, Norwegian painters traded the emotions of Romanticism for more slice-of-life detail. This was the end of the Romantic period and the beginning of Realism. With the advent of photography, painters went beyond simple realism and into extreme realism.

❺ **Eilif Peterssen, *Christian II*, 1875:** The Danish king signs the execution order for the man who'd killed the king's beloved mistress. With camera-like precision, the painter captures the whole story of murder, anguish, anger, and bitter revenge in the king's set jaw and steely eyes.

• *Go through Room 15 and into Room 16. Take time to browse the paintings.*

OSLO

Vulnerability

Death, disease, and suffering were themes seen again and again in art from the late 1800s. The most serious disease during this period was tuberculosis (which killed Munch's mother and sister).

❻ **Christian Krohg, *Sick Girl*, 1880:** Christian Krohg (1852-1925) is known as Edvard Munch's inspiration, but to Norwegians, he's famous in his own right for his artistry and giant personality. This extremely realistic painting shows a child dying of tuberculosis, as so many did in Norway in the 19th century. The girl looks directly at you. You can almost feel the cloth, with its many shades of white.

• *And just to the right of this painting, find...*

❼ **Krohg, *Albertine to See the Police Surgeon*, c. 1885-1887:** Krohg had a sharp interest in social justice. In this painting, Albertine, a sweet girl from the countryside, has fallen into the world of prostitution in the big city. She's the new kid on the Red Light block in the 1880s, as Oslo's prostitutes are pulled into the police clinic for their regular checkup. Note her traditional dress and the disdain she gets from the more experienced girls. Krohg has buried his subject in this scene. His technique requires the viewer to find her, and that search helps humanize the prostitute.

• *Facing these paintings in Room 16 is...*

❽ **Erik Werenskiold, *Peasant Burial*, 1883-1885:** While Monet and the Impressionists were busy abandoning the realistic style, Norwegian artists continued to embrace it. In this painting, you're invited to participate. A dead man's funeral is attended by a group of famers and peasants, but only one is a woman—the widow. Their faces speak volumes about the life of toil here. A common thread in Norwegian art is the cycle—the tough cycle—of life. There's also an interest in everyday experiences.

• *Continue through Room 17 and into Room 18.*

Atmosphere

Landscape painters were often fascinated by the phenomena of nature, and the artwork in this room takes us back to this ideal from the Romantic Age. Painters were challenged by capturing atmospheric conditions at a specific moment, since it meant making quick sketches outdoors, before the weather changed yet again.

• *On the right wall as you enter is...*

❾ Harald Sohlberg, *Winter Night in the Mountains*, 1914: Harald Sohlberg was inspired by this image while skiing in the

mountains in the winter of 1899. Over the years, he attempted to re-create the scene that inspired this remark: "The mountains in winter reduce one to silence. One is overwhelmed, as in a mighty, vaulted church, only a thousand times more so."

• *Follow the crowds into Room 19, the Munch room.*

Turmoil

Room 19 is filled with works by Norway's single most famous painter, Edvard Munch (see sidebar). Norway's long, dark winters and social isolation have produced many gloomy artists, but none gloomier than Munch. He infused his work with emotion and expression at the expense of realism. After viewing the paintings in general, take a look at these in particular (listed in clockwise order).

❿ Edvard Munch, *Self Portrait with a Cigarette*, 1895: This painting may not be on view, but the description is worth reading regardless, to set the context for the Munch collection. In this self-portrait, Munch is spooked, haunted—an artist working, immersed in an oppressive world. Indefinable shadows inhabit the background. His hand shakes as he considers his uncertain future. (Ironic, considering he created his masterpieces during this depressed period.) After eight months in a Danish clinic, he found peace—and lost his painting power. Afterward, Munch never again painted another strong example of what we love most about his art.

⓫ Munch, *Madonna*, 1894-1895: Munch had a tortured relationship with women. He never married. He dreaded and struggled with love, writing that he feared if he loved too much, he'd lose his

OSLO

Edvard Munch (1863-1944)

Edvard Munch (pronounced "moonk") is Norway's most famous and influential painter. His life was rich, complex, and sad. His father was a doctor who had a nervous breakdown. His mother and sister both died of tuberculosis. He knew suffering. And he gave us the enduring symbol of 20th-century pain, *The Scream.*

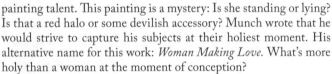

He was also Norway's most forward-thinking painter, a man who traveled extensively through Europe, soaking up the colors of the Post-Impressionists and the curves of Art Nouveau. He helped pioneer a new style—Expressionism—using lurid colors and wavy lines to "express" inner turmoil and the angst of the modern world.

After a nervous breakdown in late 1908, followed by eight months of rehab in a clinic, Munch emerged less troubled—but a less powerful painter. His late works were as a colorist: big, bright, less tormented...and less noticed.

painting talent. This painting is a mystery: Is she standing or lying? Is that a red halo or some devilish accessory? Munch wrote that he would strive to capture his subjects at their holiest moment. His alternative name for this work: *Woman Making Love.* What's more holy than a woman at the moment of conception?

⑫ Munch, *The Scream*, 1893: Munch's most famous work shows a man screaming, capturing the fright many feel as the

human "race" does just that. The figure seems isolated from the people on the bridge—locked up in himself, unable to stifle his scream. Munch made four versions of this scene, which has become *the* textbook example of Expressionism. On one, he graffitied: "This painting is the work of a madman." He explained that the painting "shows today's society, reverberating within me...making me want to scream." He's sharing his internal angst. In fact, this Expressionist masterpiece is a breakthrough painting; it's angst personified.

⓭ Munch, *Dance of Life,* **1899-1900:** In this scene of five dancing couples, we glimpse Munch's notion of femininity. To him, women were a complex mix of Madonna and whore. We see Munch's take on the cycle of women's lives: She's a virgin (discarding the sweet flower of youth), a whore (a jaded temptress in red), and a widow (having destroyed the man, she is finally alone, aging, in black). With the phallic moon rising on the lake, Munch demonizes women as they turn men into green-faced, lusty monsters.

⓮ Munch, *Puberty,* **1894-1895:** One of the artist's most important non-*Scream* canvases reveals his ambivalence about women (see also his *Madonna,* earlier). This adolescent girl, grappling with her emerging sexuality, covers her nudity self-consciously. The looming shadow behind her—frighteningly too big and amorphous—threatens to take over the scene. The shadow's significance is open to interpretation—is it phallic, female genitalia, death, an embodiment of sexual anxiety...or Munch himself?

⓯ Munch, *The Sick Child,* **1896:** The death of Munch's sister in 1877 due to tuberculosis likely inspired this painting. The girl's face melts into the pillow. She's becoming two-dimensional, halfway between life and death. Everything else is peripheral, even her despairing mother saying good-bye. You can see how Munch scraped and repainted the face until he got it right.

• *Our tour is over, but there's more to see in this fine collection. Take a break from Nordic gloom and doom by visiting Rooms 15 and 23 (adjoining each other, in the middle of the museum)—with works by Impressionist and Post-Impressionist artists...even Munch got into the spirit with his Parisian painting, titled* Rue Lafayette. *You'll see lesser-known, but still beautiful, paintings by non-Norwegian big names such as Picasso, Modigliani, Monet, Manet, Van Gogh, Gauguin, Renoir, and Cézanne.*

Near the National Gallery
Royal Palace (Slottet)
Set at the top of Karl Johans Gate, the Neoclassical Royal Palace is home to Norway's King Harald V and Queen Sonja. Completed in 1849, it was extensively (and expensively) renovated in 2001. To quell controversy the public is now invited inside each summer with a one-hour guided tour.

Cost and Hours: 135 NOK, English tours 4/day late June-mid-Aug, tickets go on sale in March and fill fast—it's smart to book in advance at www.ticketmaster.no, or by calling 81 53 31 33, www.kongehuset.no.

National Historical Museum (Historisk Museum)
Directly behind the National Gallery and just below the palace is a fine Art Nouveau building offering an easy (if underwhelming)

peek at Norway's history. It includes the country's top collection of Viking artifacts, displayed in low-tech, old-school exhibits with barely a word of English.

Cost and Hours: 100 NOK, same ticket covers Viking Ship Museum for 48 hours; open Tue-Sun 10:00-17:00, mid-Sept–mid-May 11:00-16:00; closed Mon year-round; Frederiks Gate 2, tel. 22 85 19 00, www.khm.uio.no.

Visiting the Museum: The ground floor has medieval and Viking Age artifacts from around Norway. Ogle the gorgeous carved doors from stave churches (with their filigree-like details). Look for the little door to the easy-to-miss Viking section, where you'll find the museum's hidden highlight: the only intact, authentic Viking helmet ever found in Scandinavia (with an eye mask; it's unceremoniously jammed into a crowded display case). Upstairs is an exhibit about life for the Sami (previously known to outsiders as Laplanders) and other Arctic cultures. It's fun to peek in the cutaway igloo for a glimpse at Inuit lifestyles. There's also a modest anthropological exhibit about indigenous peoples of the Americas. In this overview of the past, a few Egyptian mummies and Norwegian coins through the ages are tossed in for good measure.

FROGNER PARK

The sprawling Frogner Park anchors an upscale neighborhood of the same name, 1.5 miles west of the city center. Here you'll find a breathtaking sculpture park and two museums. The Frognerbadet swimming pool is nearby (see "Escapes from the City," later).

▲▲▲Vigeland Park

Within Oslo's vast Frogner Park is Vigeland Park, containing a lifetime of work by Norway's greatest sculptor, Gustav Vigeland

(see sidebar). In 1921, he made a deal with the city. In return for a great studio and state support, he'd spend his creative life beautifying Oslo with this sculpture garden. From 1924 until his death in 1943 he worked on-site, designing 192 bronze and granite statue groupings—600 figures in all, each nude and unique. Vigeland even planned the landscaping.

Today the park is loved and respected by the people of Oslo (no police, no fences—and no graffiti). At once majestic, hands-on, entertaining, and deeply moving, why this sculpture park isn't considered one of Europe's top artistic

Gustav Vigeland (1869-1943)

Gustav Vigeland's father was a carpenter in the city of Mandal, in southern Norway. Vigeland grew up carving wood, and showed promise. And so, as a young man, he went to Oslo to study sculpture, then supplemented his education with trips abroad to Europe's art capitals. Back home, he carved out a successful, critically acclaimed career feeding newly independent Norway's hunger for homegrown art.

During his youthful trips abroad, Vigeland had frequented the studio of Auguste Rodin, admiring Rodin's naked, restless, intertwined statues. Like Rodin, Vigeland explored the yin/yang relationship of men and women. Also like Rodin, Vigeland did not personally carve or cast his statues. Rather, he formed them in clay or plaster, to be executed by a workshop of assistants. Vigeland's sturdy humans capture universal themes of the cycle of life—birth, childhood, romance, struggle, child-rearing, growing old, and death.

sights, I can only guess. In summer, this is a tempting destination in the late afternoon—after the museums have closed and there's still plenty of daylight to go. (But if you want to visit the nearby Vigeland Museum, be aware that it closes at 17:00.) Vigeland Park is more than great art: It's a city at play. Appreciate its urban Norwegian ambience.

Cost and Hours: The garden is always open and free. The park is safe (cameras monitor for safety) and lit in the evening.

Getting There: Tram #12—which leaves from the central train station, Rådhusplassen in front of City Hall, Aker Brygge, and other points in town—drops you off right at the park gate (Vigelandsparken stop). Tram #19 (with stops along Karl Johans Gate) takes you to Majorstuen, a 10-minute walk to the gate (or you can change at Majorstuen to tram #12 and ride it one stop to Vigelandsparken).

Information and Services: For an illustrated guide and fine souvenir, consider the 120-NOK book in the **visitors center** (Besøkssenter) on your right as you enter. The modern **$$ cafeteria** has sandwiches and light meals (indoor/outdoor seating, daily 9:00-20:30 in summer, shorter hours off-season), plus books, gifts, and pay WCs.

➲ Self-Guided Tour: The park is huge, but this visit is a snap. Here's a quick, four-stop, straight-line, gate-to-monolith tour.

• *Begin by entering the park through the grand gates, from Kirkeveien (with the tram stop). In front of the visitors center, look at the...*

Gustav Vigeland Statue: Vigeland has his hammer and chisel in hand...and is drenched in pigeon poop. Consider his messed-up life. He lived with his many models. His marriages failed. His

children entangled his artistic agenda. He didn't age gracefully. He didn't name his statues, and refused to explain their meanings. While those who know his life story can read it clearly in the granite and bronze, I'd forget Gustav's troubles and see his art as observations on the bittersweet cycle of life in general—from a man who must have had a passion for living.

• Now walk 100 yards toward the fountain and the pillar.

Bridge: The 300-foot-long bridge is bounded by four granite columns: Three show a man fighting a lizard, the fourth shows a woman submitting to the lizard's embrace. Hmmm. (Vigeland was familiar with medieval mythology, where dragons represent man's primal—and sinful—nature.)

But enough lizard love; the 58 bronze statues along the bridge are a general study of the human body. They capture the joys of life (and, on a sunny day, so do the Norwegians and tourists filling the park around you). Many deal with relationships between people. In the middle, on the right, find the circular statue of a man and woman going round and round—perhaps the eternal attraction and love between the sexes. But directly opposite, another circle feels like a prison—man against the world, with no refuge.

On your left, see the famous *Sinnataggen*, the hot-headed little boy and a symbol of the park. (Notice his left hand is worn shiny from too many hand-holdings.) It's said Vigeland gave a boy chocolate and then took it away to get this reaction. Look below the angry toddler, to the lower terrace—with eight bronze infants circling a head-down fetus.

• Continue through a rose garden to the earliest sculpture unit in the park.

Fountain: Six giants hold a fountain, symbolically toiling with the burden of life, as water—the source of life—cascades steadily around them. Twenty tree-of-life groups surround the fountain. Four clumps of trees (on each corner) show humanity's relationship to nature and the seasons of life: childhood, young love, adulthood, and winter.

Take a quick swing through life, starting on the right with youth. In the branches you'll see a swarm of children (Vigeland

called them "geniuses"): A boy
sits in a tree, boys actively climb
while most girls stand by quiet-
ly, and a girl glides through the
branches wide-eyed and ready
for life...and love. Circle clockwise to the next stage: love
scenes. In the third corner, life

becomes more complicated: a sad woman in an animal-like tree, a
lonely child, a couple plummeting downward (perhaps falling out
of love), a man desperately clinging to his tree, and finally an angry
man driving away babies. The fourth corner completes the cycle, as
death melts into the branches of the tree of life and you realize new
geniuses will bloom.

The 60 bronze reliefs circling the basin develop the theme
further, showing man mixing with nature and geniuses giving the
carousel of life yet another spin. Speaking of another spin, circle
again and follow these reliefs.

The pattern in the pavers surrounding the basin is a maze—
life's long and winding road with twists, dead ends, frustrations,
and, ultimately, a way out. If you have about an hour to spare, enter
the labyrinth (on the side nearest the park's entrance gate, there's a
single break in the black border) and follow the white granite path
until (on the monolith side) you finally get out. (Tracing this path
occupies older kids, affording parents a peaceful break in the park.)
• *Or you can go straight up the steps to the...*

Monolith: The centerpiece of the park—a teeming monolith
of life surrounded by 36 groups of granite statues—continues Vige-

land's cycle-of-life motif. The figures are
hunched and clearly earthbound, while
Vigeland explores a lifetime of human
relationships. At the center, 121 figures
carved out of a single block of stone rock-
et skyward. Three stone carvers worked
daily for 14 years, cutting Vigeland's full-
size plaster model into the final 180-ton,
50-foot-tall erection.

Circle the plaza, once to trace the
stages of life in the 36 statue groups, and a
second time to enjoy how Norwegian kids
relate to the art. The statues—both young
and old—seem to speak to children.

Vigeland lived barely long enough to see his monolith raised.
Covered with bodies, it seems to pick up speed as it spirals skyward. Some people seem to naturally rise. Others struggle not to
fall. Some help others. Although the granite groups around the

monolith are easy to understand, Vigeland left the meaning of the monolith itself open. Like life, it can be interpreted many different ways.

From this summit of the park, look a hundred yards farther, where four children and three adults are intertwined and spinning in the Wheel of Life. Now, look back at the entrance. If the main gate is at 12 o'clock, the studio where Vigeland lived and worked—now the Vigeland Museum—is at 2 o'clock (see the green copper tower poking above the trees). His ashes sit in the top of the tower in clear view of the monolith. If you liked the park, visit the Vigeland Museum (described next), a delightful five-minute walk away, for an intimate look at the art and how it was made.

▲▲Vigeland Museum

This palatial city-provided studio was Gustav Vigeland's home and workplace for the last two decades of his life. The high south-facing

windows provided just the right light. Vigeland, who had a deeply religious upbringing, saw his art as an expression of his soul. He once said, "The road between feeling and execution should be as short as possible." Here, immersed in his work, Vigeland supervised his craftsmen like a father, from 1924 until his death in 1943.

Today it's filled with plaster casts and studies of many of the works you'll see in the adjacent park—shedding new light on that masterpiece, and allowing you to see familiar pieces from new angles. It also holds a few additional works, and explains Vigeland's creative (and technical) process. While his upstairs apartment is usually closed to the public, it is open a few times a year—check the website to find out when.

Cost and Hours: 80 NOK; Tue-Sun 10:00-17:00, Sept-April 12:00-16:00, closed Mon year-round; bus #20 or tram #12 to Frogner Plass, Nobels Gate 32, tel. 23 49 37 00, www.vigeland.museum.no.

Visiting the Museum: It's all on one floor, roughly arranged chronologically, which you'll see in an easy clockwise loop. **Rooms I-III** explain Vigeland's development, including his early focus on biblical themes. In *Accused* (1891), Cain flees with his family, including their dog. But gradually, Vigeland grew more interested in the dynamics that dictate relationships in families, and between men and women. In these first rooms, look for two particularly touching sculptures in marble (a medium you won't often see used by Vigeland): *Mother and Child* (1909) and *Young Man and Woman* (1906).

Room IV is a long hall of portrait busts, which Vigeland often created without payment—he considered this task an opportunity to practice. While most of the busts don't depict famous people, you will see King Oscar II and Arctic explorer Fridtjof Nansen. **Room V** continues this theme, with a few portraits (mostly full-body) of more recognizable figures: Beethoven, Ibsen, Wergeland, Bjørnson.

Room VI, with a 1942 self-portrait, explains the process by which Vigeland created his statues. See his tools displayed in a case, and read the explanation: Using the "sand casting" method, Vigeland would make a small plaster model, which guided his workers in creating a metal "skeleton." Vigeland would then bring the skeleton to life with soft clay—which he enjoyed using because its pliability allowed him to be spontaneous in his creativity. Once the clay piece was finished, plaster and sand were used to create a plaster cast, used for the final bronze piece. For his stone works, they used a "pointing machine" to painstakingly measure the exact nuances of Vigeland's contours. Examples of using both methods (including five different versions of the famous "angry baby" bronze) are displayed around the room.

Room VII holds temporary exhibits, while **Room VIII** features the full-sized plaster models for the park's bronze fountain. The large **Room IX** has more pieces from the park, including a one-fifth-scale model of the fountain (used to win the Oslo City Council's support for the project) and the four dragon statues that top the bridge's pillars (high up and difficult to see in the park, but fascinating up close).

Room X is the dramatic climax of the museum, with a model of the entire park, and the life-size plaster models for the Monolith—in three pieces, making it easy to scrutinize the details. You'll also see wrought-iron chained dragons—originally designed as a feature for the park gates—and several plaster models for the statues that surround the Monolith. Notice the many little "freckles" on these statues, left behind by the pointer used by craftsmen to replicate Vigeland's work. The museum finishes with more temporary exhibits (in Rooms XI and XII).

Nearby: Across the street from the Vigeland Museum is the **Oslo City Museum** (Oslo Bymuseum)—a modest, hard-to-be-thrilled-about exhibit that tells the story of Oslo. For a quick overview of the city while escaping the rain, watch the 15-minute English video (free, Tue-Sun 11:00-16:00, closed Mon, in Frogner Manor Farm across street from Vigeland Museum, tel. 23 28 41 70, www.oslomuseum.no).

BYGDØY NEIGHBORHOOD

This thought-provoking and exciting cluster of sights, worth ▲▲, is on a parklike peninsula just across the harbor from downtown Oslo. It provides a busy and rewarding half-day (at a minimum) of sightseeing.

Here, within a short walk, are six major sights (listed in order of importance): the **Norwegian Folk Museum,** an open-air museum with traditional wooden buildings from all corners of the country, a stave church, and a collection of 20th-century urban buildings; the **Viking Ship Museum,** showing off the best-preserved Viking ships in existence; the **Fram Museum,** showcasing the modern Viking spirit with the *Fram,* the ship of Arctic-exploration fame, and the *Gjøa,* the first ship to sail through the Northwest Passage; the **Kon-Tiki Museum,** starring the *Kon-Tiki* and the *Ra II,* in which Norwegian explorer Thor Heyerdahl proved that early civilizations—with their existing technologies—could have crossed the oceans; the **Norwegian Maritime Museum,** interesting mostly to old salts, has a wonderfully scenic movie of Norway; and the **Norwegian Holocaust Center,** memorializing the Holocaust in Norway.

Getting to Bygdøy: Sailing from downtown to Bygdøy is fun, fast, and gets you in a seafaring mood. Ride the Bygdøy **ferry**—marked *Public Ferry Bygdøy Museums*—from pier 3 in front of City Hall (45 NOK one-way at the ticket desk, 60 NOK on board; 65 NOK round-trip at the ticket desk; covered by Oslo Pass; 3/hour, 10-15-minute trip; runs mid-May-Aug daily 8:55-20:55, fewer sailings spring and fall, doesn't run mid-Oct-mid-March). Boats generally leave from downtown at :05, :25, and :45 past each hour. In summer, avoid the nearby (much more expensive) tour boats.

For a less memorable approach, you can take **bus** #30 (from train station, National Theater, or in front of City Hall, direction: Bygdøy; 20-minute trip).

Returning to Oslo: Note that after 17:00, bus and boat departures back to downtown are sparse. If returning by ferry, get to the dock a little early—otherwise the boat is likely to be full, and you'll have to wait for the next sailing.

Getting Around Bygdøy: The Norwegian Folk and Viking Ship museums are a 10-minute walk from the ferry's first stop (Dronningen). The other boating museums (Fram, Kon-Tiki, and Maritime) are at the second ferry stop, in an area called Bygdøynes. The Holocaust Center is off Fredriksborgveien, about halfway between these two museum clusters. All Bygdøy sights are within

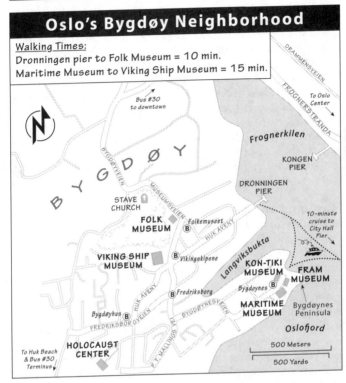

Oslo's Bygdøy Neighborhood

Walking Times:
Dronningen pier to Folk Museum = 10 min.
Maritime Museum to Viking Ship Museum = 15 min.

a pleasant (when sunny) 15-minute walk of each other. The walk gives you a picturesque taste of suburban Oslo.

City bus #30 connects the sights four times hourly in this order: Norwegian Folk Museum, Viking Ship Museum, Kon-Tiki Museum, Norwegian Holocaust Center. (For the Holocaust Center, you'll use the Bygdøyhus stop a long block away; tell the bus driver you want the stop for the "HL-Senteret.") The bus turns around at its final stop (Huk), then passes the sights in reverse order on its way back to the city center.

Planning Your Day: If the weather's good, hit the Folk Museum first (before it gets too hot). If it's ugly out—but may get better—begin with the mostly indoor boat museums at Bygdøynes. The marginally interesting Holocaust Center is a bit of a detour, and skippable if you're short on time. The Bygdøynes museums offer a 10 percent discount if you buy tickets for all three at the same time; decide before you buy your first ticket, and save a few bucks. The major museums all have free lockers, Wi-Fi, and WCs.

Eating at Bygdøy: Each of the museum areas has **$** food options. At the boat museum cluster (Bygdøynes), you'll find the **Framheim Café** inside the Fram Museum; the little **Cargo Café**

window with hot dogs and ice cream outside the Kon-Tiki Museum; and two more substantial eateries at the Maritime Museum: an **indoor café** with sandwiches and soup, and the outdoor **Fjordterrassen Café,** with hot dogs and deep-fried fish and veggie burgers, and tables overlooking the harbor. The Norwegian Folk Museum has a decent **Kafe Arkadia** at its entrance, and a fun little **farmers market** stall across the street (produce, drinks, yogurt—just enough to forage a healthy lunch). The Viking Ship Museum has an outdoor **snack window** selling shrimp and salmon sandwiches. The Holocaust Center has a small **café** upstairs.

Beach at Bygdøy: A popular beach is located at Huk, on the southwest tip of the peninsula.

Museums on Bygdøy
▲▲Norwegian Folk Museum (Norsk Folkemuseum)
Brought from all corners of Norway, 150 buildings have been re-assembled here on 35 acres. While Stockholm's Skansen was the first museum of this kind to open to the public, this collection is a bit older, started in 1881 as the king's private collection (and the inspiration for Skansen). The folk museum is most lively (and worth ▲▲▲) June through mid-August, when buildings are open and staffed with attendants in period clothing (who'll happily answer your questions—so ask many). And during peak season you'll also see craftspeople doing their traditional things and barnyard animals roaming about. Otherwise, the indoor museum is fine, but the park is just a pleasant walk past lots of locked-up log cabins.

Cost and Hours: 130 NOK, daily 10:00-18:00—grounds open until 20:00; mid-Sept-mid-May park open Mon-Fri 11:00-15:00, Sat-Sun until 16:00 but most historical buildings closed; Museumsveien 10, bus #30 stops immediately in front, tel. 22 12 37 00, www.norskfolkemuseum.no.

Visiting the Museum: Think of the visit in three parts: the park sprinkled with old buildings, the re-created old town, and the folk-art museum. As you enter, you'll cut through the courtyard with the museum to reach the open-air sections.

Upon arrival, pick up the site map and review the list of the day's activities, concerts, and guided tours (on a video screen near the ticket desk). In summer, there are two guided tours in English per day; the Telemark Farm hosts a small daily fiddle-and-folk-dance show; and a folk music-and-dance show is held each Sunday. If you don't take a tour, invest in a guidebook and ask questions of the informative attendants stationed in buildings throughout the park.

The **park** is loaded with mostly log-built, sod-roofed cabins from various parts of Norway (arranged roughly geographically). Be sure to go inside the buildings. The evocative Gol stave church,

at the top of a hill at the park's edge, is worth the climb. Built in 1212 in Hallingdal and painstakingly reconstructed here, it has a classic design and, inside, beautiful-yet-primitive wood paintings on the apse walls (c. 1452). If you won't make it to a stave church elsewhere on your trip, this is a must. (For more on stave churches, see page 9.)

Back near the entrance building, the **old town** has a variety of homes and shops that focus on urban lifestyles. It's worth exploring the tenement building, in which you can explore intimate, fully furnished apartments from various generations and lifestyles—1905, 1930, 1950, 1979, and even a Norwegian-Pakistani apartment.

In the **museum,** the ground floor beautifully presents woody, colorfully painted, and exactingly carved folk art; traditional Norwegian knitting; and weapons. Upstairs are exquisite-in-a-peasant-kind-of-way folk costumes. I'd skip the sleepy collection of Norwegian church art (in an adjoining building). But don't miss the best Sami culture exhibit I've seen in Scandinavia (across the courtyard in the green building, behind the toy exhibit). Everything is thoughtfully explained in English. A new exhibit showing various slices of Oslo life is scheduled to open in 2019.

▲▲Viking Ship Museum (Vikingskiphuset)

In this impressive museum, you'll gaze with admiration at two finely crafted, majestic oak Viking ships dating from the 9th and

10th centuries, and the scant remains of a third vessel. Along with the two well-preserved ships, you'll see the bones of Vikings buried with these vessels and remarkable artifacts that may cause you to consider these notorious raiders in a different light. Over a thousand years ago, three things drove Vikings on their far-flung raids: hard economic times in their bleak homeland, the lure of prosperous and vulnerable communities to the south, and a mastery of the sea. There was a time when most frightened Europeans closed every prayer with, "And deliver us from the Vikings, Amen." Gazing up at the prow of one of these sleek, time-stained vessels, you can almost hear the screams and smell the armpits of those redheads on the rampage.

Cost and Hours: 100 NOK, ticket also covers the National

Historical Museum in downtown Olso for 48 hours; daily 9:00-18:00, Oct-April 10:00-16:00; Huk Aveny 35, tel. 22 13 52 80, www.khm.uio.no.

Visitor Information: The museum doesn't offer tours, but everything is well-described in English. You can use the free Wi-Fi to download a free, informative audio tour app. You probably don't need the little museum guidebook—it repeats exactly what's already posted on the exhibits.

Visiting the Museum: Focus on the two well-preserved ships, starting with the *Oseberg*, from A.D. 834. With its ornate carving and impressive rudder, it was likely a royal pleasure craft. It seems designed for sailing on calm inland waters during festivals, but not in the open ocean.

The *Gokstad*, from A.D. 950, is a practical working boat, capable of sailing the high seas. A ship like this brought settlers to the west of France (Normandy was named for the Norsemen). And in such a vessel, explorers such as Eric the Red hopscotched from Norway to Iceland to Greenland and on to what they called Vinland—today's Newfoundland in Canada. Imagine 30 men hauling on long oars out at sea for weeks and months at a time. In 1892, a replica of this ship sailed from Norway to America in 44 days to celebrate the 400th anniversary of Columbus *not* discovering America.

You'll also see the ruins of a third vessel, the **Tune Ship** (c. A.D. 910), which saw service only briefly before being used as the tomb for an important chieftain. In this hall, every 20 minutes, the lights dim and a wrap-around film plays on the walls around the ship for five minutes—with dramatic virtual footage of the Vikings and their fleet.

The ships tend to steal the show, but don't miss the hall displaying **jewelry and personal items** excavated along with the ships. The ships and related artifacts survived so well because they were buried in clay as part of a gravesite. Many of the finest items were not actually Viking art, but goodies they brought home after raiding more advanced (but less tough) people. Still, there are lots of actual Viking items, such as metal and leather goods, that give insight into their culture. Highlights are the cart and sleighs, ornately carved with scenes from Viking sagas.

▲▲▲Fram Museum (Frammuseet)

Under its distinctive A-frame roof, this museum holds the 125-foot, steam- and sail-powered ship that took modern-day Vikings Roald Amundsen and Fridtjof Nansen deep into the Arctic and Antarctic, farther north and south than any vessel had gone before. In an adjacent A-frame is Amundsen's *Gjøa,* the first ship to sail through the Northwest Passage. Together, the exhibit spins a fascinating tale of adventure, scientific exploration, and human determination...all at subzero temperatures.

Cost and Hours: 100 NOK; daily June-Aug 9:00-18:00, May and Sept 10:00-17:00, Oct and March-April until 16:00; Nov-Feb Mon-Fri 10:00-15:00, Sat-Sun until 16:00; Bygdøynesveien 36, tel. 23 28 29 50, www.frammuseum.no.

OSLO

Visiting the Museum: Stepping into the museum, you're immediately bow-to-bow with the 128-foot *Fram.* Before diving in, remember that there are two parts to the museum: The *Fram,* which you're looking at, and to the left through a tunnel, the smaller *Gjøa.* I'd see the *Gjøa* first, because it's a better lead-up to the main event, and because it features a short film that's a fine introduction to the entire museum.

Crossing through the tunnel to the *Gjøa,* you'll learn about the search for the Northwest Passage (that long-sought-after trade route through the Arctic from the Atlantic to the Pacific). Exhibits tell the story of how Roald Amundsen and a crew of six used this motor- and sail-powered ship to successfully navigate the Northwest Passage (1903-1906). Exhibits describe their ordeal as well as other Arctic adventures, such as Amundsen's 1925 flight to 88 degrees north (they had to build a runway out of ice to take off and return home); and his 1926 airship (zeppelin) expedition from Oslo over the North Pole to Alaska. This section also features a 100-seat cinema showing an excellent 15-minute film about the exploration of the earth's polar regions (shows every 15 minutes).

Now return to the *Fram,* and peruse the exhibits—actual artifacts and profiles of the brave explorers and their crew. The upper floor focuses on Nansen's voyages to the North Pole on the *Fram,* including an early kayak, a full-size stuffed polar bear, and a model of the ship. Here you can cross a gangway to explore the *Fram*'s claustrophobic but fascinating interior. A simulated "Northern Lights Show," best viewed from the *Fram*'s main deck, is presented every 20 minutes.

Exhibits on the middle floor focus on Admundsen, who picked up where Nansen left off and explored the South Pole. You'll see an actual dogsled Admundsen's team used, and a small model of the motorized sled used by the rival Scott expedition. Also featured are a tent like the one Amundsen used, reconstructed shelves from his Arctic kitchen, models of the *Fram,* and a "polar simulator" plunging visitors into a 15° Fahrenheit environment.

The Fram Museum: From Pole to Pole

The Fram Museum tells the tale of two great Norwegian explorers, Fridtjof Nansen and Roald Amundsen.

Early polar explorers focused on the Northwest Passage, believing the Arctic could hold a highly lucrative trade route between the Atlantic and the Pacific oceans. Englishman John Franklin famously led a failed expedition looking for the Northwest Passage in 1845; two ships and 129 men were never seen again. Many others attempted and failed—more than a thousand sailors were lost in the search.

A generation later, with the Northwest Passage conquered by Amundsen, explorers (inspired by tales of Franklin and his ilk) became determined to reach the North Pole.

Fridtjof Nansen (1861-1930) prepared for his North Pole expedition by crossing the inland ice of Greenland in six weeks in 1888—hand-pulling sledges all the way—and then spent the winter learning from Inuit people he met. Nansen also commissioned the *Fram,* which was purpose-built for Arctic exploration—with its rounded hull, it was designed to be stuck in the ice without being crushed. (The downside was that it got tossed around in fierce waves.) It even had a windmill that could power electric lights. In the end, the *Fram* went on three major expeditions. In each one, the crew set out knowing they'd be living in subzero temperatures for three to five years.

The *Fram*'s maiden voyage was Nansen's search for the North Pole (1893-1896). He believed that, due to the natural drifting of the northern ice cap, a ship encased in ice would simply be carried by currents to the North Pole. For three years, the *Fram* drifted, trapped in the Arctic ice. While he didn't reach the North Pole, Nansen made better progress than anyone before him.

Then, **Otto Sverdrup** (1854-1930) took the helm of the *Fram* and advanced Nansen's progress (riding icebergs from 1898 until 1902), but he didn't make it all the way, either.

Finally, **Roald Amundsen** (1872-1928)—who had already successfully sailed the Northwest Passage—made plans to reach the North Pole in the *Fram* in 1910. Amundsen's crew (and financiers) believed he was heading north. But when word came that American explorer Frederick Cook had already accomplished that feat, Amundsen decided to head south instead. He sailed the *Fram* to Antarctica, and set out to reach the South Pole (1910-1912). Amundsen and his team were in a race to the pole with Englishman Robert Falcon Scott and his men, who had arrived at a different location aboard the ship *Terra Nova.* Amundsen beat Scott to the South Pole by about a month. And, unlike Scott, Amundsen made it home alive.

The *Fram* expeditions coincided with the nascent Norwegian independence movement—and became a proud patriotic symbol of the Norwegian people.

▲▲Kon-Tiki Museum (Kon-Tiki Museet)

Next to the *Fram* is a museum housing the *Kon-Tiki* and the *Ra II*, the ships built by the larger-than-life anthropologist, seafarer, and adventurer Thor Heyerdahl (1914-2002). Heyerdahl and his crew used these ships—constructed entirely without modern technology—to undertake tropical voyages many had thought impossible. Both ships are well-displayed and described in English. This museum—more lighthearted than the other boat-focused exhibits—puts you in a castaway mood.

Cost and Hours: 100 NOK, daily 9:30-18:00, March-May and Sept-Oct 10:00-17:00, Nov-Feb until 16:00, Bygdøynesveien 36, tel. 23 08 67 67, www.kon-tiki.no.

Background: Thor Heyerdahl believed that early South Americans could have crossed the Pacific to settle Polynesia. To prove his point, in 1947 Heyerdahl and five crewmates constructed the *Kon-Tiki* raft out of balsa wood, using only premodern tools and techniques—and adorned with a giant image of the sun god Kon-Tiki on the sail. They set sail from Peru on the tiny craft, surviving for 101 days on fish, coconuts, and sweet potatoes (which were native to Peru). About 4,300 miles later, they arrived in Polynesia. (While Heyerdahl proved that early South Americans *could* have made this trip, anthropologists doubt they did.) The *Kon-Tiki* story became a best-selling book and award-winning documentary (and helped spawn the "Tiki" culture craze in the US). Funded by the *Kon-Tiki* success, Heyerdahl went on to explore Easter Island (1955), and then turned his attention to another voyage—this time across the Atlantic. In 1970, Heyerdahl's *Ra II* made a similar 3,000-mile journey from Morocco to Barbados—on a vessel made of reeds—to prove that Africans could have populated the Americas.

Visiting the Museum: You'll see both the *Kon-Tiki* and the *Ra II*, and learn about Heyerdahl's other adventures (including Easter Island and the *Ra I*, which sank partway into its journey). Everything's well-described in English and very kid-friendly. In the basement, you'll see the bottom of the vessel with a life-size model of a whale shark (the largest fish on earth) and other marine life that the crew observed at sea. Nearby, a small theater continuously plays a 10-minute documentary about the voyage; every day at 12:00, they show the full-length (67-minute), Oscar-winning 1950 documentary film *Kon-Tiki*.

▲Norwegian Maritime Museum (Norsk Maritimt Museum)

If you're into the sea and seafaring, this museum is a salt lick, providing a wide-ranging look at Norway's maritime heritage through exhibits, art, and a panoramic film soaring over Norway's long and varied coastline.

OSLO

Cost and Hours: 100 NOK; daily 10:00-17:00; Sept-mid-May Tue-Sun until 16:00, closed Mon; Bygdøynesveien 37, tel. 22 12 37 00, www.marmuseum.no.

Visiting the Museum: On the ground floor, you'll see a collection of small vessels, temporary exhibits, and an exhibit called *At Sea (Til Sjøs)*, exploring what life is like on the ocean, from Viking days to the present. If you appreciate maritime art, the collection in the gallery should float your boat. Downstairs is *The Ship (Skipet)*, tracing two millennia of maritime development. You'll see a 2,200-year-old dugout boat, heft various materials used to make ships, and pilot model boats in a little lagoon. Nearby, watch the wrap-around, 20-minute movie *The Ocean: A Way of Life* (look for *Supervideografen* signs). Dated but still dramatic—and quite relaxing—it swoops you scenically over Norway's diverse coast, showing off fishing townscapes, shiplap villages, industrial harbors, and breathtaking scenery from here all the way to North Cape in a comfy theater (starts at the top and bottom of the hour). Upstairs, past the library, the *Norway Is the Sea* exhibit considers how technology has transformed the way Norwegians earn their living at sea.

Norwegian Holocaust Center (HL-Senteret)

Located in the stately former home of Nazi collaborator Vidkun Quisling—whose name is synonymous with "complicit in atrocities"—this museum and study center offers a high-tech look at the racist ideologies that fueled the Holocaust. It's designed primarily for Norwegians, but you can borrow a tablet with English translations of the exhibits. The ground floor displays historical documents about the rise of anti-Semitism and personal effects from Holocaust victims. The exhibits continue downstairs; near the end of the exhibit, the names of 760 Norwegian Jews killed by the Nazis are listed in a bright, white room. Out front, the *Innocent Questions* glass-and-neon sculpture shows an old-fashioned punch card, reminding viewers of how the Norwegian puppet government collected seemingly innocuous information before deporting its Jews.

Cost and Hours: 70 NOK; daily 10:00-18:00; Sept-May Mon-Fri 10:00-16:00, Sat-Sun from 11:00; Huk Aveny 56—take bus #30 to the Bygdøyhus stop and follow brown *HL-Senteret* signs, tel. 22 84 21 00, www.hlsenteret.no.

GRÜNERLØKKA AND GRØNLAND DISTRICTS

Oslo's Grünerløkka district is trendy, and workaday Grønland is emerging as a fun spot. The Akers River bisects Grünerløkka. You can connect the dots by taking my self-guided "Up Akers River and Down Grünerløkka Walk."

In Cold Blood

Norway likes to think of itself as a quiet, peaceful nation on the edge of Europe—after all, its legislators award the Nobel Peace Prize. So the events of July 22, 2011—when an anti-immigration fanatic named Anders Behring Breivik set off a car bomb in Oslo, killing eight, and then traveled to a summer camp where he shot and killed 69 young people and counselors—had a profound effect on the country's psyche.

Unlike other European nations, Norway had escaped 21st-century terrorism until Breivik's attack. When the public learned that the man behind the bombing and gunfire was a native Norwegian—dressed in a policeman's uniform—who hunted down his victims in cold blood, it became a national nightmare. Though Norwegians are often characterized as stoic, there was a huge outpouring of grief. Bouquets flooded the square in front of Oslo Cathedral.

Arrested after the shootings, Breivik was described by police as a gun-loving fundamentalist obsessed with what he saw as the "threat" of multiculturalism and immigration to Norwegian values. His targets were the Norwegian government and politically active youths—some only 14 years old—at an island summer camp sponsored by Norway's center-left party.

Norway has a big and growing immigrant community. More than 11 percent of today's citizens are not ethnic Norwegians, and a quarter of Oslo's residents are immigrants. These "new Norwegians" have provided a much-needed and generally appreciated labor force, filling jobs that wealthy natives would rather not do.

Horrified by Breivik's actions, many Norwegians went out of their way to make immigrants feel welcome after the attack. But there is some resentment in a country that is disinclined to be a melting pot. There have been scuffles between Norwegian gangs and immigrant groups. Another source of friction is the tough love Norwegians feel they get from their government compared to the easy ride offered to needy immigrants: "They even get pocket money in jail!"

The country strengthened its immigration laws in 2014, but Norway seems determined not to let the July 22 massacre poison its peaceful soul. Calls for police to start carrying weapons or to reinstate the death penalty were quickly rejected. "Breivik wanted to change Norway," an Oslo resident told me. "We're determined to keep Norway the way it was."

OSLO

Akers River

This river, though only about five miles long, powered Oslo's early industry: flour mills in the 1300s, sawmills in the 1500s, and Norway's Industrial Revolution in the 1800s. A walk along the river not only spans Oslo's history, but also shows the contrast the city offers. The bottom of the river (where this walk doesn't go)—bordered by the high-rise Oslo Radisson Blu Plaza Hotel and the "Little Pakistan" neighborhood of Grønland—has its share of drunks and drugs, reflecting a new urban reality in Oslo. Farther up, the river valley becomes a park as it winds past decent-size waterfalls and red-brick factories. The source of the river (and Oslo's drinking water) is the pristine Lake Maridal, situated at the edge of the Nordmarka wilderness. The idyllic recreation scenes along Lake Maridal are a favorite for nature-loving Norwegians.

▲Grünerløkka

The Grünerløkka district is the largest planned urban area in Oslo. It was built in the latter half of the 1800s to house the legions of workers employed at the factories powered by the Akers River. The first buildings were modeled on similar places built in Berlin. (German visitors observe that there's now more turn-of-the-20th-century Berlin here than in present-day Berlin.) While slummy in the 1980s, today it's trendy. Locals sometimes refer to it as "Oslo's Greenwich Village." Although that's a stretch, it is a bustling area with lots of cafés, good spots for a fun meal, and few tourists.

Getting There: Grünerløkka can be reached from the center of town by a short ride on tram #11, #12, or #13, or by taking the interesting walk described next.

▲Trendy Riverside Oslo: Up Akers River and Down Grünerløkka Walk

While every tourist explores the harborfront and main drag of Oslo, few venture north into this neighborhood that evokes the Industrial Revolution. Once housing poor workers, it now attracts Norwegian hipsters and foodie tourists. This hike up the Akers River, finishing in the stylish Grünerløkka district, shines a different, more livable, and more appealing light on Oslo than the staid and touristy central zone. Allow about an hour at a brisk pace, including a fair bit of up and down and a 20-minute detour en route.

While there are a few "sights" along this walk, they're all skippable—making this a fun experience on a sunny early evening, after the museums have closed, when Oslo's young people are out enjoying their riverside park. (Several excellent dining opportunities are along or near this walk.)

Begin the walk by leaving Karl Johans Gate where it crests (alongside the Parliament building, by the T-bane stop), and head

OSLO

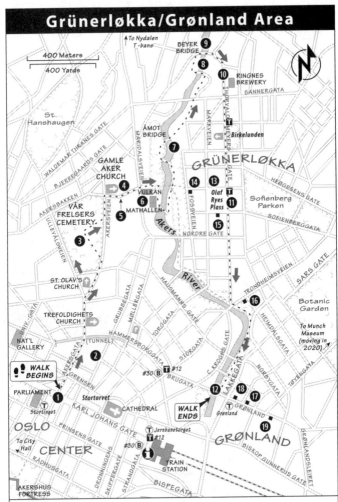

Grünerløkka/Grønland Area

Walk

❶ Akersgata

❷ July 2011 Bombing Site

❸ Vår Frelsers Cemetery

❹ Gamle Aker Church

❺ Telthusbakken Road

❻ Mathallen Oslo & Vulkan Depot

❼ Åmotbrua (Bridge)

❽ Big Waterfall

❾ Fabrikkjentene Statue & Honse-Lovisas Hus

❿ Thorvald Meyers Gate

⓫ Olaf Ryes Plass

⓬ Vaterlands Bridge

Eateries & Nightlife

⓭ Olaf Ryes Plass Eateries

⓮ Tim Wendelboe Coffee

⓯ Ryes Bar

⓰ Südøst Asian Crossover Rest.

⓱ Punjab Tandoori & Asylet

⓲ Istanbul & Dattera Til Hagen

⓳ Olympen Brown Pub

up ❶ **Akersgata**—Oslo's "Fleet Street," lined with major newspaper companies.

After two blocks, at **Apotekergata,** you'll notice stout barriers blocking car traffic, and may see some construction work to the right. Continue into the big plaza. ❷ Behind the tall, blocky building, on Grubbegata, was where a car bomb went off on July 22, 2011 (see the "In Cold Blood" sidebar). Four buildings in the area suffered structural damage—including the long, low-lying one to the left (it's slated to be torn down and replaced; if it's still there, notice the Picasso mural on the side). You may also see (on the right as you face the big building) a small visitors center marked *22. juli-senteret,* with photographs and information about the event. Along the street, notice the row of newspaper headlines under shattered glass. These were displayed in a newspaper office's window just down Akersgata, and have been preserved here—symbolizing how, for Oslo residents, time stood still on that fateful Friday morning.

Continuing straight past this somber site, you'll approach the massive brick Trefoldighets Church. Passing that, angle right onto the uphill street called **Akersveien,** along the side of the pointy-steepled St. Olav's Church. Hiking up this quiet street, you'll pass some traditional wooden houses. This is what much of "Christiania" (as Oslo was then called) looked like in the early 20th century; after World War II, most of this classic architecture was torn down in favor of modern construction.

After passing a square with a big pool, watch on the left for the entrance gate to the ❸ **Vår Frelsers (Our Savior's) Cemetery.** Stop at the big metal map just inside the gate to chart your course through the cemetery: You'll go through the light-green Æres-lunden section—with the biggest plots and VIP graves (including Munch, Ibsen, Bjørnson, and many of the painters whose works you can see in the National Gallery)—then veer right to return to Akersveien, using the exit at the far end (#13).

Once oriented, head into the cemetery and bear right, into the elevated, walled area. The tall, green, canopied grave belongs to **Henrik Wergeland** (1808-1845), Norway's national poet and instrumental in creating its May 17th celebrations (including the children's parade). Wergeland is beloved not only for his poetry, but as a champion of civil rights: He spent his life fighting a clause in the Norwegian constitution that denied the rights of citizenship to Jews. A few years after his death, it was removed.

Go up the path to the right of Wergeland, into the uppermost part of the cemetery. Bear left with the path, then turn left again.

You'll pass the grave of painter Christian Krohg on your left, then reach the grave of the great Expressionist painter, **Edvard Munch** (1863-1944).

At Munch's 10 o'clock, walk under the drooping tree to the tall, obelisk-topped tomb—that of **Henrik Ibsen** (1828-1906), the great Norwegian playwright. Notice the hammer engraved in his tomb, an allusion to an Ibsen poem that spoke of a man chipping away inside a cave. This represents the determination of Ibsen the artist—who would walk the streets of Oslo, lost in thought, painstakingly crafting his next masterpiece in his mind.

Facing Ibsen's grave, turn left and walk toward the yellow house, exiting through the nearby gate. Turn left and walk 100 yards up Akersveien to the Romanesque ❹ **Gamle Aker Church** (from the 1100s)—the oldest building in Oslo. The church, which fell into ruins and has been impressively rebuilt, is rarely open and is pretty bare inside except for a pulpit and baptismal font from the 1700s.

On the little terrace just below the church, notice the **stone marker** indicating 639 kilometers to Nidaros Cathedral in Trondheim—the burial place of the great Norwegian king/saint, Olav II (995-1030). Olav was instrumental in Christianizing Norway, and his tomb in Trondheim was the focus of Norway's main medieval pilgrimage route. Walking half the length of Norway by foot offered forgiveness of sins. Like the Camino de Santiago in northern Spain, this pilgrimage route—long forgotten—is again en vogue, not only for spiritual reasons, but for anyone who simply wants a long walk with time to think. If you're up for a slightly longer walk than this one, the modern pilgrimage office is in the pink, half-timbered building across the street.

From the church, backtrack 20 yards, head left at the red hydrant, and go downhill on the steep ❺ **Telthusbakken** road toward the huge, gray former grain silos (now student housing). This delightful lane is lined with colorful old wooden houses: Constructed by people who were too poor to meet the no-wood fire-safety building codes within the city limits, so they built in what used to be suburbs. Also notice the little neighborhood garden patches on the right (through the fence).

At the bottom of Telthusbakken, you'll reach busy **Maridalsveien** street. Cross it and turn left to the trendy, modern Vulkan shopping center. Follow the driveway just in front of Vulkan as it curls down behind the building and to the recommended ❻ **Mathallen**—a foodie paradise, with more than a dozen stalls selling every kind of cuisine imaginable, and lots of outdoor tables filling an inviting plaza. (For more on Mathallen—including several great eateries here—see "Eating in Oslo," later.)

Find the **bridge** over the river at the near end of Mathallen (just follow the sound of the waterfall). You'll pop out into a beautiful little square. Turn left just before the playground, and walk along the river (with the silo housing on your right). At the waterfall, look down on your left to see fish ladders—which allow salmon and sea trout to make their way back upstream to spawn. Farther along, enjoy a little stretch of **boardwalk** that's cantilevered to stick out over the waterfall.

The lively **Grünerløkka** district is just to your right. But if you have 20 minutes and a little energy, detour upstream first, then hook back down. Continuing along the river, you'll pass a log bridge on your left, then a few rusty *lur* horns on your right, before you come to yet another **bridge**—this one loaded down with "love locks." Cross this bridge, turn right, and continue following the riverside path uphill.

Just above the next waterfall, cross ❼ **Åmotbrua,** a big white springy suspension footbridge from 1852 (moved here in 1958).

Keep hiking uphill along the river. At the base of the next ❽ **big waterfall,** cross over again to the large brick buildings, hiking up the stairs to the **Beyer Bridge** (above the falls) and ❾ *Fabrikkjentene,* a statue of four women laborers. They're pondering the textile factory where they and 700 others toiled long and hard. This gorge was once lined with the water mills that powered Oslo through its 19th-century Industrial Age boom.

Look back (on the side you just left) at the city's two biggest former textile factories. Once you could tell what color the fabric was being dyed each day by the color of the river. Just beyond them, between the two old factories, is a small light-gray building housing the **Labor Museum** (Arbeidermuseet, free; Tue-Sun 11:00-16:00, closed Mon; mid-Aug-late June Sat-Sun only; borrow English handout). Inside you'll see old photos that humanize the life of laborers there, and an 1899 photo exhibit by Edvard Munch's sister, Inger Munch.

The tiny red house just over and below the bridge—the **Honse-Lovisas Hus** cultural center—makes a good rest-stop (Tue-Sun 11:00-16:00, closed Mon, coffee and waffles). Continue past the red house to the red-brick Ringnes Brewery and follow ❿ **Thorvald Meyers Gate** downhill directly into the heart of Grünerløkka. First you'll go through a few blocks of modern, tidy apartment buildings. Then you'll pass a park (Birkelunden) with a tram stop and a gazebo. The next stretch of Thorvald Meyers Gate is lined with several inviting bars and cafés with outdoor seating. And a few short blocks farther is Grünerløkka's main square, ❶ **Olaf Ryes Plass**—a happening place to grab a meal or drink (see "Eating in Oslo," later). Trams take you from here back to the center.

• *To continue exploring, you could keep going straight past Olaf Ryes Plass and continue walking until you reach a T-intersection with a busy road (Trondheimsveien). From there (passing the recommended Südøst Asian Crossover Restaurant) you can catch a tram back to the center, or drop down to the riverside path and follow it downstream to ❷ Vaterlands bridge in the **Grønland** district. From here the train station is a five-minute walk down Stenersgata.*

Grønland

With the Industrial Revolution, Oslo's population exploded. The city grew from an estimated 10,000 in 1850 to 250,000 in 1900. The T-bane's Grønland stop deposits you in the center of what was the first suburb to accommodate workers of Industrial Age Oslo. If you look down side streets, you'll see fine 19th-century facades from this period. While the suburb is down-and-dirty like working-class and immigrant neighborhoods in other cities, Grønland is starting to emerge as a trendy place for eating out and after-dark fun. Locals know you'll get double the food and lots more beer for the kroner here (see "Eating in Oslo," later). If you'd enjoy a whiff of Istanbul, make a point to wander through the underground commercial zone at the Grønland station (easy to visit even if you're not riding the T-bane).

EAST OF DOWNTOWN
▲Edvard Munch Museum (Munch Museet)

The only Norwegian painter to have had a serious impact on European art, Munch (pronounced "moonk") is a surprise to many who visit this fine museum—displaying the emotional, disturbing, and powerfully Expressionistic work of this strange and perplexing man. In 2020, the museum is scheduled to move to a brand-new, state-of-the-art location in the Lambda building, on a little spit in the harbor next to the Opera House; before then, you may find it at its original location a mile east of downtown (Tøyengata 53; ride the T-bane to Tøyen or bus #20 to Munchmuseet). Either way, you'll see an extensive collection of paintings, drawings, lithographs, and photographs.

If the collection is still in the inconveniently located old building—or if it's out of view entirely during the transition—never fear. You can see an arguably better (more concise and thoughtfully arranged) collection of a dozen great Munch paintings, including *The Scream*, at the National Gallery (described earlier and also slated to soon close and move to a new location). In this time of flux, if you must see Munch, check at the TI for a location that's open. For more on Munch, see page 48.

Cost and Hours: Likely 100 NOK; daily 10:00-17:00, early May-early Oct until 16:00; confirm hours and location, tel. 23 49 35 00, www.munchmuseet.no.

▲Ekeberg Sculpture Park

In 2013, this piece of wilderness—on a forested hill over town, with grand city views—was transformed into a modern sculpture park. The art collector who financed the park loves women and wanted his creation to be a "celebration of femininity." While that vision was considered a bit ill-advised and was scaled back, the park is plenty feminine and organic.

Getting There: The park, always open and free, is a 10-minute tram ride southeast of the center (at the train station, catch tram #18 from platform E, or #19 from platform C; take either one in the direction of Ljabru). Ride just a few stops to Ekebergparken, right at the park's entrance.

Background: This location (literally "Oak Hill") is historic: There's evidence that Stone Age people lived here 7,000 years ago; a spot in this park is said to be where Edvard Munch was first inspired to paint *The Scream* (the viewpoint is marked *Utsiktspunkt Skrik* on maps); and in World War II, it held a Nazi military cemetery. In 2013, real estate tycoon Christian Ringnes (grandson of Norwegian brewery tycoons, who—like Coors in Denver and Carlsberg in Copenhagen—have lots of money for grand city projects) paid to turn the wooded area into a park. Norwegians tend to be skeptical of any fat cat giving something to the city...what's the real motive? They note that the park's popularity attracts more business to the fancy Ringnes-owned restaurant within. Others disagreed with the decision to replace nature with a man-made park. But critics are getting over their concerns, and today the people of Oslo are embracing this lovely 63-acre mix of forest and contemporary art.

Visiting the Park: A visit here involves lots of climbing on trails through the trees. While some people come for the statues (35 in all, including some by prominent artists such as Dalí, Rodin, Renoir, Vigeland, and Damien Hirst), others simply enjoy a walk in nature...and most agree that the views of Oslo's fast-emerging harbor scene (the Opera House and Barcode Project) may be the highlight. From the tram stop, hike up to the little cluster of buildings (including the visitors center, where you can pick up a map and join a 1.5-hour guided walk in English—see schedule at www.ekebergparken.com). In this area, you can see the first of the sculptures. For views and more art, keep heading up the hill to the restaurant...and beyond. Maps, suggesting various walking routes, are posted throughout the park.

Nearby: The faint **ruins of medieval Oslo** (free, always open) are between the harbor and Ekeberg Park—you can get a peek of them as you rumble past on the tram. While underwhelming for most, history buffs can spend a few minutes wandering a park with a few scant foundations of the 11th-century town—back when it was 3,000 people huddled around a big stone cathedral, seat of the Norwegian bishop. The arcade of a 13th-century Dominican monastery still stands (office of today's Lutheran bishop). To get there, hop off at the St. Halvards Plass tram stop; the ruins are across the street from the bus stop.

ESCAPES FROM THE CITY

Oslo is surrounded by a vast forest dotted with idyllic little lakes, huts, joggers, bikers, and sun-worshippers. One of the easiest escapes is simply to grab a beach towel and ride T-bane line #6 to its last stop, Sognsvann, and join the lakeside scene of Norwegians at play. A pleasant trail leads around the lake. To go farther afield, consider these options.

▲Holmenkollen Ski Jump and Ski Museum

The site of one of the world's oldest ski jumps (from 1892), Holmenkollen has hosted many championships, including the 1952 Winter Olympics. To win the privilege of hosting the 2011 World Ski Jump Championship, Oslo built a bigger jump to match modern ones built elsewhere—futuristic, cantilevered, and Olympic-standard. For skiers and winter-sports fans, a visit here is worth ▲▲.

Cost and Hours: 130-NOK ticket includes museum and viewing platform at top of jump; zipline-600 NOK, ski simulator-95 NOK; daily 9:00-20:00, May and Sept 10:00-17:00, Oct-April until 16:00; tel. 22 92 32 64, www.skiforeningen.no.

Getting There: T-bane line #1 gets you out of the city, through the hills, forests, and mansions that surround Oslo, and to the jump (4/hour, 25 minutes, direction: Frognerseteren). From the Holmenkollen station, you'll hike steeply up the road 15 minutes to the ski jump. (Getting back down is more like 10 minutes. Note T-bane departure times before you leave.) For more details—including a slightly longer, but more scenic, approach—see "Near the Ski Jump," later.

Visiting Holmenkollen: You'll enter the complex directly under the ramp. First you'll tour the **ski museum,** which traces the evolution of the sport, from 4,000-year-old rock paintings to crude

1,500-year-old wooden sticks to the slick and quickly evolving skis of modern times, including a fun exhibit showing the royal family on skis. You'll see gear from Roald Amundsen's famous trek to the South Pole, including the stuffed remains of Obersten ("The Colonel"), one of his sled dogs. Exhibits show off lots and lots of historic skis, gear, and video clips of great moments in skiing. Kids love the downhill ski-breeze simulator...basically a superpowered fan that blasts you in the face with fierce wind.

Near the end of the museum exhibits, look for the sign up to the **ski jump.** The tilted elevator takes you up to the top (on a sunny day, you may have to wait your turn for the elevator). Stand right at the starting gate, just like an athlete, and get a feel for this daredevil sport. The jump empties into a 30,000-seat amphitheater. Climb the stairs up to the rooftop deck; when it's clear, you'll see one of the best possible views of Oslo. While the view is exciting from the top, even more thrilling is the **zip-line** ride that sends daredevils screaming (literally) down over the jump to the landing area at the very bottom in 30 heart-stopping seconds.

As you ponder the jump, consider how modern athletes continually push the boundaries of their sport. The first champion here in 1892 jumped 21 meters (nearly 69 feet). In 1930 it took a 50-meter jump to win. In 1962 it was 80 meters, and in 1980 the champ cracked 100 meters. And, most recently, a jump of 140 meters (459 feet) took first place.

To cap your Holmenkollen experience, you can step into the **simulator** (or should I say stimulator?) and fly down the ski jump and ski in a virtual downhill race. My legs were exhausted after the five-minute terror. It's located at the lower level of the complex, near the entry of the ski museum. Outside, have fun watching a candid video of those shrieking inside.

Near the Ski Jump

For an easy downhill jaunt through the Norwegian forest, with a woodsy coffee or meal break in the middle, stay on the T-bane past Holmenkollen to the end of the line at Frognerseteren. From there, follow signs five minutes downhill on the gravel path to the recommended **Frognerseteren Hovedrestaurant,** a fine traditional eatery with a sod roof, reindeer meat on the griddle, an affordable cafeteria, and a city view over more sod rooftops.

From the restaurant, head down to the little sod-roofed village and look for the *Holmenkollen 1.6* sign to the right. Follow the wide, reddish gravel path through the woods (don't be distracted by the many side-paths, which are for mountain bikers—speaking of which, keep an eye out for bicycles zipping across your path). After about 20 minutes, you'll come to a paved roller-ski course (use the gravel path alongside), then pass between the wooden Holmenkol-

len village church and the top of a different ski jump (Midtstubak-
ken). Soon you'll see the glassy swoop of Holmenkollen on your
right; the entrance to the jump is at the base of the ramp.

On your way back to the Holmenkollen T-bane stop, you'll
pass the recommended **Holmenkollen Restaurant,** with a similar view, but without Frognerseteren's pewter-and-antlers folk
theme—or pretense. For details on both restaurants, see "Eating
in Oslo," later.

Oslofjord Island Beaches

On a hot day, it seems the busy ferry scene at Oslo's harborfront
is primarily designed to get locals out of their offices and onto the
cool, green islands across the harbor so they can take a dip in the
fjord, enjoy a little beach time, or simply stroll and enjoy views of
the city. The larger Hovedøya offers good beaches, the ruins of a
Cistercian monastery from 1147, some old cannons from the early
1800s, a marina, and a café. Little Gressholmen has good swimming, easy wandering to a pair of connected islands, and Gressholmen Kro, a rustic café dating to the 1930s.

Getting to the Islands: From Aker Brygge, catch ferry #B1,
#B2, or #B3 to Hovedøya, or ferry #B4 to Gressholmen (both cov-
ered by city transit passes and Oslo Pass, ticket machines at dock).
For schedules and fare info, check www.ruter.no.

Beach at Bygdøy: There's also a beach at Huk on the Bygdøy
peninsula; take the direct boat from pier 3 in front of City Hall or
bus #30. Once there, if you head left, you'll find a clothed beach,
and to the right is a nude beach.

Mountain Biking

Mountain-biking possibilities are endless (as you'll discover if you
go exploring without a good map). Consider taking your bike on
the T-bane (free outside of rush hour, otherwise half the normal
adult fare) to the end of line #1 (Frognerseteren, 30 minutes from
National Theater) to gain the most altitude possible. Then follow
the gravel roads (mostly downhill but with some climbing) past
several dreamy lakes to Sognsvann at the end of T-bane line #6.
Farther east, from Maridalsvannet, a bike path follows the Akers
River all the way back into town. (The TI has details.) While Oslo
isn't much on bike rentals, you can rent quality bikes at Viking Biking (listed under "Helpful Hints," earlier).

Amusement Parks and Wet Fun

The giant **Tusenfryd** amusement complex, just out of town, offers a world of family fun. It's sort of a combination Norwegian
Disneyland/Viking Knott's Berry Farm, with more than 50 rides,
plenty of entertainment, and restaurants (closed off-season, tel. 64

OSLO

97 66 99, www.tusenfryd.no, ride bus #500 from behind Oslo's train station).

Oslo also offers a variety of water play. Located near Vigeland Park, the **Frognerbadet** has three outdoor pools, a waterslide, high dives, a cafeteria, and lots of young families (open mid-May-late Aug, closed off-season, Middelthunsgate 28, tel. 23 27 54 50).

Tøyenbadet, a modern indoor/outdoor pool complex with a 330-foot-long waterslide, also has a gym and sauna (northeast of downtown at Helgengate 90, tel. 23 30 44 70). Oslo's free botanical gardens are nearby.

NEAR OSLO

▲Eidsvoll Manor

During the Napoleonic period, control of Norway changed from Denmark to Sweden. This ruffled the patriotic feathers of Norway's Thomas Jeffersons and Ben Franklins, and on May 17, 1814, Norway's constitution was written and signed in this stately mansion (in the town of Eidsvoll Verk, north of Oslo). While Sweden still ruled, Norway had more autonomy than ever. To get ready for the bicentennial of Norway's constitution, the manor itself was restored to how it looked in 1814. A visitors center in the nearby Wergeland House tells the history of Norway's march to independence with 21st-century high-tech touches. Your ticket also includes an English tour, offered every day year-round at 12:30.

Cost and Hours: 125 NOK; daily 10:00-17:00; Sept-April Tue-Fri 10:00-15:00, Sat-Sun 11:00-16:00, closed Mon; tel. 63 92 22 10, www.eidsvoll1814.no.

Getting There: Eidsvoll is 45 minutes from Oslo by car (take road E-6 toward Trondheim, turn right at *Eidsvolls Bygningen* sign, free parking). You can also take the train to the Eidsvoll Verk station (2/hour, 30 minutes plus 20-minute walk). If you're driving from Oslo to Lillehammer and the Gudbrandsdal Valley, the manor is right on the way and worth a stop.

Drøbak

This delightful fjord town is just an hour from Oslo by bus (2/hour, bus #500 from behind the train station) or ferry (70 NOK one-way, 2/day weekends only spring and fall, also 1/day weekdays mid-June-mid-Aug, check at pier 1 or ask at Oslo TI). Consider taking the 1.25-hour boat trip down, exploring the town, having dinner, and taking the bus back (either trip is covered by a 2-zone, 53-NOK ticket). TI tel. 64 93 50 87, www.visitdrobak.no.

For holiday cheer year-round, stop into **Tregaarden's Julehuset** Christmas shop, right off Drøbak's main square (closed Christmas-Feb, tel. 64 93 41 78, www.julehus.no). Then wander out past the church and cemetery on the north side of town to a pleasant park. Looking out into the fjord, you can see the old **Oscarsborg Fortress,** where Norwegian troops fired cannons and torpedoes to sink Hitler's warship, *Blücher.* The attack bought enough time for Norway's king and parliament to escape capture and eventually set up a government-in-exile in London during the Nazi occupation of Norway (1940-1945). Nearby, a monument is dedicated to the commander of the fortress, and one of *Blücher*'s anchors rests aground (the other is at Aker Brygge in Oslo). A 100-NOK round-trip summer ferry shuttles visitors from the town harbor.

OSLO

Eating in Drøbak: With outdoor seating, **$$$$ Restaurant Skipperstuen** is a pricey but good option for dinner overlooking the fjord and all the Oslo-bound boat traffic (Mon-Sat 12:00-22:00, Sun until 20:00; off-season closed Mon-Tue; Havnebakken 11, tel. 64 93 07 03, www.skipperstuen.no).

Shopping in Oslo

Shops in Oslo are generally open 10:00-18:00 or 19:00. Many close early on Saturday and all day Sunday. Shopping centers are open Monday through Friday 10:00-21:00, Saturday 9:00-18:00, and are closed Sunday. Remember, when you make a purchase of 315 NOK or more, you can get the 25 percent tax refunded when you leave the country. Here are a few favorite shopping opportunities many travelers enjoy, but not on Sunday, when they're all closed. For locations, see the map on page 24.

Norway Designs, just outside the National Theater, shows off the country's sleek, contemporary designs in clothing, kitchenware, glass, textiles, jewelry—and high prices (Stortingsgata 12, T-bane: Nationaltheatret, tel. 23 11 45 10).

Paleet is a mall in the heart of Oslo, with 30 shops on three levels and a food court in the basement (Karl Johans Gate 37, tel. 23 08 08 11).

Dale of Norway, considered Norway's biggest and best maker of traditional and contemporary sweaters, offers its complete collection at their "concept store" in downtown Oslo (Karl Johans Gate 45, tel. 97 48 12 07).

Heimen Husfliden has a superb selection of authentic Norwegian sweaters, *bunads* (national costumes), traditional jewelry, and other Norwegian crafts (top quality at high prices, Rosenkrantz Gate 8, tel. 23 21 42 00).

GlasMagasinet is one of Oslo's oldest and fanciest department stores (top-end, good souvenir shop, near the cathedral at Stortorvet 9, tel. 22 82 23 00).

The Husfliden Shop, in the basement of the GlasMagasinet department store (listed earlier), is popular for its Norwegian-made sweaters, yarn, and colorful Norwegian folk crafts (tel. 22 42 10 75).

The Oslo Sweater Shop has competitive prices for a wide range of Norwegian-made sweaters, including Dale brand (in Radisson Blu Scandinavia Hotel at Tullinsgate 5, tel. 22 11 29 22).

Byporten, the big, splashy mall adjoining the central train station, is filled with youthful and hip shops, specialty stores, and eateries (Jernbanetorget 6, tel. 23 36 21 60).

The street named **Bogstadveien** is considered to have the city's trendiest boutiques and chic, high-quality shops (stretches from behind the Royal Palace to Majorstuen near Vigeland Park).

Oslo's Flea Market makes Saturday morning a happy day for those who brake for garage sales (at Vestkanttorvet, March-Nov only, two blocks east of Frogner Park at the corner of Professor Dahl's Gate and Neubergsgate).

Oslo Flaggfabrikk sells quality flags of all shapes and sizes, including the long, pennant-shaped *vimpel,* seen fluttering from flagpoles all over Norway (a 11.5-foot *vimpel* dresses up a boat or cabin wonderfully, near City Hall at Hieronymus Heyerdahlsgate 1, entrance on Tordenskioldsgate—on the other side of the block, tel. 22 40 50 60).

Vinmonopolet stores are the only places where you can buy wine and spirits in Norway. The most convenient location is at the central train station. Another location, not far from Stortinget, is at Rosenkrantz Gate 11. The bottles used to be kept behind the counter, but now you can actually touch the merchandise. Locals say it went from being a "jewelry store" to a "grocery store." (Light beer is sold in grocery stores, but strong beer is still limited to Vinmonopolet shops.)

Sleeping in Oslo

Oslo's hotel rates are particularly susceptible to supply-and-demand fluctuation. You may find deals on weekends and during some parts of the summer, but even then, conventions or special meetings can cause hotel prices to double overnight. Since it's so hard to predict trends, the only way to know is to check hotel websites, or a booking engine, for the dates you want to visit, and see who's offering a discount. For convenience and modern comfort, I like the Thon Budget Hotels. For lower prices, consider a cheap hotel or a hostel.

NEAR THE TRAIN STATION AND KARL JOHANS GATE

These accommodations are within a 15-minute walk of the station. While some streets near the station can feel a bit sketchy, these

Sleep Code

Hotels are classified based on the average price of a typical en suite double room with breakfast in high season.

$$$$	**Splurge:** Most rooms over 1,500 NOK
$$$	**Pricier:** 1,200-1,500 NOK
$$	**Moderate:** 900-1,200 NOK
$	**Budget:** 600-900 NOK
¢	**Hostel/Backpacker:** Under 600 NOK
RS%	**Rick Steves discount**

Unless otherwise noted, credit cards are accepted, and free Wi-Fi is available. Comparison-shop by checking prices at several hotels (on each hotel's own website, on a booking site, or by email). For the best deal, *always book directly with the hotel.* Ask for a discount if paying in cash; if the listing includes **RS%**, request a Rick Steves discount.

hotels are secure and comfortable. Parking in a central garage will run you about 250-300 NOK per day.

Thon Hotels

This chain of business-class hotels (found in big cities throughout Norway) knows which comforts are worth paying for, and which are not. They offer little character, but provide maximum comfort per *krone* in big, modern, conveniently located buildings. Each hotel has a cheery staff and lobby, tight but well-designed rooms, free Wi-Fi, free coffee in the lobby, and a big buffet breakfast. All are nonsmoking and have elevators and central air-conditioning.

Thon's **$$$$** "City Hotels" are a cut above their **$$$** "Budget Hotels" and are generally more expensive. Because Thon Hotels base their prices on demand, their rates vary wildly (my price ratings are based on average summer rates). You may be able to find a City hotel that's discounted below the cost of the Budget hotels. Both Budget and City hotels are usually cheaper during the summer. In Budget hotels, all rooms lack phones and minifridges; also, rooms with double beds are a bit bigger than twin-bedded rooms for the same price.

Book by phone or online (central booking tel. 81 55 24 00, www.thonhotels.no). For the best prices, check the "price calendar" on the Thon Hotels website. Booking via the Thon website gets you a 10 percent "Thon WebDeal" discount (with some exceptions) if you prepay, and with no option to change or cancel your reservation 24 hours after booking. Of the more than a dozen Thon Hotels in Oslo, I find the following most convenient:

Thon City Hotel Rosenkrantz Oslo offers 152 modern, comfortable, stylish rooms in a central location two blocks off Karl Jo-

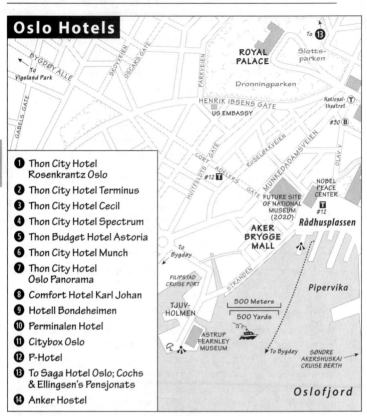

OSLO

Oslo Hotels

1. Thon City Hotel Rosenkrantz Oslo
2. Thon City Hotel Terminus
3. Thon City Hotel Cecil
4. Thon City Hotel Spectrum
5. Thon Budget Hotel Astoria
6. Thon City Hotel Munch
7. Thon City Hotel Oslo Panorama
8. Comfort Hotel Karl Johan
9. Hotell Bondeheimen
10. Perminalen Hotel
11. Citybox Oslo
12. P-Hotel
13. To Saga Hotel Oslo; Cochs & Ellingsen's Pensjonats
14. Anker Hostel

hans Gate. Its eighth-floor lounge offers views of the Royal Palace park. They offer a free light supper every evening for guests—making this an even better value than it seems. If you want to splurge, this is the place to do it (Rosenkrantz Gate 1, tel. 23 31 55 00, www.thonhotels.no/rosenkrantzoslo, rosenkrantzoslo@thonhotels.no).

Thon City Hotel Terminus is similar but just a five-minute walk from the station; along with the Rosenkrantz, it offers a free light evening meal for guests (Steners Gate 10, tel. 22 05 60 00, www.thonhotels.no/terminus, terminus@thonhotels.no).

Thon City Hotel Cecil, ideally located near the Parliament building a block below Karl Johans Gate, has 110 efficient, comfortable rooms ringing a tall, light-filled, breakfast-room atrium (Stortingsgata 8, tel. 23 31 48 00, www.thonhotels.no/cecil, cecil@thonhotels.no).

Thon City Hotel Spectrum has 187 rooms just behind Oslo Spektrum concert arena. It's on a pedestrianized street, next door to a handy grocery store. Rooms facing the street can be noisy on weekends (Brugata 7; leave station out north entrance toward bus terminal, go across footbridge and down the stairs on the left,

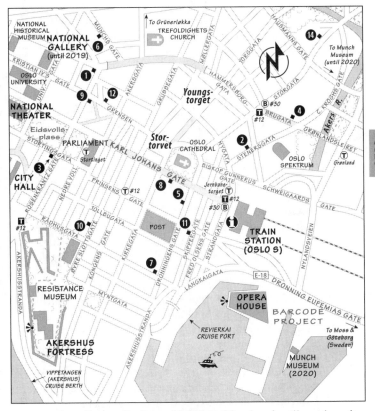

pass by tall glass Radisson Blu Plaza Hotel and walk to the other side of the park; tel. 23 36 27 00, www.thonhotels.no/spectrum, spectrum@thonhotels.no).

Thon Budget Hotel Astoria, with 180 rooms, has the least charm of my recommended Thon Hotels, but it's well-located and perfectly serviceable (2 blocks in front of station, 50 yards off Karl Johans Gate, Dronningens Gate 21, tel. 24 14 55 50, www. thonhotels.no/astoria, astoria@thonhotels.no).

Thon City Hotel Munch has 180 rooms in a location that's quiet but still relatively central, a few blocks from the National Gallery. Some rooms have hardwood floors, others have carpets. Because it's transitioning from "Budget" to "City" class, its prices are a bit lower and therefore a good value (Munchs Gate 5, tel. 23 21 96 00, www.thonhotels.no/munch, munch@thonhotels.no).

Thon City Hotel Oslo Panorama was a 15-story attempt at a downtown condominium building (the condos didn't work, so now it's a 118-room hotel). While higher rooms are more expensive, even those reserving a cheap room often get bumped up. If you request anything higher than the fourth floor, you'll likely enjoy a bigger room, perhaps with a tiny balcony and/or a kitchenette (just off Dronningens Gate at Rådhusgata 7, about 6 blocks from station, tel. 23 31 08 00, www.thonhotels.no/oslopanorama, oslopanorama@thonhotels.no).

More Hotels near the Train Station

$$$$ Comfort Hotel Karl Johan fills a mod building with 181 tight rooms, across from the cathedral near the train-station end of Karl Johans Gate. It feels new (from 2016), with sleek, somewhat minimalist decor and a trendy lobby that tries a little too hard to be hip and funky. Light sleepers should request a quiet room (elevator, Karl Johans Gate 12, tel. 23 01 03 50, www.nordicchoicehotels. com).

$$$ Hotell Bondeheimen ("Farmer's Home") is a historic hotel run by the farmers' youth league, *Bondeungdomslaget*. It once housed the children of rural farmers attending school in Oslo. Its 145 rooms have all the comforts of a modern hotel (elevator, Rosenkrantz Gate 8, tel. 23 21 41 00, www.bondeheimen.com, bookingoffice@ bondeheimen.com). This almost-100-year-old building is also home to the Kaffistova cafeteria (see "Eating in Oslo") and the Heimen Husfliden shop (see "Shopping in Oslo").

$$ Perminalen Hotel, designed for military personnel on leave, also rents 15 rooms to tourists. It's perfectly central, spartan, and inexpensive. Spliced invisibly into a giant office block on a quiet street, they have the same fair prices all year—making it an excellent deal when the city is busy and rates are sky-high. All of the doubles are bunk beds (some seventh-floor rooms have tiny balconies, elevator, tram #12, #13, or #19 from station to Øvre Slottsgate stop, Øvre Slottsgate 2, tel. 24 00 55 00, www.perminalen. com, post.perminalen@iss.no). They also have single beds in dorms segregated by sexes (with lockers and breakfast). Its cheap mess hall is open nightly for dinner, and for lunch on weekdays.

$$ Citybox Oslo has 217 simple, basic rooms at a good price, in a nondescript urban zone a short walk from the train station. While services are minimal (self-check-in), the public areas are inviting (breakfast extra, Prinsens Gate 6, tel. 21 42 04 80, www. citybox.no).

$$ P-Hotel rents 93 cheaply designed, well-worn but affordable rooms. It's a lesser value than the polished Thon hotels, but may have rooms when others are full (or charging higher rates). You get a basic breakfast delivered each morning. Avoid late-night street noise by requesting a room high up or in the back (some sixth-floor rooms have balconies, Grensen 19, T-bane: Stortinget, tel. 23 31 80 00, www.p-hotels.com, oslo@p-hotels.no).

THE WEST END

This pleasant, refined-feeling residential neighborhood is a long walk or a short tram ride from downtown, tucked between the Royal Palace and Frogner Park. The busy main drag of this area is Hegdehaugsveien, lined with tram tracks, busy shops, and restaurants and cafés. The pensions listed here are affordable, but are plagued by street and tram noise—try requesting a quiet room. Saga Hotel is quieter and more upscale.

$$$$ Saga Hotel Oslo feels elegant, with a trendy lobby and gold-trim furnishings. The 47 rooms are comfortable, and the location—in a posh residential area—is appealing (Eilert Sundts Gate 39, tel. 22 55 44 90, www.sagahotels.no).

$$ Ellingsen's Pensjonat rents 24 bright, cheery rooms with fluffy down comforters. About half of their rooms have shared bathrooms, which cost less. It's in a residential neighborhood four blocks behind the Royal Palace (breakfast extra, nonsmoking, tram #19 from central station to Rosenborg stop, near Uranienborg church at Holtegata 25, tel. 22 60 03 59, www.ellingsenspensjonat. no, post@ellingsenspensjonat.no, Peter and Emelie).

$ Cochs Pensjonat is cheap and cozy, with 90 dated, simple rooms, many with kitchenettes (cheaper rooms with shared bath, discounts for breakfast at nearby cafés, elevator; T-bane: Nationaltheatret, exit to Parkveien, and 10-minute walk through park; or more-convenient tram #11 to Homansbyen or #17 or #18 to Dalsbergstien; Parkveien 25, tel. 23 33 24 00, www.cochs.no, booking@cochs.no, three generations of the Skram family).

PRIVATE HOMES

To find a room in a private home, which can save you money but at the cost of being farther from the center, try Airbnb or www.bbnorway.com. Sleeping downtown puts you close to the main sights, but carefully check reviews for noise troubles (many loud discos are in the center). The upscale area behind the Royal Palace (Frogner and Majorstuen neighborhoods) gives you a posh address in Oslo. And for proximity to the trendy dining scene, look in the part of Grünerløkka near the river.

HOSTELS

¢ Anker Hostel, a huge student dorm open to travelers of any age, offers 250 rooms, including 34 of Oslo's best cheap doubles. The hostel also offers bunks in dorm rooms. Though it comes with the ambience of a bomb shelter, each of its rooms is spacious, simple, clean, and has a small kitchen (sheets and towels extra, elevator, no breakfast, pay parking; tram #12 or #13, or bus #30 or #31 from central station, bus and tram stop: Hausmannsgate; or 15-minute walk from station; Storgata 55, tel. 22 99 72 00, www.ankerhostel. no, hostel@anker.oslo.no).

¢ **Haraldsheim Youth Hostel (IYHF),** a huge, modern hostel open all year, comes with a grand view, 315 beds—most of them in four-bed rooms...and a long commute (2.5 miles out of town). They also offer private rooms (sheets extra, from Oslo's central train station catch bus #31 or tram #17 to Sinsenkrysset, or T-bane lines #4 or #5 to Sinsen, then 5-minute uphill hike to Haraldsheim-veien 4, tel. 22 22 29 65, www.haraldsheim.no, oslo.haraldsheim@ hihostels.no). Eurailers can train to the hostel with their rail pass (2/hour, to Grefsen and walk 10 minutes).

SLEEPING ON A TRAIN OR BOAT

Norway's trains and ferries offer ways to travel while sleeping. The eight-hour night train between Bergen and Oslo leaves at about 23:00 in each direction (nightly except Sat). The overnight cruise between these Nordic capitals is a clever way to avoid a night in a hotel and to travel while you sleep, saving a day in your itinerary (see "Oslo Connections," later).

Eating in Oslo

Eating out is expensive in Oslo. How do average Norwegians afford their high-priced restaurants? They don't eat out much. This is one city in which you might want to settle for simple or ethnic meals—you'll save a lot and miss little. Many menus list small and large plates. Because portions tend to be large, choosing a small plate or splitting a large one makes some otherwise pricey options reasonable. You'll notice many locals just drink free tap water, even in fine restaurants.

Splurge for a hotel that includes breakfast, or pay for it if it's optional. At around 80 NOK, a Norwegian breakfast fit for a Viking is a good deal. Picnic for lunch or dinner. Basements of big department stores have huge, first-class supermarkets with lots of alternatives to sandwiches for picnic dinners. The little yogurt tubs with cereal come with collapsible spoons. Wasa crackers and meat, shrimp, or cheese spread in a tube are cheap and pack well. The central station has a Joker supermarket with long hours. Some supermarkets have takeout food that is discounted just before closing—showing up just before 20:00 or so to buy some roast chicken could be your cheapest meal in Oslo. My favorite meals in Oslo are picnic dinners harborside.

Oslo's One-Time Grills

Norwegians are experts at completely avoiding costly restaurants. "One-time grills," or *engangsgrill,* are the rage for locals on a budget. For about 25 NOK, you get

a disposable outdoor cooker consisting of an aluminum tray, easy-to-light charcoal, and a flimsy metal grill. All that's required is a sunny evening, a grassy park, and a group of friends. During balmy summer evenings, the air in Oslo's city parks is thick with the smell of disposable (and not terribly eco-friendly) grills. It's fun to see how prices for this kind of "dining" aren't that bad in the supermarket: Norwegian beer-28 NOK/half-liter, potato salad-30 NOK/tub, cooked shrimp-50 NOK/half kilo, "ready for grill" steak-two for 120 NOK, *grill pølse* hot dogs-75 NOK per dozen, *lomper* (Norwegian tortillas for wrapping hot dogs)-20 NOK per stack, and the actual grill itself.

Bars are also too expensive for the average Norwegian. Young night owls drink at home before *(forspiel)* and after *(nachspiel)* an evening on the town, with a couple of hours, generally around midnight, when they go out for a single drink in a public setting. A beer in a bar costs about $10 for a half-liter (compared to $6 in Ireland and $2 in the Czech Republic), while they can get a six-pack for about twice that price in a grocery store.

You'll save by getting takeaway food from a restaurant rather than eating inside. (The tax on takeaway food is 12 percent, while restaurant food is 24 percent.) Fast-food restaurants ask if you want to take away or not before they ring up your order on the cash register. Even McDonald's has a two-tiered price list.

Oslo is awash with little budget eateries (modern, ethnic, fast food, pizza, department-store cafeterias, and so on). **Deli de Luca,** a cheery convenience store chain that's notorious for having a store on every key corner in Oslo, is a step up from the similarly ubiquitous 7-Elevens and Narvesens. Most are open 24/7, selling sandwiches, pastries, sushi, and to-go boxes of warm pasta or Asian noodle dishes. You can fill your belly here for about 80 NOK. Some outlets (such as the one at the corner of Karl Johans Gate and Rosenkrantz Gate) have seating on the street or upstairs. Beware: Because this is still a *convenience* store, not everything is well-priced. Convenience stores—while convenient—charge double what supermarkets do.

Restaurant Price Code

I've assigned each eatery a price category, based on the average cost of a typical main course. Drinks, desserts, and splurge items (steak and seafood) can raise the price considerably.

$$$$ **Splurge:** Most main courses over 175 NOK
$$$ **Pricier:** 125-175 NOK
$$ **Moderate:** 75-125 NOK
$ **Budget:** Under 75 NOK

In Norway, a Deli de Luca or other takeout spot is **$**; a sit-down café is **$$**; a casual but more upscale restaurant is **$$$**; and a swanky splurge is **$$$$**.

KARL JOHANS GATE STRIP

Strangely, **Karl Johans Gate**—the most Norwegian of boulevards—is lined with a strip of good-time American chain eateries and sports bars where you can get ribs, burgers, and pizza, including T.G.I. Fridays and the Hard Rock Café. **$$ Egon Restaurant** offers a daily 110-NOK all-you-can-eat pizza deal (available Tue-Sat 11:00-18:00, Sun-Mon all day)—though the rest of their menu is overpriced. Each place comes with great sidewalk seating and essentially the same prices.

$$$$ Grand Café is perhaps the most venerable place in town, with genteel decor described on page 28. They have a seasonal menu, with high-end Nordic, French, and international dishes. Reserve a window, and if you hit a time when there's no tour group, you're suddenly a posh Norwegian (Mon-Fri 11:00-23:00, Sat-Sun 12:00-23:00, Karl Johans Gate 31, tel. 98 18 20 00).

$ Deli de Luca, just across from the Grand Café, offers good-value food and handy seats on Karl Johans Gate. For a fast meal with the best people-watching view in town, you may find yourself dropping by here repeatedly (for 70 NOK you can get a calzone, or a portion of chicken noodles, beef noodles, or chicken vindaloo with rice—ask to have it heated up, open 24/7, Karl Johans Gate 33, tel. 22 33 35 22).

$$ Kaffebrenneriet is a good local coffeehouse chain serving quality coffee drinks and affordable sandwiches, salads, and pastries. Convenient locations include in the park along Karl Johans Gate at #24, closer to the cathedral and train station at Karl Johans Gate 7, behind the cathedral at Storgata 2, facing the back of the Parliament building at Akersgata 16, and next to City Hall at Hieronymus Heyerdahls Gate 1. Most have similar hours (typically Mon-Fri 7:00-19:00, Sat 9:00-18:00, closed Sun).

$$ United Bakeries, next to the Paleet mall, is a quiet bit of Norwegian quality among sports bars, appreciated for its 80-NOK sandwiches, salads, light weekday lunches, and fresh pastries

Norwegian Cuisine

Traditional Norwegian cuisine doesn't rank very high in terms of excitement. But the typical diet of meat, fish, and potatoes is evolving to incorporate more diverse products, and the food here is steadily improving. Fresh produce, colorful markets, and efficient supermarkets abound in Europe's most expensive corner.

In this land of farmers and fishermen, traditional recipes are built on ingredients like potatoes, salmon, or beef. A favorite tart/sweet condiment is lingonberry jam, which cuts through a heavy, salty meat dish. Some traditional places also serve *lefse*—a soft flatbread made from potatoes, milk, and flour.

Norway's national dish is *Fårikål*, a lamb or mutton stew with cabbage, peppercorns, and potatoes. This dish is so popular that the last Thursday in September is *Fårikål* day in Norway. There's really no need for a recipe, so every stew turns out differently—and every grandma claims hers is the best.

Because of its long, cold winters, Norway relies heavily on the harvesting and preservation of fish. Smoked salmon, called *røkt laks,* is prepared by salt-curing the fish and cold-smoking it, ensuring the temperature never rises above 85°F. This makes the texture smooth and almost raw. *Bacalao* is another favorite: salted and dried cod that is rehydrated and rinsed in water before cooking. You'll often find *bacalao* served with tomatoes and olives. Stockfish (*tørrfisk*), usually cod, is hung on wooden racks to air-dry (rather than salt-cure), creating a kind of "fish jerky" that goes well with beer. *Klippfisk* is yet another variation, which is partly air-dried on rocks along the shoreline, then further salt-cured.

Some Norwegians serve lutefisk around Christmas time, but you'll rarely see this salty, pungent dish on the menu. Instead, try the more pleasant *fiskekake,* a small white fish cake made with cream, eggs, milk, and flour. You can find these patties year-round.

For a break from seafood, try local specialties such as reindeer meatballs, or pork-and-ground beef meat cakes called *kjøttkaker.* True to Scandinavian cuisine, *kjøttkaker* are usually slathered in a heavy cream sauce.

Dessert and coffee after a meal are essential. *Bløtkake,* a popular delight on Norway's Constitution Day (May 17), is a layered cake drizzled with strawberry juice, covered in whipped cream, and decorated with fresh strawberries. The cloudberry (*multe*), which grows in the Scandinavian tundra, makes a unique jelly that tastes delicious on vanilla ice cream, or even whipped into a rich cream topping for heart-shaped waffles. Norwegians are proud of their breads and pastries, and you'll never be too far from a bakery that sells an almond-flavored *kringle* or a cone-shaped *krumkake* cookie filled with whipped cream.

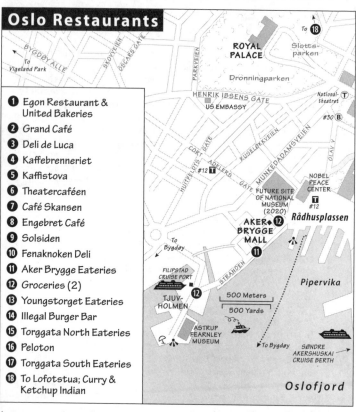

Oslo Restaurants

1 Egon Restaurant & United Bakeries
2 Grand Café
3 Deli de Luca
4 Kaffebrenneriet
5 Kaffistova
6 Theatercaféen
7 Café Skansen
8 Engebret Café
9 Solsiden
10 Fenaknoken Deli
11 Aker Brygge Eateries
12 Groceries (2)
13 Youngstorget Eateries
14 Illegal Burger Bar
15 Torggata North Eateries
16 Peloton
17 Torggata South Eateries
18 To Lofotstua; Curry & Ketchup Indian

(seating inside and out, Mon-Fri 7:30-20:00, Sat 9:00-18:00, Sun 11:00-17:00).

$$$ **Kaffistova,** a block off the main drag, is where my thrifty Norwegian grandparents always took me. And it remains almost unchanged since the 1970s. This alcohol-free cafeteria still serves simple, hearty, and typically Norwegian (read: bland) meals for a good price (big portions of Norwegian meatballs, Mon-Fri 11:00-21:00, Sat-Sun until 19:00, Rosenkrantz Gate 8, tel. 23 21 41 00).

$$$$ **Theatercaféen,** since 1900 the place for Norway's illuminati to see and be seen (note the celebrity portraits adorning the walls), is a swanky splurge steeped in Art Nouveau elegance (Mon-Sat 11:00-23:00, Sun 15:00-22:00, in Hotel Continental at Stortingsgata 24, across from National Theater, tel. 22 82 40 50).

NEAR AKERSHUS FORTRESS

$$$$ **Café Skansen** is a delightful spot for a quality meal—especially in good weather, when its leafy, beer garden-like terrace fills with a convivial, mostly local crowd. Or huddle in the old-time interior, and dig into classic Norwegian dishes. They serve more

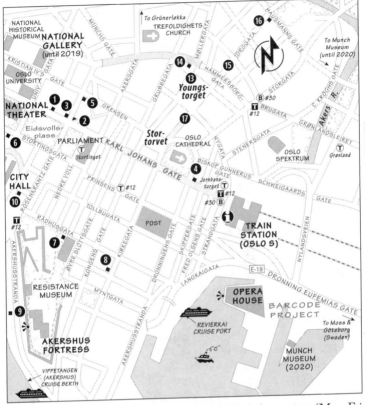

affordable lunches until 16:00, and good salads anytime (Mon-Fri 11:00-23:00, Sat-Sun 12:00-22:00, Rådhusgata 32, tel. 24 20 13 11).

$$$$ Engebret Café is a classic old restaurant in a 17th-century building in the Christiania section of town below the fortress. Since 1857, it's been serving old-fashioned Norse food (reindeer is always on the menu) in a classic old Norwegian setting. In good weather, you can sit out on the delightful square with a gurgling fountain (Mon-Fri 11:30-23:00, Sat from 17:00, closed Sun and most of July, Bankplassen 1, tel. 22 82 25 25).

$$$$ Solsiden ("Sunny Side"), filling a glassed-in former warehouse on the embankment just under the fortress, is a local favorite for a harborfront splurge. You'll dig into fish and seafood meals in an open, unpretentious, nautical-themed, blue-and-white interior that doesn't distract from the cooking. Think of this as a less posh-feeling alternative to the Aker Brygge scene across the harbor. Reserve ahead, and ask for a table with a view (May-mid-Sept daily 16:30-22:00, in peak times they do two dinner seatings—at 20:00 and 22:30, Akershusstranda 13, tel. 22 33 36 30, www.solsiden.no).

Top-End Picnic Shopping: Near City Hall, **Fenaknoken** is a characteristic deli specializing in gourmet Norwegian products—from salmon and lefse to moose salami and dried fish. If you value authentic quality products over price, this is the place to assemble a blowout Norwegian picnic to enjoy out along the harbor (Mon-Fri 10:00-17:00, Sat until 13:30, closed Sun, Tordenskioldsgate 12, tel. 22 42 34 57, www.fenaknoken.no).

HARBORSIDE DINING IN AKER BRYGGE

Aker Brygge, the harborfront development near City Hall, is popular with businesspeople and tourists. While it isn't cheap, its inviting cafés and restaurants with outdoor, harborview tables make for a memorable waterfront meal. Before deciding where to eat, walk the entire lane (including the back side), considering both the brick-and-mortar places (some with second-floor view seating) and the various floating options. Nearly all are open for lunch and dinner.

$$$$ Lekter'n Lounge, right on the water, offers the best harbor view (rather than views of strolling people). This trendy bar has a floating dining area open only when the weather is warm. It serves hamburgers, fish-and-chips, salads, mussels, and shrimp buckets (all outdoors, Stranden 3, tel. 22 83 76 46). If you go just for drinks, the sofas make you feel right at home, and a DJ adds to the ambience.

$$$$ Rorbua ("Fisherman's Cabin") is a lively yet cozy eatery tucked back into this otherwise modern stretch of restaurants. The specialty is food from Norway's north, such as whale and reindeer. Inside, it's extremely woody with a rustic charm and candlelit picnic tables surrounded by harpoons and old B&W photos. While the à la carte dinners start at around 300 NOK, a hearty daily special with coffee for 175 NOK is one of the city's best restaurant deals (daily 12:30-23:00, Stranden 71, tel. 22 83 64 84).

$$$$ Lofoten Fiskerestaurant serves fish amid a dressy yacht-club atmosphere at the end of the strip. While it's beyond the people-watching action, it's comfortable even in cold and blustery weather because of its heated atrium, which makes a meal here practically outdoor dining. Reservations are a must, especially for a harborside window table (daily 11:00-23:00, Stranden 75, tel. 22 83 08 08, www.lofoten-fiskerestaurant.no).

Budget Tips: If you're on a budget, try a hot dog from a *pølse* stand or get a picnic from a nearby grocery store and grab a bench along the boardwalk. The **Co-op Mega** grocery store—in the middle of the mall a few steps behind all the fancy restaurants—has salads, warm takeaway dishes (sold by weight), and more (turn in about midway down the boardwalk, Mon-Sat 8:00-22:00, Sun 9:00-20:00). Farther down is a **Joker mini-grocery,** just over the bridge and to the right on Lille Stranden in Tjuvholmen (Mon-Sat 8:00-22:00, Sun from 11:00).

NEAR YOUNGSTORGET

Central Oslo's most appealing dining zone percolates just a 10-minute stroll north of Karl Johans Gate, around the otherwise nondescript urban square named Youngstorget. This aptly named square feels fresh and trendy, although it's tucked between all-business high-rises and Thon hotels. The square itself has several fine options, but the streets leading off it are also worth a browse—especially Torggata, lined with a couple dozen eclectic options more tempting than anything in the touristy downtown.

On Youngstorget

First, check out the hipster **food carts** that are often parked in the middle of the square, which can be a great spot for a quick, affordable al fresco bite. But to settle in for a more serious meal, you have plenty of choices.

Three good options cluster at the base of the towering, red-brick headquarters of the Arbeiderpartiet (Labor Party). **$$$ Fiskeriet** started as a small fish counter (with stacks of dried cod) before expanding into a full-blown restaurant. It has a concise but tempting menu of simple fish-focused dishes, including fish-and-chips, and seating either in the tiled interior or out on the square (Mon-Fri 11:00-21:00, Sat from 12:00, closed Sun, Youngstorget 2b, tel. 22 42 45 40, www.fiskeriet.com). Next door, **$$$$ Taverna'n** is an industrial-strength eatery with a big, rustic/trendy interior plus outdoor dining, a fun energy, and a menu of pastas, fish dishes, grill meals, and pizza—which they call "skorpe" (Mon-Fri 11:00-late, Sat from 12:00, Sun 13:00-22:00, Youngstorget 1, tel. 40 01 74 37). Rounding out the scene is **$$ Internasjonalen,** a bar with a checkerboard-tile-and-red-leather interior, a wall of lit-up liquor bottles, inviting outdoor tables on the square, and cheap sandwiches (Mon-Sat 10:00-late, Sun from 16:00, Youngstorget 2a, tel. 46 82 52 40).

From any of the above, you can gaze across the square to the pinkish, crenellated former police station that was headquarters for the notorious Nazi security service during the occupation—and where traitor Vidkun Quisling surrendered to Norwegian police at war's end. Its former stables, in the arcades just below, are filled with more bars and eateries (cozy **Fyret** has a great selection of aquavit and open-face sandwiches, while **Politiker'n** has ample outdoor seating). And finally, if you were to hike up to the old police station and turn right (at the uphill corner of the square), you'd find **$$$ Illegal Burger Bar**—the best-regarded of Oslo's many trendy burger joints, with a long, creative menu of gourmet burgers (daily 14:00-late, Møllergata 23, tel. 22 20 33 02).

On Torggata, North of Youngstorget

For even more options, simply stroll from Youngstorget up Torggata and comparison-shop menus, ignoring the American fast-food chains and keeping an eye out for these places (listed in order as you head north): A short block up Badstugata (on the left) is the high-end **$$$$ Arakataka**, serving refined New Nordic dishes in an elegant setting (450-NOK tasting *menu*, daily from 16:00, Mariboes Gate 7b, tel. 23 32 83 00, www.arakataka.no). Nearby is **$$ Pisco**, with affordable Peruvian and Latin American meals, and across the street is **Tilt Bar**, a pinball-themed dive filling what used to be the old public bathhouse. Back on Torggata at #18, you'll pass **$$$ Troys Burger** (Mon-Sat from 11:00, Sun from 14:00). A block farther up, on the corner at #30, **$$$ Taco República** has impressively authentic and delicious Mexican food in a tight, lively, colorful, casual setting. As servings are small, you may need several dishes to fill up (Tue-Thu 16:00-22:00, Fri 15:00-24:00, Sat from 12:00, Sun 14:00-22:00, closed Mon, tel. 40 05 76 65). Just past that, at #32, **$$ Crowbar** is an industrial-mod microbrewery with an easy-to-miss self-service counter upstairs serving cheap falafel and kebabs (Sun-Fri 15:00-late, Sat from 13:00, tel. 21 38 67 57). And finally, up at the corner (at #36), **$$$ Peloton** is a casual and inviting *sykkelcafe*—a bright, cheery "bicycle café" serving pizza and long list of beers, with a bike shop in the back (Mon 8:00-18:00, Tue-Fri until 24:00, Sat 10:00-24:00, Sun 12:00-23:00, tel. 92 15 61 81).

On Torggata, South of Youngstorget

The stretch of Torgatta to the south, where it connects Youngstorget to Karl Johans Gate, feels less residential and more shopping-oriented. But it's also lined with a fun variety of eateries as well—most of which double as hard-partying nightspots into the wee hours. **$$$ Cafe Sør**, a few steps south of Youngstorget, has a cool ramshackle vibe and an affordable menu of salads and sandwiches. It becomes a lively dance club after hours (Mon-Sat 10:00-late, Sun from 12:00, Torggata 11, tel. 41 46 30 47). Nearby, the *Strøget* sign marks the entrance to a courtyard that's jammed with lively eateries, bars, cafés, and clubs. This courtyard is a fun place to browse for a meal or drink by day, or to find a lively nightlife scene after hours. In here, **$$$$ Habibi** has an old cafeteria vibe, a menu of Palestinian mezes, and warbling Middle Eastern music. **Angst** is an achingly hip bar with brooding, atmospheric decor and a live DJ after 23:00.

DINING NEAR VIGELAND PARK

$$$$ Lofotstua Restaurant feels transplanted from the far northern islands it's named for. Kjell Jenssen and his son, Jan Hugo, proudly serve up fish Lofoten-style. Evangelical about fish, they will patiently explain to you the fine differences between all the local varieties, with the help of a photo-filled chart. They serve only the freshest catch, perfectly—if simply—prepared. And if you want meat, they've got it: whale or seal (Mon-Fri 15:00-21:30, closed Sat-Sun, generally closed in July, 5-minute walk from Vigeland Park's main gate, tram #12, in Majorstuen at Kirkeveien 40, tel. 22 46 93 96). This place is packed daily in winter for their famous lutefisk.

$$$ Curry and Ketchup Indian Restaurant is filled with locals enjoying hearty, decent meals for about 130 NOK. This happening place requires no reservations and feels like an Indian market, offering a flavorful meal near Vigeland's statues (daily 14:00-23:00, a 5-minute walk from Vigeland Park's main gate, tram #12, in Majorstuen at Kirkeveien 51, tel. 22 69 05 22).

TRENDY DINING AT THE BOTTOM OF GRÜNERLØKKA

These spots are located on the map on page 67.

Oslo's Foodie Epicenter: Mathallen and Vulkan

This fast-emerging zone, on the bank of the Akers River (and covered on my "Akers River and Grünerløkka Walk"), has recently put Oslo on the foodie map. In the appealing Akers River valley, several old brick industrial buildings and adjoining new construction house a busy hive of culinary activity that's an easy walk or tram ride from downtown (it's a 5-minute walk from the tram stop at Olaf Ryes Plass, described later).

The anchor of this area is **Mathallen Oslo**—once a 19th-century factory, now spiffed up and morphed into a riverside market with a mix of produce stalls and enticing eateries all sharing food-circus-type seating in the middle (Tue-Wed and Sat 10:00-19:00, Thu-Fri until 20:00, Sun 11:00-17:00, closed Mon, some restaurants open longer, www.mathallenoslo.no).

Inside, and ringing the perimeter, you'll find a world of options: tapas, Italian, sushi, tacos and tequila, pizza, Asian street food, Paradis gourmet ice cream, and so on. Most places have high-quality meals in the 150-200-NOK range. **$$$ Ma Poule** is a French wine bar with tasty light meals. **$$$ Atelier Asian Tapas** dishes up small plates and full meals. Or browse the market vendors: **Ost & Sånt** is a high-end Norwegian farm cheese counter with generous free samples. **Smelt Ostesmørbrød** sells fresh breads, pastries, and sandwiches. **The Cupcake & Pie Co.** serves sweet and savory pies. Upstairs, don't miss the taco shop and the sprawling **Hitchhiker** wine bar.

More places face the outside of the hall, including—overlooking the bridge—**$$$$ Lucky Bird** fried chicken and ribs, **$$$$ Smelteverket** ("global tapas" with wonderful views over the river), and more. Still can't decide? For me, the winner may be **$$$$ Vulkanfisk,** with indoor and outdoor seating and a tempting menu of relatively well-priced and elegantly executed fish and seafood dishes: mussels, fish-and-chips, fish soup, garlic scampi, etc. (Tue-Sat 10:00-22:00, Sun until 20:00, closed Mon, tel. 21 39 69 58, www.vulkanfisk.no). For just a drink, consider the suntrap outdoor patio bar in **Dansens Hus** (the national dance theater), facing Vulkanfisk from across the street.

Just uphill is the **Vulkan Depot,** a small shopping mall with a trendy food court including Sapporo Ramen Bar, an Italian grocery store, a florist, a pharmacy, the Aetat co-working space (where independent contractors can rent a desk), and a big Rema 1000 supermarket.

Olaf Ryes Plass

Grünerløkka's main square (and the streets nearby) is lined with inviting eateries and has a relaxed, bohemian-chic vibe. To get here, hop on tram #11, #12, or #13. The top edge of the square has several pubs selling beer-centric food to a beer-centric crowd. Before choosing, simply wander and survey your options: Quesadilla (Mexican fare), Parkteatret (a classic café), Fontés (tapas), Eldhuset (barbecue), the charming little Grünerhaven café kiosk in the park itself, and perhaps the most appealing choice, **$$$ Villa Paradiso Pizzeria.** Youthful and family-friendly, it has a rustic interior and a popular terrace overlooking the square and people scene (Olaf Ryes Plass 8, tel. 22 35 40 60). Just past Villa Paradiso, a block to the west (toward the Mathallen scene described earlier), sits Oslo's most renowned third-wave coffee shop, named simply **Tim Wendelboe** for its celebrity-barista owner. If you're a coffee pilgrim wanting to caffeinate in style...do it here (Mon-Fri 8:30-18:00, Sat-Sun 11:00-17:00, Grüners Gate 1).

The bottom of the leafy square is more focused on nightlife, including **Ryes** (a dive bar famous for its cheap happy-hour beer and 1950s Americana theme). From here, it's fun to stroll south on lively Thorvald Meyers Gate back toward downtown, passing a few cheap international eateries (**Miss Gin** Vietnamese street food,

Bislett kebab house, and **Trattoria Popolare,** with affordable pastas and sprawling outdoor seating perfectly situated to catch the sun's final rays). Eventually you'll run into the place described next.

Between Olaf Ryes Plass and Downtown: Originally a big bank, **$$$$ Südøst Asian Crossover Restaurant** now fills its vault with wine (which makes sense, given Norwegian alcohol prices). Today it's popular with young Norwegian professionals as a place to see and be seen. It's a fine mix of Norwegian-chic, high-ceilinged, woody ambience inside with a trendy menu, and a big riverside terrace outdoors with a more casual menu. Diners enjoy its setting, smart service, and modern creative Asian-fusion cuisine. Reservations are wise, especially on weekends. They're particularly popular on Sundays, when they offer an all-you-can-eat buffet for a relatively affordable 200 NOK (daily 11:00-24:00, Sun buffet until 21:00, at bottom of Grünerløkka, tram #11, #12, or #17 to Trondheimsveien 5, tel. 23 35 30 70).

EATING CHEAP AND SPICY IN GRØNLAND

The street called Grønland leads through this colorful immigrant neighborhood (a short walk behind the train station or T-bane: Grønland; see the map on page 67). After the cleanliness and orderliness of the rest of the city, the rough edges and diversity of people here can feel like a breath of fresh air. Whether you eat here or not, the street is fun to explore. In Grønland, backpackers and immigrants munch street food for dinner. Cheap and tasty *börek* (savory phyllo pastry with feta, spinach, or mushroom) is sold hot and greasy to go for 25 NOK.

$$ Punjab Tandoori is friendly and serves hearty meals (lamb and chicken curry, tandoori specials). I like eating outside here with a view of the street scene (daily 11:00-23:00, Grønland 24).

$$ Istanbul Restaurant is clean and simple, with a decorative interior, outdoor seating, cheap kebabs, and affordable plates of Turkish food (Mon-Fri 10:00-24:00, Sat-Sun from 11:00, Grønland 14, tel. 23 40 90 22).

$$$ Asylet is more expensive and feels like it was here long before Norway ever saw a Pakistani. This big, traditional eatery—like a Norwegian beer garden—has a rustic, cozy interior and a cobbled backyard filled with picnic tables (burgers, pub food, hearty dinner salads, daily 11:00-23:30, Grønland 28, tel. 22 17 09 39).

$$$ Dattera Til Hagen feels like a college party. It's a lively scene filling a courtyard with graffiti, picnic tables, and benches under strings of colored twinkle lights. If it's too cold, hang out inside. Locals like it for the tapas, burgers, salads, and Norwegian microbrews on tap (daily 11:00-late, Grønland 10, tel. 22 17 18 61). On weekends after 22:00, it becomes a disco.

$$$$ Olympen Brown Pub is a dressy dining hall that's a

blast from the past. You'll eat in a spacious, woody saloon with big dark furniture, faded paintings of circa-1920 Oslo lining the walls, and huge chandeliers. It's good for solo travelers, because sharing the long dinner tables is standard practice. They serve hearty, pricey plates and offer a huge selection of beers. Traditional Norwegian cuisine is served downstairs, while upstairs on the rooftop, the food is grilled (daily 11:00-late, Grønlandsleiret 15, tel. 22 17 28 08).

NEAR THE SKI JUMP, HIGH ON THE MOUNTAIN

You can combine a trip into the forested hills surrounding the city with lunch or dinner and get a chance to see the famous Holmenkollen Ski Jump up close (described earlier, under "Sights in Oslo").

Frognerseteren Hovedrestaurant, nestled high above Oslo (and 1,387 feet above sea level), is a classy, sod-roofed old restaurant. Its packed-when-it's-sunny terrace, offering a commanding view of the city, is a popular stop for its famous apple cake and coffee. The **$$ self-service café** is affordable for hearty plates of classic Norwegian dishes, with indoor and outdoor seating (Mon-Sat 11:00-22:00, Sun 11:00-21:00). The elegant view **$$$$ restaurant** is quite expensive and more formal, with antler chandeliers—ideally, reserve ahead for evening dining (reindeer specials, Mon-Fri 12:00-22:00, Sat from 13:00, Sun 13:00-21:00, tel. 22 92 40 40, www.frognerseteren.no).

$$$$ Holmenkollen Restaurant, below the ski jump and a five-minute hike above the Holmenkollen T-bane stop, is a practical alternative to Frognerseteren. Woody but modern, it's slightly cheaper and also has a grand Oslofjord view, but without the folk charm and affordable self-service option. I'd eat here only if you need a solid meal near the ski jump and aren't heading up to Frognerseteren (Tue-Sat 12:00-21:00, Sun 13:00-19:00, Holmenkollveien 119, tel. 22 13 92 00).

Oslo Connections

BY TRAIN, BUS, OR CAR

For train information, call 61 05 19 10 and press 9 for English. For international trains, press 3. Even if you have a rail pass, reservations are required (or strongly recommended) for express and other long-distance journeys. If you have a first-class rail pass, you can get a free "Komfort" class seat reservation for long-distance trains if you book it in Norway; if you have a second-class pass, you'll pay about 50 NOK for a reservation, or 90 NOK to upgrade to "Komfort." Note that private trains (like the Flåmsbana Myrdal-Flåm connection for the "Norway in a Nutshell" route) are not fully covered by rail passes (for details on this complex connection, see the Norway in a Nutshell chapter).

Be warned that international connections from Oslo are often in flux. Schedules can vary depending on the day of the week, so carefully confirm the specific train you need and purchase any required reservations in advance. Most trips from Oslo to Copenhagen require a change in Sweden.

From Oslo by Train to Stockholm: The speedy X2000 train zips from downtown to downtown in about 5.5 hours, runs several times daily, and requires reservations (160 NOK in first class, 65 NOK in second class; first class often comes with a hot meal, fruit bowl, and unlimited coffee). Note that through 2020, construction on this line will likely interrupt service, in which case you'll take the slower SJ InterCity train (recommended 35-NOK reservation in either class). There may also be (slower) connections possible with a change in Göteborg.

By Train to Bergen: Oslo and Bergen are linked by a spectacularly scenic train ride (3-5/day, 7 hours, overnight possible daily except Sat). Many travelers take it as part of the **Norway in a Nutshell** route, which combines train, ferry, and bus travel in an unforgettably beautiful trip. For information on times and prices, see the Norway in a Nutshell chapter.

By Train to: Lillehammer (almost hourly, 2.5 hours), **Kristiansand** (5/day, 4.5 hours, overnight possible), **Stavanger** (5/day, 8 hours, overnight possible), **Copenhagen** (2/day, 8.5 hours, transfer at Göteborg, more with multiple changes).

By Bus to Stockholm: Taking the bus to Stockholm is cheaper but slower than the train (3/day, 8 hours, www.swebus.se).

By Car to the Jotunheimen Mountains: See "Route Tips for Drivers" on page 164.

BY PLANE
Oslo Airport
Oslo Lufthavn, also called Gardermoen, is about 30 miles north of the city center and has a helpful 24-hour information center (airport code: OSL, tel. 91 50 64 00, www.osl.no).

The fastest and cheapest way to get into the city center is by **train.** Exiting the baggage claim, turn left and head to the far end of the building. Here you'll see two options: local trains (NSB) take about 25 minutes to downtown (93 NOK, 2/hour, covered by rail passes, cheaper if you have an Oslo Pass, buy ticket at machines or pay a little extra to buy it at the counter); the private, competing Flytoget train is only a few minutes faster but costs nearly double (180 NOK, 4/hour, runs roughly 5:00-24:00, not covered by rail passes, www.flytoget.no; simply swipe your credit card at the gate, then swipe it again when you get off). Monitors show the next several departures; unless you are in a big hurry or enjoy paying double, I'd stick with the NSB trains. Note that for either type of train, some departures only go as far as the central train station, while others continue—for no extra charge—to the National Theater station (which is closer to most recommended hotels). Unfortunately, this isn't clearly indicated on the screen; to spare yourself a transfer (or save some extra walking), ask whether your train continues to the National Theater.

Flybuss airport buses stop directly outside the arrival hall and make several downtown stops, including the central train station (180 NOK one-way, 3/hour, 40 minutes, tel. 67 98 04 80)—but since it costs more than the train and takes twice as long, it's hard to justify taking the bus.

Taxis take about 45 minutes to downtown, and vary in price depending on the company; figure 600-900 NOK on weekdays, more on weekends or after hours. An interactive screen at the information desk (near the trains) lets you comparison-shop prices and order a cab. Given the high price and long trip, I'd take a taxi only if you're traveling with a group or have lots of luggage.

Sandefjord Airport Torp

Ryanair, WizzAir, and other discount airlines use this airport (airport code: TRF, tel. 33 42 70 00, www.torp.no), 70 miles south of Oslo. You can take a bus into downtown Oslo (220 NOK, www.torpekspressen.no). If you're going from Oslo *to* Sandefjord, note that buses depart Oslo's central bus terminal (next to the train station) about three hours before all flight departures.

BY CRUISE SHIP

Oslo has three cruise ports, described next. For more in-depth cruising information, pick up my *Rick Steves Scandinavian & Northern European Cruise Ports* guidebook.

Getting Downtown: To varying degrees, all of Oslo's cruise ports are within walking distance of the city center—but from the farthest-flung port, Filipstad, your best option is to take advantage of your cruise line's shuttle bus, even if you have to pay for it (most drop off by the Nobel Peace Center, near City Hall on the harborfront). No public transit serves the ports, but Open Top Sightseeing's hop-on, hop-off bus tours meet arriving cruise ships at or near all ports (pricey but con-  venient; see "Tours in Oslo," near the beginning of this chapter). A taxi into town from any of the ports costs 150 NOK minimum.

Once you arrive at the City Hall/harbor area, you can simply walk up the street behind City Hall to find Karl Johans Gate, and the National Gallery; hop on tram #12 (ride it toward Majorstuen to reach Vigeland Park—get off at the Vigelandsparken stop; or ride it toward Disen to reach the train station—use the Jernbanetorget stop); or take the shuttle boat from below City Hall across the harbor to the museums on Bygdøy.

Port Details: Akershus, right on the harbor below Akershus Fortress, has two berths: **Søndre Akershuskai,** a bit closer to town, and **Vippetangen,** at the tip of the peninsula. Both are within an easy 10-minute walk of City Hall (just stroll with the harbor on your left). **Revierkai,** around the east side of the Akershus Fortress peninsula, faces Oslo's striking, can't-miss-it Opera House. From the Opera House, cross the busy street to the train station and the start of my self-guided "Oslo Walk," or head up the street called Rådhusgata to City Hall.

Filipstad is just west of downtown, next to the Tjuvholmen development (around the far side of Aker Brygge from City Hall). From here, it's best to take the cruise-line shuttle bus into town. But if you do choose to hoof it, it's a dull 20-minute walk: Exiting the port, turn right at the roundabout, then head to the busy highway and follow the path to the right and signs to *sentrum*. Your ship's upper deck provides the perfect high-altitude vantage point for scouting your options before disembarking.

BY OVERNIGHT BOAT TO COPENHAGEN

Consider connecting Oslo and Copenhagen by cruise ship. The boat leaves daily from Oslo at 16:30 (arrives in Copenhagen at 9:45 the following morning; going the other way, it departs Copenhagen at 16:30 and arrives in Oslo at 9:45; about 17 hours sailing each way). The boat leaves Oslo from the far (Opera House) side of the Akershus Fortress peninsula (take bus #60 to Vippetangen from the train station, 2-4/hour, get off at Vippetangen stop and follow signs to DFDS ticket office at Akershusstranda 31). Boarding is from 15:15 to 16:15. From Oslo, you'll sail through the Oslofjord—not as dramatic as Norway's western fjords, but impressive if you're not going to Bergen. On board are gourmet restaurants, dinner and breakfast buffets, cafés, nightclubs, tax-free shops, a casino, children's activities, a sauna, hot tub, and swimming pool. This is fun and convenient, but not as swanky as the Stockholm-Helsinki cruise.

You can take this cruise one-way or do a round-trip from either city. Book online or by phone (from Norway, call DFDS Seaways' Denmark office: Mon-Fri 9:00-16:30, closed Sat-Sun, tel. 00 45 33 42 30 10, www.dfdsseaways.us). Book in advance for the best prices. For more specifics and sample prices, see "By Boat" on page 229.

NORWAY IN A NUTSHELL

A Scenic Journey to the Sognefjord

While Oslo and Bergen are the big draws for tourists, Norway is first and foremost a place of unforgettable natural beauty. There's a certain mystique about the "land of the midnight sun," but you'll get the most scenic travel thrills per mile, minute, and dollar by going west from Oslo rather than north.

Norway's greatest claims to scenic fame are her deep, lush fjords. Three million years ago, an ice age made this land as inhabitable as the center of Greenland. As the glaciers advanced and cut their way to the sea, they gouged out long grooves—today's fjords.

The entire west coast is slashed by stunning fjords, and the Sognefjord—Norway's longest (120 miles) and deepest (1 mile)—is tops. The seductive Sognefjord has tiny but tough ferries, towering canyons, and isolated farms and villages marinated in the mist of countless waterfalls.

A series of well-organized and spectacular bus, train, and ferry connections—appropriately nicknamed "Norway in a Nutshell"—lays Norway's beautiful fjord country before you on a scenic platter. With the Nutshell, you'll delve into two offshoots of the Sognefjord, which make an upside-down "U" route: the Aurlandsfjord and the Nærøyfjord. You'll link the ferry ride to the rest of Norway with two trains and a bus: The main train is an express route that takes you through stark and icy scenery above the tree line. To get from the express train down to the ferry, you'll catch an old-fashioned slow train one way (passing waterfalls and forests) and a bus the other way (offering fjord views and more waterfalls). All connections are designed for tourists, explained in English, convenient, and easy. At the start of the fjord, you'll go through the town of Flåm (a transit hub), then pass briefly by the workaday town of

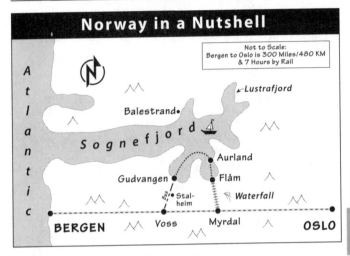

Norway in a Nutshell

Not to Scale:
Bergen to Oslo is 300 Miles/480 KM
& 7 Hours by Rail

A t l a n t i c

Lustrafjord

Balestrand•

S o g n e f j o r d

Aurland

Gudvangen   Flåm

Stal-
heim   Waterfall

BERGEN   Voss   Myrdal   OSLO

Aurland and the hamlet of Undredal (by taking the Nutshell trip segments at your own pace, you can visit the latter two fjord towns on your own; all are described in this chapter).

This region enjoys mild weather for its latitude, thanks to the warm Gulf Stream. (When it rains in Bergen, it just drizzles here.) But if the weather is bad, don't fret. I've often arrived to gloomy weather, only to enjoy sporadic splashes of brilliant sunshine all day long.

Recently the popularity of the Nutshell route has skyrocketed. And the 2005 completion of the longest car tunnel in the world (15 miles between Flåm and Lærdal) rerouted the main E-16 road between Bergen and Oslo through this idyllic fjord corner. All of this means that summer comes with a crush of crowds, dampening some of the area's magic. Unfortunately, many tourists are overcome by Nutshell tunnel-vision, and spend so much energy scurrying between boats, trains, and buses that they forget to simply enjoy the fjords. Relax—you're on vacation.

PLANNING YOUR TIME

Even the blitz tourist needs a day for the Norway in a Nutshell trip. With more time, sleep in a town along the fjord, and customize your fjord experience to include sights outside the Nutshell.

Day 1: The Nutshell works well as a single day (one-way between Oslo and Bergen, or as a long day-trip loop from either city). If you're without a car and want to make efficient use of your time, organize your trip so that it begins in Oslo and ends in Bergen (or vice versa).

Day 2: If you have enough time, spend the night somewhere on the Sognefjord—either along the Nutshell route itself (in Flåm

"Norway in a Nutshell" in a Nutshell

The essential five Nutshell segments (all described in detail in this chapter) are:

Oslo to Myrdal Train (Norwegian State Railways, NSB): 2 departures each morning—6:25 (recommended) and 8:25 (for sleepyheads), 5 hours. Confirm times online or locally.

Myrdal to Flåm Train (Flåmsbana): Hourly departures, generally timed for arrival of Oslo train, 1 hour.

Flåm to Gudvangen Fjord Cruise: Almost hourly departures, 1.5-2 hours.

Gudvangen to Voss Bus: Departures timed with boat arrivals, 75 minutes.

Voss to Bergen Train: Hourly departures, 75 minutes.

Nutshell travelers originating in Bergen can use this route in reverse.

or Aurland; accommodations listed later), or in another, even more appealing fjordside town (such as Balestrand or Solvorn, both described in the next chapter).

With More Time: The Sognefjord deserves more than a day. If you can spare the time, venture off the Nutshell route. You can easily connect to some non-Nutshell towns (such as Balestrand) via ferry or express boat. Drivers can improve on the Nutshell by taking a northern route: From Oslo, drive through the Gudbrandsdal Valley, go over the Jotunheimen Mountains, then along the Lustrafjord to Kaupanger; from there, you can experience the Sognefjord on a car ferry ending in Gudvangen, and drive the remainder of the Nutshell route to Bergen. (Most of these sights, and the ferry connections, are covered in the next two chapters.) For more tips, see the "Beyond the Nutshell" sidebar.

Orientation to the Nutshell

The most exciting single-day trip you could make from Oslo or Bergen is this circular train/boat/bus/train jaunt through fjord country.

Local TIs (listed throughout this chapter) are well-informed about your options, and they sell tickets for various segments of the trip. At TIs, train stations, and hotels, look for souvenir-worthy brochures with photos, descriptions, and exact times.

Route Overview

The basic idea is this: Take a train halfway across the mountainous spine of Norway, make your way down to the Sognefjord for a boat cruise, then climb back up out of the fjord to rejoin the main train line. Each of these steps is explained in the self-guided "Nutshell Tour" in this chapter. Transportation along the Nutshell route is carefully coor-

dinated. If any segment of your journey is delayed, the transportation for the next segment will wait for you (because everyone on board is catching the same connection).

Doing the Nutshell one-way between Oslo and Bergen (or vice versa) is most satisfying—you'll see the whole shebang, and it's extremely efficient if you're connecting the two cities anyway. It's also possible to do most of the route in a round-trip loop from either Bergen or Oslo. Doing the round-trip from Bergen is cheaper, but it doesn't include the majestic train ride between Myrdal and Oslo. The round-trip from Oslo includes all the must-see sights but it's a very long day (you leave Oslo at 6:25 and don't get back until 22:35).

When to Go

The Nutshell trip is possible all year. In the summer (June-Aug), the connections are most convenient, the weather is most likely to be good...and the route is at its most crowded. Outside of this time, sights close and schedules become more challenging. Some say the Nutshell is most beautiful in winter, though schedules are severely reduced.

Nutshell Itineraries
Oslo-Bergen

You must take one of two morning departures (6:25 or 8:25) to do the entire trip from Oslo to Bergen in a day. I recommend the earlier departure to enjoy an hour more free time in Flåm and generally fewer crowds. This itinerary shows typical sample times for summer travel; confirm exact times before your trip (www.nsb.no for trains, www.kringom.no for buses and ferries):

- Train from Oslo to Myrdal: 6:25-11:34
- Flåmsbana train from Myrdal to Flåm: 12:13-13:10
- Free time in Flåm: 13:10-15:15

- Boat from Flåm to Gudvangen: 15:15-17:30
- Bus from Gudvangen to Voss: 17:45-19:00
- Train from Voss to Bergen: 19:38-21:00

If you leave Oslo on the later train, you can either arrive in Bergen at the same time (with less free time in Flåm) or have more time in Flåm and Voss and arrive later (22:30).

Other Options

Here are other one-day options for doing the Nutshell in the summer. Confirm specific times before your trip.

Bergen-Oslo: Train departs Bergen-8:43, arrives Voss-9:56; bus departs Voss-10:10, arrives Gudvangen-11:20; boat departs Gudvangen-11:45, arrives Flåm-13:15; Flåmsbana train departs Flåm-16:05, arrives Myrdal-17:03; train departs Myrdal-17:54, arrives Oslo-22:35.

Day-Trip Loop from Oslo: Train departs Oslo-6:25, arrives Myrdal-11:34; Flåmsbana train departs Myrdal-12:13, arrives Flåm-13:10; boat departs Flåm-14:00, arrives Gudvangen-15:30; bus departs Gudvangen-15:40, arrives Voss-16:55; train departs Voss-17:11, arrives Oslo-22:35.

Day-Trip Loop from Bergen: Train departs Bergen-8:43, arrives Voss-9:56; bus departs Voss-10:10, arrives Gudvangen-11:20; boat departs Gudvangen-11:45, arrives Flåm-13:15; Flåmsbana train departs Flåm-14:50, arrives Myrdal-15:46; train departs Myrdal-17:30, arrives Bergen-19:56.

Buying Tickets

The easiest way to purchase Nutshell tickets is to buy a package from Fjord Tours—it will save you time and the trouble of planning your itinerary. However, you're locked into their schedule and the package price can be more expensive than buying individual tickets.

On your own, you can often find discounts for the train and can choose the cheapest ferry—possibly saving up to 500 NOK. You also have more flexibility—you choose how much time you spend in Flåm and what time you arrive in Bergen or Oslo. However, you have to plan your itinerary and buy tickets for each leg of your journey—that's five separate tickets for a one-way trip between Oslo and Bergen.

If you have a rail pass, or if you're a student or a senior (68 or older), you'll save money by booking the Nutshell on your own.

Whether you are doing a package deal or buying tickets on your own, in summer book well in advance—four to five weeks is best. Train tickets on the Nutshell route from or back to Oslo can sell out in high season (June-Aug), as can some departures on the ferry from Flåm.

Nutshell Route & Beyond

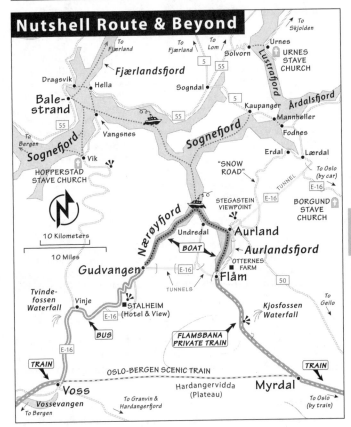

Package Deals

Fjord Tours sells the Nutshell package at all Norwegian State Railways (NSB) stations, including Oslo and Bergen, or through their offices in Norway (tel. 55 55 76 60, www.fjordtours.com, booking@fjordtours.com). With these packages, all your departures are fixed. You can choose between two different types of ferries: Classic, about a 2-hour ride on an old car ferry that just carries foot passengers; or Premium, 1.5 hours on a hybrid catamaran. Unless you are in a hurry (though why hurry through the fjords?), take the Classic ferry.

Here are the prices (as of press time) for Nutshell packages on the Classic ferry:

- One-way from Bergen or Oslo-1,690 NOK
- Round-trip from Oslo via Voss-2,760 NOK
- Round-trip from Bergen via Myrdal-1,440 NOK
- Round-trip from Flåm-1,010 NOK

Packages on the Premium ferry cost 250-500 NOK extra.

Beyond the Nutshell

The Sognefjord is the ultimate natural thrill Norway has to offer, and there's no doubt that the Nutshell route outlined in this chapter is the most efficient way to see it quickly. Unfortunately, its trains, buses, and boats are thronged with other visitors who have the same idea.

Travelers with a bit more time, and the willingness to chart their own course, often have a more rewarding Sognefjord experience. It's surprisingly easy to break out of the Nutshell and hit the northern part of the Sognefjord (for example, using the Bergen-Vik-Balestrand-Aurland-Flåm express boat, described on page 139).

In the next chapter, you'll find some tempting stopovers on the north bank of the Sognefjord, including adorable fjordside villages (such as Balestrand and Solvorn), evocative stave churches (Hopperstad and Urnes), and a chance to get up close to a glacier (at the Nigard Glacier).

Read up on your options, then be adventurous about mixing and matching the fjordside attractions that appeal to you most. Ideally, use the Nutshell as a springboard for diving into the Back Door fjords of your travel dreams.

Fjord Tours also sells a Nutshell round-trip from Oslo that includes a night train, a "Sognefjord in a Nutshell" tour, and a "Sognefjord and Nærøyfjord in a Nutshell" tour—see www.fjordtours.com for details.

On Your Own

Specific information on buying tickets for each leg of the Nutshell route is explained later, under their individual listings. In general, you can buy train tickets (including the Flåmsbana) at the NSB train stations in Oslo or Bergen or online at www.nsb.no. For the best deal, look for nonrefundable "minipris" tickets. You can buy Flåm-Gudvangen ferry tickets with one of two companies: The Fjords (more sailings, www.visitflam.com) or Lustrabaatane (cheaper prices, www.lustrabaatane.no). You can't buy tickets in advance for the Gudvangen-Voss bus; there's always room but you must pay the driver in cash. If you're a student or senior, always ask about discounts.

Rail Pass Discounts: If you have any rail pass that includes Norway, the Oslo-Bergen train is covered (except a 50-NOK reservation fee for second class; free for first-class passholders); you also get a 30 percent discount on the Flåmsbana train. You still have to pay full fare for the boat cruise and the Gudvangen-Voss bus. Your total one-way cost between Oslo and Bergen: about 650 NOK with a first-class pass, 700 NOK with a second-class pass.

Travel Tips

Luggage: Transporting luggage on the Nutshell is no big deal, as the connections require almost no walking: At Myrdal, you just cross the platform; in Flåm, you walk 50 yards from the train to the dock; in Gudvangen, the bus meets the ferry at the dock; in Voss, the bus drops you at the train station. If you want to check your bag during your free time in Flåm, use the baggage-check cabin at the head of the train track, across the lane from the boat dock.

An alternative to carrying your luggage is **Porterservice AS.** They pick up your luggage at your hotel, transport it via the train between Oslo and Bergen, and drop it off at your next hotel by 21:00 (250 NOK/piece, mobile 90 61 00 09, www.porterservice. no).

Eating: Options along the route aren't great—on the Nutshell I'd consider food just as a source of nutrition and forget about fine dining. You can buy some food on the fjord cruises (hot dogs, burgers, and pizza) and the Oslo-Bergen train. Depending on the timing of your layovers, Myrdal, Voss, or Flåm are your best lunch-stop options (the Myrdal and Flåm train stations have decent cafeterias, and other eateries surround the Flåm and Voss stations)—although you won't have a lot of time there if you're making the journey all in one day. Your best bet is to pack picnic meals and munch en route. If catching an early train in Oslo, the station has a handy grocery store open at 5:00 (6:00 on Sun).

Cruise-Ship Passengers: Tiny Flåm—in the heart of Nutshell country—is an increasingly popular destination for huge cruise ships. If arriving in Flåm by cruise ship, see my *Scandinavian & Northern European Cruise Ports* book for details on how to approach the Nutshell during your day in port.

Nutshell Tour

If you only have one day for this region, it'll be a thrilling one—worth ▲▲▲. The following self-guided segments of the Nutshell route are narrated from Oslo to Bergen. If you're going the other way, hold the book upside down.

▲▲Oslo-Bergen Train (Via Myrdal)

The Oslo-Bergen route—called "Bergensbanen" by Norwegians—is simply the most spectacular train ride in northern Europe. The entire railway, an amazing engineering feat completed in 1909, is 300 miles long; peaks at 4,266 feet, which, at this Alaskan latitude, is far above the tree line; goes under 18 miles of snow sheds; trundles over 300 bridges; and passes through 200 tunnels in just under seven hours. To celebrate the Bergensbanen centennial in 2009, Norwegian TV mounted cameras on the outside of the train and broadcast the entire trip—and more than a million Norwegians tuned in (search for "Bergensbanen" on YouTube and you can watch it too).

Cost and Reservations: Here are the one-way fares for various segments: Oslo-Bergen-950 NOK, Oslo-Myrdal-781 NOK, Myrdal-Voss-126 NOK, Myrdal-Bergen-309 NOK, Voss-Bergen-204 NOK. You can save money on these fares if you book "minipris" tickets in advance at www.nsb.no. If you have difficulty paying for your ticket with a US credit card online, use PayPal or call 61 05 19 10—press 9 for English, and you'll be given a web link where you can finish your transaction. In peak season, get reservations for this train four to five weeks in advance.

Second-class rail-pass holders pay just 50 NOK to reserve, and first-class passholders pay nothing. If you have a second-class rail pass or ticket, you can pay 90 NOK to upgrade to "Komfort" class, with more legroom, extra comfortable seats, free coffee and tea, and an outlet for your laptop (book online or ask the conductor when you board).

Schedule: This train runs three to five times per day, including two morning departures (overnight possible except Sat). The segment from Oslo to Myrdal takes about five hours; going all the way to Bergen takes seven hours.

Route Narration: The scenery crescendos as you climb over Norway's mountainous spine. After a mild three hours of deep woods and lakes, you're into the barren, windswept heaths and glaciers. Here's what you'll see traveling westward from Oslo: Leaving Oslo, you pass through a six-mile-long tunnel and stop in Drammen, Norway's fifth-largest town. The scenery stays low-key and woodsy up Hallingdal Valley until you reach Geilo, a popular ski resort. Then you enter a land of big views and tough little cabins. Finse, at about 4,000 feet, is the highest stop on the line. At several towns, the conductor may announce how many minutes the train will be stopped there. This gives you a few fun moments to get out, stretch, take a photograph, and look around.

Before Myrdal, you enter the longest high-mountain stretch of railway in Europe. Much of the line is protected by snow tun-

nels. The scenery gets more dramatic as you approach Myrdal (MEER-doll). Just before Myrdal, look to the right and down into the Flåm Valley, where the Flåmsbana branch line winds its way down to the fjord. Nutshell travelers get off at Myrdal.

▲▲Myrdal-Flåm Train (Flåmsbana)

The little 12-mile spur line leaves the Oslo-Bergen line at Myrdal (2,800 feet), which is nothing but a scenic high-altitude train junc-

tion with a decent cafeteria. Before boarding, pick up the free, multilingual souvenir pamphlet with lots of info on the trip (or see www. flaamsbana.no). Video screens onboard and sporadic English commentary on the loudspeakers explain points of interest, but there's not much to say—it's all about the scen-

ery. If you're choosing seats, you'll enjoy slightly more scenery if you sit on the left going down.

Cost and Reservations: 360 NOK one-way (rail-pass holders pay 250 NOK), 480 NOK round-trip. You can book one-way tickets on www.nsb.no; the cheapest round-trip tickets are on www. visitflam.com. You also can buy tickets onboard the train or at the Flåmsbana stations in Flåm. Train staff in Oslo may tell you that the Flåmsbana is booked—don't worry, it very rarely fills. Even if it's standing-room only, you can usually squeeze in. Simply get to Myrdal and hop on the train.

However, morning trains ascending from Flåm to Myrdal (when there are several cruise ships in port) can sell out. In summer, if you want to leave Flåm in the morning, try buying your ticket the night before or right when the Flåm ticket office opens (at 7:00). The best plan is to buy your Flåmsbana ticket at the same time you buy your other train tickets.

Schedule: The train departs in each direction nearly hourly.

Route Narration: From Myrdal, the Flåmsbana train winds down to Flåm (sea level) through 20 tunnels (more than three

miles' worth) in 55 thrilling minutes. It's party time on board, and the engineer even stops the train for photos at the best waterfall, Kjosfossen. According to a Norwegian legend, Huldra (a temptress) lives behind these falls and tries to lure men to the rocks with her singing... look out for her...and keep a wary eye on your partner.

The train line is an even more impressive feat of engineering when you realize it's not a cogwheel train—it's held to the tracks only by steel wheels, though it does have five separate braking systems.

▲▲▲Flåm-Gudvangen Fjord Cruise

The Flåmsbana train deposits you at Flåm, a scenic, functional transit hub at the far end of the Aurlandsfjord. If you're doing the Nutshell route nonstop, follow the crowds and hop on the sightseeing boat that'll take you to Gudvangen. With minimal English narration, the boat takes you close to the goats, sheep, waterfalls, and awesome cliffs.

Cruise Options: There are two boat companies to choose from— The Fjords (www.visitflam.com) and Lustrabaatane (www.lustrabaatane.com). The Fjords has a Classic option that takes more than two hours. It stops at Aurland, Undredal, Dyrdal, and Styvi, which is handy if you want to hop off and on along the way—though you'll need to buy separate tickets for each leg of your trip, and it'll end up costing you more (be sure to notify the ticket seller where you want to get off, to make certain they'll stop). The other option is their Premium ferry, a hybrid catamaran that's faster, silent, and more expensive. It takes about 1.5 hours nonstop between Flåm and Gudvangen.

The cheapest option is the Lustrabaatane ferry—a slow boat that takes about two hours—similar to the Classic ferry, but with no stops.

I much prefer the slower boats because the price is lower, you have more time to savor the scenery, and the bus connection in Gudvangen is immediate and reliable.

Cost and Reservations: For the whole route (Flåm-Gudvangen), you'll pay 250-645 NOK one-way depending on the ferry (435-705 NOK round-trip).

Reservations may be necessary on busy days in summer. Buy your ticket in Flåm as soon as you know which boat you want or in advance at each boat company's website. Beware: The ticket desk at the Flåm Visitors Center is The Fjords boat desk, and they'll sell you a boat ticket implying it's your only option. Tickets for Lustrabaatane are sold at the nearby TI.

Schedule: In summer (June-Aug), boats run multiple times daily in both directions—Classic ferry (2/day), Premium ferry (5/day), Lustrabaatane ferry (2/day). Specific departure times can vary, but generally boats leave Flåm starting at 8:00, with a last departure at 19:00. From Gudvangen, the first boat is generally

The Facts on Fjords

The process that created the majestic Sognefjord began during an ice age about three million years ago. A glacier up to 6,500 feet thick slid downhill at an inch an hour, following a former river valley on its way to the sea. Rocks embedded in the glacier gouged out a steep, U-shaped valley, displacing enough rock material to form a mountain 13 miles high. When the climate warmed up, the ice age came to an end. The melting glaciers retreated and the sea level rose nearly 300 feet, flooding the valley now known as the Sognefjord. The fjord is more than a mile deep, flanked by 3,000-foot mountains—for a total relief of 9,300 feet. Waterfalls spill down the cliffs, fed by runoff from today's glaciers. Powdery sediment tinges the fjords a cloudy green, the distinct color of glacier melt.

Why are there fjords on the west coast of Norway, but not, say, on the east coast of Sweden? The creation of a fjord requires a setting of coastal mountains, a good source of moisture, and a climate cold enough for glaciers to form and advance. Due to the earth's rotation, the prevailing winds in higher latitudes blow from west to east, so chances of glaciation are ideal where there is an ocean to the west of land with coastal mountains. When the winds blow east over the water, they pick up a lot of moisture, then bump up against the coastal mountain range, and dump their moisture in the form of snow—which feeds the glaciers that carve valleys down to the sea.

You can find fjords along the northwest coast of Europe—including western Norway and Sweden, Denmark's Faroe Islands, Scotland's Shetland Islands, Iceland, and Greenland; the northwest coast of North America (from Puget Sound in Washington state north to Alaska); the southwest coast of South America (Chile); the west coast of New Zealand's South Island; and on the continent of Antarctica.

As you travel, bear in mind that, while we use the word "fjord" to mean only glacier-cut inlets, Scandinavians often use it in a more general sense to include bays, lakes, and lagoons that weren't formed by glacial action.

at 9:30, with a last departure at 17:45. See www.kringom.no for schedules covering both ferry lines.

Your only concern is that the Nutshell bus from Gudvangen to Voss may not meet the last departure of the day (check locally); the worst-case scenario is that you'd need to catch the regular commuter bus to Voss, which makes more stops and doesn't take the razzle-dazzle Stalheimskleiva corkscrew road.

Route Narration: You'll cruise up the lovely **Aurlandsfjord,** motoring by the town of **Aurland** (a good home base, but only a few boats stop here), pass the towns of **Undredal, Dyrdal,** and **Styvi** (possible stops here on limited sailings by request), and hang a left at the stunning **Nærøyfjord.** The cruise ends at the apex of the Nærøyfjord, in **Gudvangen.**

The trip is breathtaking in any weather. For the last hour, as you sail down the Nærøyfjord, camera-clicking tourists scurry around struggling to get a photo that will catch the magic. Waterfalls turn the black cliffs into bridal veils, and you can nearly reach out and touch the cliffs of the Nærøyfjord. It's the world's narrowest fjord: six miles long and as little as 820 feet wide and 40 feet deep. On a sunny day, the ride is one of those fine times—like when you're high on the tip of an Alp—when a warm camaraderie spontaneously combusts between the strangers who've come together for the experience.

▲Gudvangen-Voss Bus

Nutshellers get off the boat at Gudvangen and take the 25-mile bus ride to Voss. Gudvangen is little more than a boat dock and giant tourist kiosk. If you want, you can

browse through the grass-roofed souvenir stores and walk onto a wooden footbridge—then catch your bus. While some buses—designed for commuters rather than sightseers—take the direct route to Voss, buses tied to the Nutshell schedule take a super-scenic detour via Stalheim (described later). If you're a waterfall junkie, sit on the left.

Cost: 115 NOK, pay on board, cash only, no rail pass discounts. Reservations are not necessary.

Schedule: Buses meet each ferry, or will show up usually within an hour. (Confirm this in advance if you plan to take the last boat of the day—the ferry crew can call ahead to be sure the bus waits for you.)

Route Narration: First the bus takes you up the **Nærøydal** and through a couple of long tunnels. Then you'll take a turnoff to drive past the landmark **Stalheim Hotel** for the first of many spectacular views back into fjord country. Though the hotel dates from 1885, there's been an inn here since about 1700, where the royal mailmen would change horses. The hotel is geared for tour groups (genuine trolls sew the pewter buttons on the sweaters), but the priceless view from the backyard is free. Drivers should be sure to stop here for the view and peruse the hotel's living room to survey the art showing this perch in the 19th century.

Leaving the hotel, the bus wends its way down a road called **Stalheimskleiva,** with a corkscrew series of switchbacks flanked by a pair of dramatic waterfalls. With its 18 percent grade, it's the steepest road in Norway.

After winding your way down into the valley, you're back on the same highway. The bus goes through those same tunnels again, then continues straight on the main road through pastoral countryside to Voss. You'll pass a huge lake, then follow a crystal-clear, surging river. Just before Voss, look to the right for the wide **Tvindefossen waterfall,** tumbling down its terraced cliff. Drivers will find the grassy meadow and flat rocks at its base ideal for letting the mist fog their glasses and enjoying a drink or snack (be discreet, as "picnics are forbidden").

Voss

The Nutshell bus from Gudvangen drops you at the Voss train station, which is on the Oslo-Bergen train line. This connection is generally not well-coordinated; you'll likely have 40 minutes or so to kill before the next train to Bergen.

Visiting Voss: A plain town in a lovely lake-and-mountain setting, Voss lacks the striking fjordside scenery of Flåm, Aurland, or Undredal, and is basically a home base for summer or winter sports (Norway's Winter Olympics teams often practice here). Voss surrounds its fine, 13th-century church with workaday streets—busy with both local shops and souvenir stores—stretching in several directions. Fans of American football may want to see the humble monument to player and coach Knute Rockne, who was born in Voss in 1888; look for the metal memorial plaque on a rock near the train station.

Voss' helpful **TI** is a five-minute walk from the train station—just head toward the church and stay on the right; the TI is down the street past the City Hall signed *Voss Tinghus* (Mon-Sat 9:00-18:00, Sun 10:00-17:00; off-season until 16:00 and closed Sat-Sun; Skulegata 14, mobile 40 61 77 00, www.visitvoss.no).

Drivers should zip right through Voss, but two miles outside town, you can stop at the **Mølstertunet Folk Museum,** which has 16 buildings showing off farm life in the 17th and 18th centuries (80 NOK; daily 10:00-17:00, Sept-mid-May until 15:00 and closed Sat; Mølstervegen 143, tel. 47 47 97 94, www.vossfolkemuseum.no).

▲Voss-Bergen Train

The least exciting segment of the trip—but still pleasantly scenic—

this train chugs 60 miles along the valley between the midsize town of Voss and Bergen. For the best scenery, sit on the right side of the train if coming from Oslo, or the left side if coming from Bergen. Between Voss and Dale, you'll pass several scenic lakes; near Bergen, you'll go along the Veafjord.

Cost: 204 NOK, fully covered by rail passes that include Norway. Reservations aren't necessary for this leg.

Schedule: Unlike the long-distance Oslo-Bergen journey, this line is also served by more frequent commuter trains (about hourly, 75 minutes).

Voss-Oslo Train: Note that if you're doing the Nutshell round-trip loop from Oslo, you should catch the train from Voss (rather than Bergen) back to Oslo. The return trip takes six hours and costs 860 NOK; reservations are strongly recommended four to five weeks ahead in peak season.

Flåm

Flåm (pronounced "flome")—where the boat and Flåmsbana train meet, at the head of the Aurlandsfjord—feels more like a transit junction than a village. But its striking setting, easy transportation connections, and touristy bustle make it appealing as a home base for exploring the nearby area.

Orientation to Flåm

Most of Flåm's services are in a modern cluster of buildings in and around the train station, including the TI, train ticket desk, public WC, cafeteria, and souvenir shops. Just outside the station, the little red shed at the head of the tracks serves as a **left-luggage desk** (daily 8:00-19:00, on your right as you depart the train, ring bell if nobody's there), and displays a chart of the services you'll find in the station. The **boat dock** for fjord cruises is just beyond the end of the tracks. Surrounding the station are a Co-op Marked **grocery store** (with a basic pharmacy and post office inside, Mon-Fri 8:00-20:00, Sat-Sun 10:00-18:00, shorter hours off-season) and a smattering of hotels, travel agencies, and touristy restaurants. Aside from a few scattered farmhouses and some homes lining the road, there's not much of a town here. (The extremely sleepy old

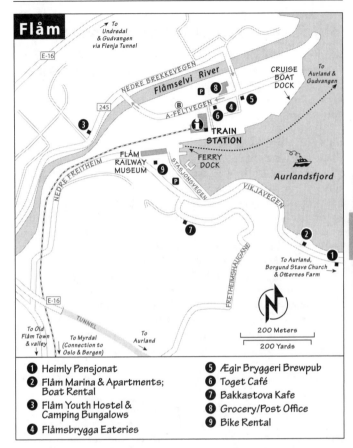

NORWAY IN A NUTSHELL

Flåm

To Undredal & Gudvangen via Flenja Tunnel

E-16

NEDRE BREKKEVEGEN

Flåmselvi River

245

A-FELTVEGEN

CRUISE BOAT DOCK

To Aurland & Gudvangen

P

8

B

6 4 5

3

i **TRAIN STATION**

FLÅM RAILWAY MUSEUM

9

STASJONSVEGEN

FERRY DOCK

Aurlandsfjord

VIKJAVEGEN

NEDRE FRETHEIM

P

7

FRETHEIMSHAUGANE

2

1

To Aurland, Borgund Stave Church & Otternes Farm

E-16

TUNNEL

To Old Flåm Town & valley

To Myrdal (Connection to Oslo & Bergen)

To Aurland

N

200 Meters
200 Yards

❶ Heimly Pensjonat
❷ Flåm Marina & Apartments; Boat Rental
❸ Flåm Youth Hostel & Camping Bungalows
❹ Flåmsbrygga Eateries

❺ Ægir Bryggeri Brewpub
❻ Toget Café
❼ Bakkastova Kafe
❽ Grocery/Post Office
❾ Bike Rental

town center—where tourists rarely venture, and which you'll pass on the Flåmsbana train—is a few miles up the river, in the valley.)

Tourist Information: Inside the train station you'll find the TI and the Flåm Visitors Center.

The **visitors center** sells tickets for The Fjords ferries to Gudvangen (but not its rival, Lustrabaatane), the Flåmsbana train, regular train tickets, and other tours in the area (daily 7:00-19:00, shorter hours Sept-April, tel. 57 63 14 00, www.visitflam.com).

At the **TI** you can purchase tickets for the Lustrabaatane ferry to Gudvangen, the express boat to Bergen, FjordSafari, Njord Seakayak Adventures, and other tours. The TI also hands out schedules for buses, boats, and trains; a diagram of the train-station area, identifying services available in each building; a map of Flåm and the surrounding area, marked with suggested walks and hikes; and information on Bergen or Oslo (daily 8:30-18:00, Oct-March 9:00-15:00, mobile 99 23 15 00, https://en.sognefjord.no).

Sights and Activities in and near Flåm

I've listed several activities in the village of Flåm. But the main reason people come here is to leave it—see the options later. Because Aurland and Flåm are close together (10 minutes away by car or bus, or 20 minutes by boat), I've also listed attractions near Aurland.

IN THE VILLAGE

Flåm's village activities are all along or near the pier.

The **Flåm Railway Museum** (Flåmsbana Museet), sprawling through the long old train station building alongside the tracks, has surprisingly good exhibits about the history of the train that connects Flåm to the main line up above. You'll find good English explanations, artifacts, re-creations of historic interiors (such as a humble schoolhouse), and an old train car. It's the only real museum in town and a good place to kill time while waiting for your boat or train (free, daily 9:00-17:00, until 20:00 in summer).

A pointless and overpriced **tourist train** does a 45-minute loop around Flåm (130 NOK).

The pleasantly woody **Ægir Bryggeri,** a microbrewery designed to resemble an old Viking longhouse, offers tastes of its five beers (150 NOK; also restaurant meals in evening with a matching beer menu).

The TI hands out a map suggesting several **walks and hikes** in the area, starting from right in town.

Consider renting a **boat** to go out on the peaceful waters of the fjord. You can paddle near the walls of the fjord and really get a sense of the immensity of these mountains. You can rent rowboats, motorboats, and paddleboats at the little marina across the harbor. If you'd rather have a kayak, **Njord Seakayak Adventures** does kayak tours, but won't rent you one unless you're certified (mobile 91 32 66 28, www.seakayaknorway.com).

FROM OR NEAR FLÅM
▲▲▲Cruising Nærøyfjord

The most scenic fjord I've seen anywhere in Norway is about an hour from Flåm (basically the last half of the Flåm-Gudvangen trip). If you've driven to Flåm, didn't book a Nutshell tour, or are staying overnight, here are several ways to cruise it.

The Fjords Tours: This private company runs several trips from Flåm; their most popular is a ferry ride to Gudvangen and a bus ride back to Flåm (435-705 NOK, 4-hour round-trip, departs Flåm at 10:00, 12:00, 16:00, and 18:00, fewer off-season, choose slower Classic ferry for best viewing).

Another offering, the World Heritage Cruise, is a boat trip up the Nærøyfjord, stopping at Bleiklindi, Bakka, Styvi, and Dyrdal. You can leave the boat to visit these villages and hop on when the boat returns. It's possible to hike about four miles between Bleiklindi and Styvi with this option (350 NOK, 3 hours, multiple departures daily June-Aug). They also do a variation on this trip with a 45-minute stop in the village of Undredal for lunch and a goat-cheese tasting (750 NOK, June-Aug only); a bus ride up to the thrilling Stegastein viewpoint (a concrete-and-wood viewing pier sticking out from a mountainside high above Aurland, 290 NOK); and more. For details, drop by the Flåm Visitors Center inside the train station, call 57 63 14 00, or see www.visitflam.com.

FjordSafari to Nærøyfjord: FjordSafari takes little groups out onto the fjord in small, open Zodiac-type boats with an English-speaking guide. Participants wear full-body weather suits, furry hats, and spacey goggles (making everyone on the boat look like crash-test dummies). As the boat rockets across the water, you'll be thankful for the gear, no matter what the weather. Their two-hour Flåm-Gudvangen-Flåm tour focuses on the Nærøyfjord, and gets you all the fjord magnificence you can imagine (790 NOK, several departures daily). Their three-hour tour is the same but adds a stop in Undredal, where you can see goat cheese being made, sample it, and wander that sleepy village (890 NOK, one departure daily May-Aug, fewer off-season, kids get discounts, mobile 99 09 08 60, www.fjordsafari.com, Maylene). Skip the 1.5-hour "basic" tour, which just barely touches on the Nærøyfjord.

▲Flåm Valley Bike Ride or Hike

For the best single-day land activity from Flåm, take the Flåms-bana train to Myrdal, then hike or mountain-bike along the road

(half gravel, half paved) back down to Flåm (2-3 hours by bike, gorgeous water-falls, great mountain scenery, and a cute church with an evocative graveyard, but no fjord views).

Walkers can hike the best two hours from Myrdal to Blomheller, and catch the train from there into the valley. Or, without riding the train, you can simply walk up the valley 2.5 miles to the church and a little farther to a waterfall. Whenever you get tired hiking up or down the valley, you can hop on the next train. Pick up the helpful map with this and other hiking options (ranging from easy to strenuous) at the Flåm TI.

Bikers can rent good mountain bikes from the cabin next to the Flåm train station (180 NOK/2-hour minimum, 350 NOK/

day, includes helmet; daily May-June 9:00-18:00, July-Sept 8:00-20:00, closed off-season). It costs 100 NOK to take a bike to Myrdal on the train.

Otternes Farms

This humble but magical cluster of four centuries-old farms is about three miles from Flåm (easy for drivers; a decent walk or bike ride otherwise). It's a ghost village perched high on a ridge, up a twisty gravel road midway between Flåm and Aurland. These traditional time-warp houses and barns date from the time before emigration decimated the workforce, coinage replaced barter, and industrialized margarine became more popular than butter—all

of which left farmers to eke out a living relying only on their goats and the cheese they produced. Until 1919 the only road between Aurland and Flåm passed between this huddle of 27 buildings, high above the fjord. First settled in 1522, farmers lived here until the 1990s.

OVER (OR UNDER) THE MOUNTAINS, TO LÆRDAL AND BORGUND

To reach these sights, you'll first head along the fjord to Aurland (described later). Of the sights below, the Lærdal Tunnel, Stegastein viewpoint, and Aurlandsvegen "Snow Road" are best for drivers. The Borgund Stave Church can be reached by car, or by bus from Flåm or Aurland.

Lærdal Tunnel

Drivers find that this tunnel makes connecting Flåm and Lærdal a snap. It's the world's longest road-vehicle tunnel, stretching 15 miles between Aurland and Lærdal as part of the E-16 highway. It also makes the wonderful Borgund Stave Church (described later) less than an hour's drive from Aurland. The downside to the tunnel is that it goes beneath my favorite scenic drive in Norway (the Aurlandsvegen "Snow Road," described next). But with about two hours, you can drive through the tunnel to Lærdal and then return via the "Snow Road," with the Stegastein viewpoint as a finale, before dropping back into Aurland.

▲▲Stegastein Viewpoint and Aurlandsvegen "Snow Road"

With a car, clear weather, and a little nerve, consider twisting up the

NORWAY IN A NUTSHELL

mountain behind Aurland on route 243 for about 20 minutes to a magnificent view over the Aurlandsfjord. A viewpoint called Stegastein—which looks like a giant, wooden, sideways number "7"—provides a platform from which you can enjoy stunning views across the fjord and straight down to Aurland. Immediately beyond the viewpoint, you leave the fjord views and enter the beautifully desolate mountaintop world of the Aurlandsvegen "Snow Road." When this narrow ribbon of a road finally hits civilization on the other side, you're a mile from the Lærdal tunnel entrance and about 30 minutes from the fine Borgund Stave Church.

▲▲Borgund Stave Church

About 16 miles east of Lærdal, in the village of Borgund, is Norway's most-visited and one of its best-preserved stave churches.

Dating from around 1180, the interior features only a few later additions, including a 16th-century pulpit, 17th-century stone altar, painted decorations, and crossbeam reinforcements.

Cost and Hours: 90 NOK, buy tickets in museum across street, daily June-Aug 8:00-20:00, May and Sept 10:00-17:00, closed Oct-April. The museum has a shop and a fine little **$$ cafeteria** serving filling and tasty lunches. Tel. 57 66 81 09, www.stavechurch.com.

Getting There: It's about a 30-minute **drive** east of Lærdal, on E-16 (the road to Oslo—if coming from Aurland or Flåm, consider taking the scenic route via the Stegastein viewpoint, described earlier). There's also a convenient **bus** connection: The bus departs Flåm and Aurland around midday (direction: Lillehammer) and heads for the church, with a return bus departing Borgund in mid-afternoon (170-NOK round-trip, get ticket from driver, about 1 hour each way with about 1 hour at the church, bus runs daily May-Sept, tell driver you want to get off at the church).

Visiting the Church: Explore the dimly lit interior, illuminated only by the original, small, circular windows up high. The oldest and most authentic item in the church is the stone baptismal font. In medieval times, priests conducting baptisms would go outside to shoo away the evil spirits from an infant before bringing it inside the church for the ritual. (If infants died before being baptized, they couldn't be buried in the churchyard, so parents would put their bodies in little coffins and hide them under the church's floorboards to get them as close as possible to God.)

Notice the X-shaped crosses of St. Andrew (the church's patron), carvings of dragons, and medieval runes. Borgund's church also comes with one of this country's best stave-church history museums, which beautifully explains these icons of medieval Norway.

Sleeping in Flåm

My recommended accommodations are away from the tacky train-station bustle, but a close enough walk to be convenient. The first two places are located along the waterfront a quarter-mile from the station: Walk around the little harbor (with the water on your left) for about 10 minutes. It's more enjoyable to follow the level, waterfront dock than to hike up the main road.

$$$$ Heimly Pensjonat, with 22 straightforward rooms, is clean, efficient, and the best small hotel in town. Sit on the porch with new friends and watch the clouds roll down the fjord. Prices include breakfast and a three-course dinner (family rooms, doubles are mostly twins, closed off-season, tel. 57 63 23 00, post@heimly. no).

$$$ Flåm Marina and Apartments, perched right on the fjord, is ideal for families and longer stays. They offer one standard double and 10 new-feeling, self-catering apartments that each sleep 2-5 people. All units offer views of the fjord with a balcony, kitchenette, and small dining area (no breakfast, café serving lunch and dinner open during high season, boat rental, laundry facilities, next to the guest harbor just below Heimly Pensjonat, tel. 57 63 35 55, www.flammarina.no, booking@flammarina.no).

¢-$$ Flåm Youth Hostel and Camping Bungalows, voted Scandinavia's most beautiful campground, is run by the friendly Håland family, who rent the cheapest beds in the area (sheets and towels included in hostel but extra in cabins, showers extra, no meals but kitchen access, laundry, apple grove, mobile 94 03 26 81, www.flaam-camping.no, camping@flaam-camping.no). It's a five-minute walk toward the valley from the train station: Cross the bridge and turn left up the main road; then look for the hostel on the right.

Eating in Flåm

Dining options beyond your hotel's dining room or kitchenette are expensive and touristy. Don't aim for high cuisine here—go practical. Almost all eateries are clustered near the train station complex. Hours can be unpredictable, flexing with the season, but you can expect these to be open daily in high season. Places here tend to close pretty early (especially in shoulder season)—don't wait too long for dinner.

The **Flåmsbrygga** complex, sprawling through a long building toward the fjord from the station, includes a hotel, the affordable **$$ Furukroa Caféteria** (daily 8:00-20:00 in season, sandwiches, fast-food meals, and pizzas), and the pricey **$$$$ Flåmstova Restaurant** (breakfast and lunch buffet, sit-down dinner service). Next door is their fun, Viking-longhouse-shaped brewpub, **$$$ Ægir Bryggeri** (daily 17:00-22:00, local microbrews, Viking-inspired meals). **$$ Toget Café,** with seating in old train cars, prides itself on using as many locally sourced and organic ingredients as possible. **$$ Bakkastova Kafe,** at the other end of town, feels cozier. Housed in a traditional Norwegian red cabin just above the Fretheim Hotel, with a view terrace, it serves sandwiches, salads, and authentic Norwegian fare (daily 12:00-16:00).

Aurland

A few miles north of Flåm, Aurland is more of a real town and less of a tourist depot. While it's nothing exciting (Balestrand is

more lively and appealing, and Solvorn is cuter—see next chapter), it's a good, easy-going fjordside home base. And thanks to its location—on the main road and boat lines, near Flåm—it's relatively handy for those taking public transportation.

Getting There: Aurland is an easy 10-minute drive or bus trip from Flåm. If you want to stay overnight in Aurland, note that every train (except the late-night one) arriving in Flåm connects with a bus or boat to Aurland (in summer: bus-11/day, 10 minutes, 60 NOK; ferry-4/day, 20 minutes, 165 NOK). The Flåm-Gud-vangen Classic ferry doesn't always have a scheduled stop at Aurland, but they're willing to stop there if you ask—so it's possible to continue the Nutshell route from Aurland without backtracking to Flåm. Boat tickets can be bought aboard the ferry in Aurland or at www.visitflam.com. The Bergen-Balestrand-Flåm express boat stops in Aurland (for details, see the next chapter).

Orientation to Aurland

From Aurland's dingy boat dock area, walk one block up the paved street into the heart of town. On your right is the Spar supermarket (handy for picnic supplies) and Marianne Bakeri and Café (at the bridge). To your left is the Vangsgården Guest House and, behind it, Aurland Fjordhotel. To reach the TI, go straight ahead and bear right, then look behind the white church (800 years old and worth a peek). The bus stop, with buses to Flåm, is in front of the TI. For attractions near Aurland, see "Sights and Activities in and near Flåm," earlier.

Tourist Information: The TI stocks English-language brochures about hikes and day trips from the area, and sells local maps (daily 9:00-16:00, closed Sat-Sun in off-season; behind the white church—look for green-and-white *i* sign; mobile 91 79 41 64, https://en.sognefjord.no).

Sleeping in Aurland

$$$$ Aurland Fjordhotel is big, modern, and centrally located. While it has a business-hotel vibe, most of its 30 rooms come with gorgeous fjord-view balconies (tel. 57 63 35 05, www.aurland-fjordhotel.com, post@aurland-fjordhotel.com, Steinar Kjerstein).

$$$ Vangsgården Guest House, closest to the boat landing, is a complex of old buildings dominating the old center of Aurland and run from one reception desk (Wi-Fi in main building, tel. 57 63 35 80, www.vangsgaarden.no, vangsgaarden@alb.no, open all year, Astrid). The main building is a simple, old guesthouse offering basic rooms and a fine old-timey living room. Their old-fashioned **Aabelheim Pension** is Aurland's best *koselig* (cozy)-like-a-farmhouse place (same prices). And lining the waterfront are their six adorable wood **$$$$** cabins with balconies, kitchen, bathroom, and two bedrooms (sleeps 2-6 people, sheets and breakfast extra, book 2 months in advance). The owners also run the recommended Duehuset Pub and rent bikes.

NEAR AURLAND

$$ Skahjem Gard is an active farm run by Aurland's former deputy mayor, Nils Tore. He's converted his old sheep barn into seven spic-and-span family apartments with private bathrooms and kitchenettes, each sleeping up to four people (sheets and towels included, two miles up the valley—road #50, follow *Hol* signs, mobile 95 17 25 67, nskahjem@online.no). It's a 25-minute walk from town, but Nils will pick up and drop off travelers at the ferry. This is best for families and foursomes with cars.

¢ Winjum Huts, about a half-mile from Aurland's dock, rents 14 basic cabins on a peaceful perch overlooking the majestic fjord. The washhouse/kitchen is where you'll find the toilets and showers. Follow the road uphill past the Aurland Fjordhotel; the huts are after the first hairpin curve (apartment available, sheets extra, showers extra, no food available—just beer, mobile 41 47 47 51).

Eating in Aurland

$$$ Marianne Bakeri and Café is a basic little bakery/café serving the best-value food in town. It's a block from the main square, at the bridge over the river. Sit inside or on its riverside terrace (sandwiches, pizza, and quiche; daily 10:00-17:00, mobile 90 51 29 78).

$$$ Duehuset Pub ("The Dove's House"), run by Vangsgården Guest House, serves up decent food in the center of town (daily 15:00-23:00, only open Fri-Sun for dinner in off-season).

The **$$$$ Aurland Fjordhotel** is your only alternative for splurges (dinner buffet, daily 19:00-22:00, shorter hours off-season, bar open later, tel. 57 63 35 05).

For cheap eats on dockside benches, gather a picnic at the **Spar** supermarket (Mon-Fri 9:00-20:00, Sat until 18:00, closed Sun).

Undredal

This almost impossibly remote community is home to about 80 people and 400 goats. A huge percentage of the town's former

population (300 people) emigrated to the US between 1850 and 1925. Undredal was accessible only by boat until 1988, when the road from Flåm opened. There's not much in the town, which is famous for its church and its goat cheese, but I'll never forget the picnic I had on the ferry wharf. While appealing, Undredal is quiet (some say better from the boat) and difficult to reach—you'll have to be patient to connect to other towns. For more information on the town, see www.undredal.no.

Getting There: The 15-minute drive from Flåm is mostly through a tunnel. By sea, you'll sail past Undredal on the Flåm-Gudvangen boat (you can request a stop). To get the ferry to pick you up in Undredal, turn on the blinking light (though some express boats will not stop).

Visiting Undredal: Undredal has Norway's smallest still-used **church,** seating 40 people for services every fourth Sunday. The original church was built in 1147 (look for the four original stave pillars inside). It was later expanded, pews added, and the interior painted in the 16th century in a way that resembles the traditional Norwegian *rosemaling* style (which came later). You can get in only with a 30-minute tour (70 NOK, June-mid-Aug daily 10:00-17:00, less in shoulder season, closed Oct-April, mobile 95 29 76 68).

Undredal's farms exist to produce **cheese.** The beloved local cheese comes in two versions: brown and white. The brown version is unaged and slightly sweet, while the white cheese has been aged and is mild and a bit salty. For samples, visit the Undredalsbui grocery store at the harbor (Mon-Fri 9:00-16:30, Sat until 15:00, Sun 12:00-16:00, shorter hours and closed Sun off-season).

Sleeping in Undredal: This sleepy town can accommodate maybe a dozen visitors a night. **$ Undredal Overnatting** rents four modern, woody, comfortable rooms and two apartments. The reception is at the café on the harbor, while the accommodations are at the top of town (sheets included, breakfast extra, tel. 57 63 30 80, www.visitundredal.no, visit@undredal.no).

MORE ON THE SOGNEFJORD

Balestrand • The Lustrafjord • Scenic Drives

Norway's world of fjords is decorated with medieval stave churches, fishing boats, cascading waterfalls, dramatic glaciers, and brightly painted shiplap villages. Travelers in a hurry zip through the fjords on the Norway in a Nutshell route (see previous chapter). Their heads spin from all the scenery, and most wish they had more time on the Sognefjord. If you can linger in fjord country, this chapter is for you.

Snuggle into the fjordside village of Balestrand, which has a variety of walking and biking options and a fun local arts scene. Balestrand is also a handy jumping-off spot for adventures great and small, including a day trip up the Fjærlandsfjord to gaze at a receding tongue of the Jostedal Glacier, or across the Sognefjord to the truly medieval-feeling Hopperstad Stave Church. Farther east is the Lustrafjord, a tranquil branch of the Sognefjord offering drivers an appealing concentration of visit-worthy sights. On the Lustrafjord, you'll enjoy enchanting hamlets with pristine fjord views (such as Solvorn), historic churches (including Norway's oldest stave church at Urnes and the humble village Dale Church in Luster), an opportunity to touch and even hike on a glacier (the Nigard), and more stunning fjord views.

This region is important to the people of Norway. After four centuries under Danish rule, the soul of the country was nearly lost. With partial independence and its own constitution in the early 1800s, the country experienced a resurgence of national pride. Urban Norwegians headed for the fjord country here in the west. Norway's first Romantic painters and writers were drawn to Balestrand, inspired by the unusual light and dramatic views of mountains plunging into the fjords. The Sognefjord, with its many branches, is featured in more Romantic paintings than any other fjord.

PLANNING YOUR TIME

If you can spare a day or two off the Norway in a Nutshell route, spend it here. Balestrand is the best home base, especially if you're

relying on public transportation (it's well-connected by express boat both to the Nutshell scene and to Bergen). If you have a car, consider staying in the heart of the Lustrafjord region in sweet little Solvorn (easy ferry connection to the Urnes Stave Church and a short drive to the Nigard Glacier). As fjord home bases go, Balestrand and Solvorn are both better—but less convenient—than Flåm or Aurland on the Nutshell route.

With one night in this area, you'll have to blitz the sights on the way between destinations; with two

nights, you can slow your pace (and your pulse) to enjoy the fjord scenery and plenty of day-trip possibilities.

Balestrand

The pleasant fjord town of Balestrand (pop. 1,300) has a long history of hosting tourists, thanks to its landmark Kviknes Hotel. But

it also feels real and lived-in, making Balestrand a nice mix of cuteness and convenience. The town is near, but not *too* near, the Nutshell bustle across the fjord—and yet it's an easy express-boat trip away if you'd like to dive into the Nuttiness. In short, consider Balestrand a worthwhile detour from the typical fjord visit—al-

lowing you to dig deeper into the Sognefjord, just like the glaciers did during the last ice age.

With two nights, you can relax and consider some day trips: Cruise up the nearby Fjærlandsfjord for a peek at a distant tongue of the ever-less-mighty Jostedal Glacier, or head across the Sognefjord to the beautiful Hopperstad Stave Church in Vik. Balestrand also has outdoor activities for everyone, from dreamy fjordside strolls and strenuous mountain hikes to wildly scenic bike rides. For dinner, splurge on the memorable *smörgåsbord*-style *store koldt bord* dinner in the Kviknes Hotel dining room, then sip coffee from its balcony as you watch the sun set (or not) over the fjord.

PLANNING YOUR TIME

Balestrand's key advantage is its easy express-boat connection to Bergen, offering an alternative route to the fjord from the typical Nutshell train-bus combo. Consider zipping here on the Bergen boat, then continuing on via the Nutshell route.

One night is enough to get a taste of Balestrand. But spending two nights buys you some time for day trips. Note that the first flurry of day trips departs early, around 7:30-8:00 (includes the boat to Vik/Hopperstad Stave Church or the full-day Fjærlandsfjord glacier excursion), and the next batch departs around noon (the half-day Fjærlandsfjord glacier excursion and the last boat to Flåm). If you wait until after 12:00 to make your choice, you'll miss the boat...literally.

Balestrand pretty much shuts down from mid-September through mid-May—when most of the activities, sights, hotels, and restaurants listed here are likely closed.

Orientation to Balestrand

Most travelers arrive in Balestrand on the express boat from Bergen or Flåm. The tidy harbor area has a TI, two grocery stores, a couple of galleries, a town history museum, and a small aquarium devoted to marine life found in the fjord. The historic wooden Kviknes Hotel and its ugly modern annex dominate Balestrand's waterfront.

Even during tourist season, Balestrand is quiet. How quiet? The police station closes on weekends. And it's tiny—from the harbor to the Balestrand Hotel is a five-minute stroll, and you can walk from the aquarium to Kviknes Hotel in less time than that.

Balestrand became accessible to the wider world in 1858 when an activist minister (from the church you see across the fjord from town) brought in the first steamer service. That put Balestrand on the Grand Tour map of the Romantic Age. Even the German *Kaiser* chose to summer here. Today, people from around the world come here to feel the grandeur of the fjord country and connect with the essence of Norway.

TOURIST INFORMATION

At the TI, located next to the Joker supermarket at the harbor, pick up the free, helpful *Outdoor Activities in Balestrand* brochure. If

MORE SOGNEFJORD

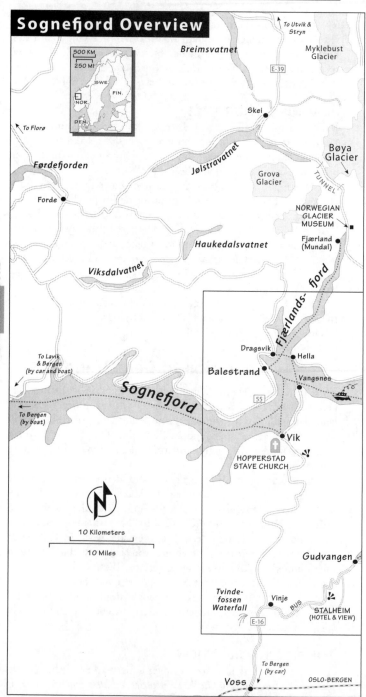

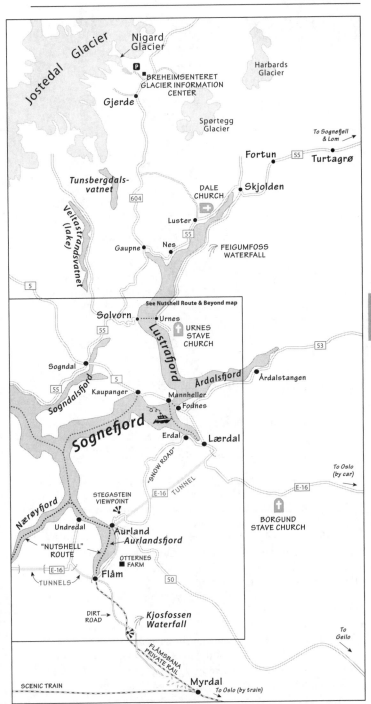

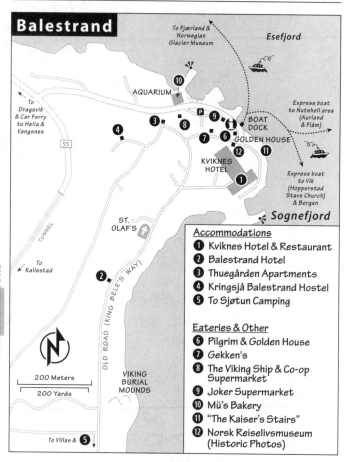

Balestrand

To Fjærland &
Norwegian
Glacier Museum

Esefjord

AQUARIUM

To
Dragsvik
& Car Ferry
to Hella &
Vangsnes

Express boat
to Nutshell area
(Aurland
& Flåm)

BOAT
DOCK

GOLDEN HOUSE

KVIKNES
HOTEL

Express boat
to Vik
(Hopperstad
Stave Church)
& Bergen

ST.
OLAF'S

Sognefjord

TUNNEL

To
Kallestad

OLD ROAD (KING BELE'S WAY)

200 Meters

200 Yards

VIKING
BURIAL
MOUNDS

To Villas &

Accommodations
1 Kviknes Hotel & Restaurant
2 Balestrand Hotel
3 Thuegården Apartments
4 Kringsjå Balestrand Hostel
5 To Sjøtun Camping

Eateries & Other
6 Pilgrim & Golden House
7 Gekken's
8 The Viking Ship & Co-op Supermarket
9 Joker Supermarket
10 Mü's Bakery
11 "The Kaiser's Stairs"
12 Norsk Reiselivsmuseum (Historic Photos)

MORE SOGNEFJORD

you're planning on a longer hike, consider the good 150-NOK hiking map. The TI has numerous brochures about the Sognefjord area and detailed information on the more challenging hikes. It offers free Wi-Fi, rents bikes (100 NOK/hour, 270 NOK/day), and sells tickets for the Norled ferry and various fjord, kayak, and fishing tours in the area (daily 10:00-16:00 in summer, closed weekends in spring and fall and all of Oct-April; mobile 94 87 75 01—answered all year, https://en.sognefjord.no).

Local Guide: Bjørg Bjøberg, who runs the Golden House (Det Gylne Hus) art gallery, knows the town well and is happy to show visitors around (1,000-1,500 NOK/2 hours per group—gather several people and divvy up the cost, mobile 91 56 28 42).

Car Rental: The **Balholm Car Rental** agency will deliver a car to your Balestrand hotel, and they'll pick it up, too (daily 8:00-20:00, tel. 41 24 82 53, www.leigebil.no, booking@leigebil.no).

Also, the Kviknes Hotel can arrange a one-day car rental for you (tel. 57 69 42 00).

Sights in Balestrand

Balestrand Harborfront Stroll

The tiny harbor stretches from the aquarium to the big, old Kviknes Hotel. Stroll its length, starting at the aquarium (described later) and little marina. Across the street, at The Viking Ship shack, a German woman named Carola sells German sausages with an evangelical zeal (see "Eating in Balestrand," later). A couple of doors down, the Spindelvev ("Spider's Web") shop sells handicrafts made by people with physical and mental disabilities. A local home for the disabled was closed in the 1980s, but many of its former residents stayed in Balestrand because the government gave them pensions and houses in town.

Then, in the ugly modern strip mall, you'll find the TI, supermarket, and a community bulletin board with the schedule for the summer cinema (the little theater, 800 yards away, runs films nightly in their original language). On the corner is the Golden House art gallery and museum (described later). Behind it—and built into solid rock—is the boxy new moss-covered home of the Norwegian Travel Museum (Norsk Reiselivsmuseum), featuring photos showing this part of Norway over the past 150 years, interactive exhibits, and souvenirs. And just beyond that is the dock where the big Bergen-Sognefjord express catamaran ties up.

Across the street is a cute white house (at #8), which used to stand at the harborfront until the big Joker supermarket and Kviknes Hotel, with its modern annex, partnered to ruin the town center. This little house was considered historic enough to be air-lifted 100 yards to this new spot. It's flanked by two other historic buildings, which house a gallery and an artisans' workshop.

Farther along, find the rust-red building that was the waiting room for the 19th-century steamer that first brought tourism to town. Walk a few steps farther, and stop at the tall stone monument erected to celebrate the North Bergen Steamship Company. Its boats first connected Balestrand to the rest of the world in 1858. In front of the monument, some nondescript concrete steps lead into the water. These are "The Kaiser's Stairs," built for the German emperor, Kaiser Wilhelm II, who made his first summer visit (complete with navy convoy) in 1899 and kept returning until the outbreak of World War I.

Behind the monument stands one of the largest old wooden buildings in Norway, Kviknes Hotel. It was built in the 1870s and faces the rare little island in the fjord, which helped give the town its name: "Balestrand" means the strand or promenade in front of an island. (The island is now connected to the hotel's front yard and is part of a playground for its guests.) Hike up the black driveway that leads from the monument to the hotel's modern lobby. Go inside and find (to your left) the plush old lounge, a virtual painting gallery. All the pieces are by artists from this area, celebrating the natural wonder of the fjord country—part of the trend that helped 19th-century Norway reconnect with its heritage. (While you're here, consider making a reservation and choosing a table for a *smörgåsbord* dinner tonight.) Leave the hotel lobby (from the door opposite to the one you entered), and head up to St. Olaf's Church (300 yards, described next). To continue this stroll, take King Bele's Way (described later) up the fjord.

St. Olaf's Church

This distinctive wooden church was built in 1897. Construction was started by Margaret Sophia Kvikne, the wife of Knut Kvikne

(of the Kviknes Hotel family; her portrait is in the rear of the nave), but she died in 1894, before the church was finished. This devout Englishwoman wanted a church in Balestrand where English services were held...and to this day, bells ring to announce services by British clergy. St. Olaf, who brought Christianity to Norway in the 11th century, was the country's patron saint in Catholic times. The church was built in a "Neo-stave" style, with lots of light from its windows and an altar painting inspired by the famous *Risen Christ* statue in Copenhagen's Cathedral of Our Lady. Here, Christ is flanked by fields of daisies (called "priests' collars" in Norwegian) and peace lilies. From the door of the church, enjoy a good view of the island in the fjord.

Cost and Hours: Free, open daily, services in English every Sun from late May through August.

Golden House (Det Gylne Hus)

This golden-colored house facing the ferry landing was built as a general store in 1928. Today it houses an art installation called "Golden Memories" and a quirky museum created by local watercolorist and historian Bjørg Bjøberg, and her husband, Arthur Adamson.

Cost and Hours: Free entry to the ground floor, 25 NOK for the second floor and the glass dome; optional private one-hour tour costs 50 NOK/person and includes all floors—

minimum 5 people, maximum 9; May-Aug daily 10:00-22:00, shorter hours late April and Sept, closed in winter; mobile 91 56 28 42, www.detgylnehus.no.

Visiting the Golden House: On the ground floor you'll find Bjørg's gallery, with her watercolors celebrating the beauty of Norway, and Arthur's paintings, celebrating the beauty of women. Upstairs is the Pilgrimage Balestrand room, focusing on their local nature pilgrimage program, along with an exhibit of historical knickknacks, contributed by locals wanting to preserve treasures from their families' past. You'll see a medicine cabinet stocked with old-fashioned pills, an antiquated tourist map, lots of skis, and WWII-era mementos. A wheel in the wall once powered a crane that could winch up goods from the fjord below (back when this store was actually on the waterfront). While there are no written English explanations, Bjørg is happy to explain things.

Unable to contain her creative spirit, Bjørg has paired an eccentric wonderland experience with her private tour of the Golden House's hidden rooms. The tour includes a 30-minute movie (at 17:00 and 18:00), either about her art and local nature, or about Balestrand in winter. Bjørg and Arthur also run the recommended on-site restaurant, Pilgrim. Diners have free access to the glass dome on top of the building, with a telescope and lovely views.

Strolling King Bele's Way up the Fjord

For a delightful walk (or bike ride), head west out of town up the "old road"—once the main road from the harbor—for about a mile. It follows the fjord's edge, passing numerous "villas" from the late 1800s. At the time, this Swiss style was popular with some locals, who hoped to introduce a dose of Romanticism into Norwegian architecture. Look for the dragons' heads (copied from Viking-age stave churches) decorating the gables. Along the walk, you'll pass a swimming area, a campground, and two burial mounds from the Viking age, marked by a ponderous statue of the Viking King Bele. Check out the wooden shelters for the mailboxes; some give the elevation (*m.o.h.* stands for "meters over *havet*"—the sea)—not too high, are they? The walk is described in the *Outdoor Activities in Balestrand* brochure (free at the TI or your hotel).

Aquarium

The tiny aquarium gives you a good look at marine life in the Sognefjord. For descriptions, borrow the English booklet at the front desk. While not thrilling, the well-explained place is a decent rainy-day option. A 15-minute slideshow starts at the top and bottom of each hour. The last room is filled with wood carvings depicting traditional everyday life in the fjordside village of Munken. The fish-filled tanks on the dock outside are also worth a look.

Cost and Hours: 70 NOK, daily 9:00-19:00, closed mid-Sept-April, tel. 57 69 13 03.

Biking

You can cycle around town, or go farther by circling the scenic Esefjord (north of town, en route to the ferry landing at Dragsvik—about 6 miles each way). Or pedal west up Sognefjord along the scenic King Bele's Way (described earlier). The roads here are relatively flat. Rental bikes are available at the TI and through Kviknes Hotel.

Kayak and Boat Tours

If you're looking for a recreational—and educational—kayak trip on the fjord, **Gone Paddling** offers a three-hour tour with an experienced guide (790 NOK, includes lunch, mobile 91 53 81 33, www.gonepaddling.no).

Balestrand Fjord Adventure specializes in Zodiac-type boat tours on the Sognefjord. Passengers wear full-body weather suits, life vests, and goggles. Join their daily round-trip cruise departing at 13:00 (650 NOK, 1.5 hours) or take the more extensive Nærøyfjord tour (1,300 NOK, 2.5 hours, 3/week, mobile 47 85 53 23, www.balestrandadventure.no).

NEAR BALESTRAND

These two side-trips are possible only if you've got the better part of a day in Balestrand. With a car, you can see Hopperstad Stave Church on the drive to Bergen.

▲▲Hopperstad Stave Church
(Hopperstad Stavkyrkje) in Vik

The most accessible stave church in the area—and perhaps the most scenically situated in all of Norway—is located just a 20-minute express-boat ride across the Sognefjord, in the town of Vik. Hopperstad Stave Church boasts a breathtaking exterior, with several tiers of dragon heads overlooking rolling fields between fjord cliffs. The interior is notable for its emptiness. Instead of being crammed full of later additions, the church is blissfully uncluttered, as it was when it was built in the mid-12th century. (For more on stave churches, see page 9.)

Cost and Hours: 70 NOK; daily 10:00-17:00, mid-June–mid-Aug from 9:00, closed Oct–mid-May; good 30-NOK color booklet in English, tel. 57 69 52 70, www.stavechurch.com/hopperstad.

Tours: Attendants will give you a free tour at your request, provided they're not too busy. (Ask where the medieval graffiti is, and they'll grab their flashlight and show you.)

Getting There: Pedestrians can ride the express passenger boat between Balestrand and Vik (89 NOK each way). The only way to get to the church and back in one day is to take the 7:50 departure from Balestrand, then return on the 11:30 departure from Vik, arriving back in Balestrand at 11:50—just in time to join a 12:00 glacier excursion (described on the next page). Because schedules can change, be sure to double-check these times at the TI or www.norled.no under "Expressboat." The church is a 20-minute walk up the valley from Vik's harbor. From the boat landing, walk up the main street from the harbor about 200 yards (past the TI, a grocery store, and hotel). Take a right at the sign for *Hopperstad Stavkyrkje,* walk 10 minutes, and you'll see the church perched on a small hill in the distance.

Since cars can't go on the express boat, **drivers** must go around the small Esefjord to the town of Dragsvik, then catch the ferry across the Sognefjord to Vangsnes (a 20-minute drive from Vik and the church).

Visiting the Church: Originally built around 1140 and retaining most of its original wood, Hopperstad was thoroughly re-

stored and taken back to basics in the 1880s by renowned architect Peter Blix. Unlike the famous stave church at Urnes (described later), which has an interior that has been rejiggered by centuries of engineers and filled with altars and pews, the Hopperstad church looks close to the way it did when it was built. You'll see only a few added features, including the beautifully painted canopy that once covered a side altar (probably dating from around 1300), and a tombstone from 1738. There are just a few colorful illustrations and some very scant medieval "graffiti" carvings and runic inscriptions.

Notice the intact chancel screen (the only one surviving in Norway), which separates the altar area from the congregation. As with the iconostasis (panel of icons) in today's Orthodox faith, this screen gave priests privacy to do the spiritual heavy lifting. Because Hopperstad's interior lacks the typical adornments, you can really grasp the fundamentally vertical nature of stave church architecture, leading your gaze to the heavens. Follow that impulse and look up to appreciate the Viking-ship rafters. Imagine the comfort this ceiling brought the church's original parishioners, whose seafaring ancestors had once sought refuge under overturned boats. For a unique angle on this graceful structure, lay your camera on the floor and shoot the ceiling.

▲Excursion to Fjærland and the Jostedal Glacier

From Balestrand, cruise up the Fjærlandsfjord to visit the Norwegian Glacier Museum in Fjærland and to see a receding tongue of the Jostedal Glacier (Jostedalbreen). Half-day (765 NOK) and full-day (800 NOK) excursions are sold by Balestrand's TI or onboard the boat. Reservations are smart (tours offered daily June-Aug only, tel. 57 63 14 00, www.visitflam.com and follow links for "Fjærlandsfjord").

While the museum and the glacier's tongue are underwhelming, it's a pleasant excursion with a dreamy fjord cruise (1.5 hours each way). To take the all-day trip, catch the 8:00 ferry; for the shorter trip, hop on the 12:00 boat. Either way, you can return on the 15:20 boat, getting you back to Balestrand at 16:50 (just in time to catch the fast boat back to Bergen). Both tours offer the same fjord ride, museum visit, and trip to the glacier. The all-day version, however, gives you a second glacier viewing point and about 2.5 hours to hang out in the town of Fjærland. (This sleepy village, famous for its secondhand book shops, is about as exciting as Walter Mondale, the former US vice president whose ancestors came from here.)

The ferry ride (no stops, no narration) is just a scenic glide with the gulls. Bring a picnic, as there's almost no food sold onboard, and some bread to toss to the gulls (they do acrobatics to catch whatever you loft into the air). You'll be met at the ferry dock (labeled *Mundal*) by a bus—and your guide, who reads a script about the glacier as you drive up the valley for about 15 minutes. You'll stop for an hour at the **Norwegian Glacier Museum** (Norsk Bremuseum). After watching an 18-minute aerial tour of the dramatic Jostedal Glacier in the theater, you'll learn how glaciers were formed, experiment with your own hunk of glacier, weigh evidence of the woolly mammoth's existence in Norway, and learn about the effect of global climate change on the fjords (way overpriced at 125 NOK, included in excursion price, daily June-Aug 9:00-19:00, April-May and Sept-Oct 10:00-16:00, closed Nov-March, tel. 57 69 32 88, www.bre.museum.no). From the museum, the bus runs you up to a café near a lake, at a spot that gives you a good look at the Bøyabreen, a tongue of the Jostedal Glacier. Marvel at how far the glacier has retreated—10 years ago, the visit was more dramatic. With global warming, glacier excursions like this become more sad than majestic. I wonder how long they'll even be able to bill this as a "glacier visit."

Considering that the fjord trip is the highlight of this journey, you could save time and money by just riding the ferry up and back (8:00-11:25). At 475 NOK for the round-trip boat ride, it's much cheaper than the tour.

Note that if you're into glaciers, a nearby arm of the Jostedal,

called the **Nigard Glacier,** is a more dramatic and boots-on experience (described later, under "Sights on the Lustrafjord"). It's
easy for drivers to reach; see "Orientation to Balestrand," earlier,
for car-rental info.

Sleeping in Balestrand

$$$$ Kviknes Hotel is the classy grande dame of Balestrand,
dominating the town and packed with tour groups. The pictur-

esque wooden hotel—and five generations of the Kvikne family—have
welcomed tourists to Balestrand
since the late 19th century. The hotel
has two parts: a new wing, and the
historic wooden section, with 25
older, classic rooms, and no elevator.
All rooms come with balconies. The
elegant Old World public spaces in the old section make you want
to just sit there and sip tea all afternoon (family rooms, closed Oct-
April, tel. 57 69 42 00, www.kviknes.no, booking@kviknes.no).
Part of the Kviknes ritual is gorging on the *store koldt bord* buffet
dinner—open to nonguests, and a nice way to soak in the hotel's
old-time elegance without splurging on an overnight (see "Eating
in Balestrand," later; cheaper if you stay at the hotel for 2 or more
nights).

$$$ Balestrand Hotel, family-run by Unni-Marie Kvikne,
her California-born husband Eric Palmer, and their three children,
is your best fjordside home. Open mid-May through early Septem-
ber, this cozy, welcoming place has 30 well-appointed, comfortable,
quiet rooms; a large, modern common area with lots of English pa-
perbacks; laundry service, balconies (in some rooms), and outdoor
benches for soaking in the scenery. The waterfront yard has inviting
lounge chairs and a mesmerizing view. When reserving, let them
know your arrival time, and they'll pick you up at the harborfront
(5-minute walk from dock, past St. Olaf's Church—or free pick-
up, tel. 57 69 11 38, www.balestrand.com, info@balestrand.com).

$ Thuegården offers five clean, bright, modern doubles with
kitchenettes, conveniently located near the ferry dock and just up
the street from the Co-op grocery store. Some rooms have balco-
nies and some come with a fjord view (discount if staying more
than 3 nights, no breakfast, office inside ground-floor hair salon,
tel. 57 69 15 95, mobile 97 19 92 63, www.thuegaarden.com,
thuegaarden@gmail.com).

¢-$$ Kringsjå Balestrand Hostel, a camp school for sixth-
graders, rents beds and rooms to budget travelers from mid-June
to mid-August. Three-quarters of their 58 beds are in doubles. All

the rooms have private bathrooms and most have view balconies (private and family rooms, includes sheets and towels, game room, tel. 57 69 13 03, www.kringsja.no, kringsja@kringsja.no).

¢ **Sjøtun Camping** rents the cheapest beds around in their 11 rustic huts (sheets extra, no breakfast, a mile west of town, mobile 95 06 72 61, www.sjotun.com, camping@sjotun.com).

Eating in Balestrand

Balestrand's dining options are limited, but good.

$$$$ Kviknes Hotel offers a splendid, spendy *store koldt bord* buffet dinner in a massive yet stately old dining room. For a memorable fjordside *smörgåsbord* experience, it doesn't get any better than this. Don't rush. Consider taking a preview tour—surveying the reindeer meat, lingonberries, and fjord-caught seafood—before you dive in, so you can budget your stomach space. Get a new plate with each course and save room for dessert. Each dish is labeled in English (575 NOK/person, May-

Sept daily 18:30-21:00, closed Oct-April). They also offer a four-course, locally sourced dinner for 695 NOK. After dinner, head into the rich lounge to pick up your cup of coffee or tea (included), which you'll sip sitting on classy old-fashioned furniture and basking in fjord views. For tips on enjoying this feast, see page 229.

$$$ Pilgrim, inside the Golden House at the harbor, dishes up Norwegian home cooking and a variety of salads. Sit outside or inside, in a dining area built to resemble a traditional Norwegian kitchen. The restaurant upstairs shows off part of owner Bjørg's antique collection (Mon-Sat 16:00-21:00, closed Sun and all of Sept-mid-May, mobile 91 56 28 42).

$$ Gekken's is an informal summer restaurant serving good-value meat, fish, and vegetarian dishes, along with burgers, fish-and-chips, and other fried fare. Sit in the simply decorated interior, or out on the shaded little terrace. Geir Arne "Gekken" Bale can trace his family's roots back 400 years in Balestrand. He has filled his walls with fascinating historic photos and paintings, making his dining hall an art gallery of sorts (May-Aug daily 12:00-22:00, closed Sept-April, above and behind the TI from the harbor, tel. 57 69 14 14).

$ The Viking Ship, the hot-dog stand facing the harbor, is proudly run by Carola. A bratwurst missionary from Germany, she claims it took her years to get Norwegians to accept the tastier bratwurst over their beloved *pølser* weenies. Eat at her picnic tables or across the street on the harbor park (fine sausages, fish-and-chips, May-Sept daily 11:00-20:00, closed Oct-April).

Picnic: The delightful waterfront park next to the aquarium has benches and million-dollar fjord views. The Co-op and Joker **supermarkets** at the harbor have basic grocery supplies, including bread, meats, cheeses, and drinks; the Co-op is bigger and has a wider selection (both open generally Mon-Fri 8:00-20:00, shorter hours on Sat, closed Sun). **$ Mü's Bakery** offers a healthy assortment of sandwiches and fresh-baked goodies (Mon-Sat 9:30-18:00, Sun until 15:00, closed mid-Sept-early May, just inside the aquarium entrance).

Balestrand Connections

Because Balestrand is separated from the Lustrafjord by the long Fjærlandsfjord, most Balestrand connections involve a boat trip.

BY BOAT

Express Passenger Boat: The easiest way to reach Balestrand is on the handy express boat, which connects to **Bergen, Vik** (near Hopperstad Stave Church), **Aurland,** and **Flåm** (see sidebar for schedules). Note that you can also use this boat to join the Nutshell trip in Flåm. From here, continue on the Nutshell boat down the Nærøyfjord to Gudvangen, where you'll join the crowd onward to Voss, then Bergen or Oslo. As you're making schedule and sightseeing decisions, consider that the Balestrand-Flåm boat skips the Nærøyfjord, the most dramatic arm of the Sognefjord.

Car Ferry: Balestrand's main car-ferry dock is at the village of **Dragsvik,** a six-mile, 15-minute drive around the adorable little Eselfjord. From Dragsvik, a car ferry makes the short crossing east to **Hella** (a 30-minute drive from Sogndal and the Lustrafjord), then crosses the Sognefjord south to **Vangsnes** (a 20-minute drive to Hopperstad Stave Church and onward to Bergen). The ferry goes at least once per hour (2/hour in peak times, fewer boats Sun, 94 NOK for car and driver).

Note that you can also drive through Sogndal to catch the **Kaupanger-Gudvangen** or **Mannheller-Fodnes** ferries (described under "Lustrafjord Connections," near the end of this chapter).

BY BUS

A local bus links Balestrand to **Sogndal** (5/day Mon-Fri, 3/day Sat-Sun, 1.5 hours, includes ride on Dragsvik-Hella ferry, get details at TI).

Express Boat Between Bergen and the Sognefjord

The made-for-tourists express boat makes it a snap to connect Bergen with Balestrand and other Sognefjord towns (for foot passengers only—no cars). In summer, the boat links Bergen, Vik, Balestrand, Aurland, and Flåm. You can also use this boat to connect towns on the Sognefjord, such as zipping from quiet Balestrand to busy Flåm, in the heart of the Nutshell action (reservations are smart—call 51 86 87 00 or visit www.norled.no and select "Expressboat"; discounts for students and seniors, tickets also sold on boat and at TI). The following times were good as of press time—confirm them locally.

Between Bergen and the Sognefjord: The boat trip between Bergen and **Balestrand** takes four hours (600 NOK, departs Bergen May-Sept daily at 8:00 and 16:30, Oct-April Sun-Fri at 16:30, Sat at 14:15; departs Balestrand May-Sept Mon-Sat at 7:00 and 16:55, some Sun at 11:30 and 16:55, Oct-April Mon-Sat at 7:50, Sun at 16:25). In summer, the 8:00 boat from Bergen continues to Flåm.

Between Flåm and Balestrand: Going by boat between Flåm and Balestrand with the Norled ferry takes about 1.5 hours (285 NOK, departs Flåm May-Sept daily at 15:30, stops at Aurland, arrives in Balestrand at 16:55; departs Balestrand daily at 11:50 arriving Flåm at 13:25; no express boats between Flåm and Balestrand Oct-April). Another option is the Visit-flam express-ferry, which also stops at Leikanger, Undredal, and Aurland (275 NOK, only runs June-mid-Aug, takes 2 hours, departs Flåm Mon-Fri at 6:00, departs Balestrand at 8:30, no boats Sat-Sun, tel. 57 63 14 00, www.visitflam.com). In peak season book ahead for any of the Flåm-Balestrand ferries.

From Oslo to Balestrand via the Nutshell: This variation on the standard Norway in a Nutshell route is called "Sognefjord in a Nutshell" (Oslo-Myrdal-Flåm-Balestrand-Bergen). From Oslo, you can take an early train to Flåm (no later than the 8:25 train as part of the Norway in a Nutshell route), then catch the 15:30 express boat to Balestrand. After your visit, you can continue on the express boat to Bergen, or return to the Nutshell route by taking the express boat to Flåm, and transferring to the next boat to Gudvangen.

The Lustrafjord

This arm of the Sognefjord is rugged country—only 2 percent of the land is fit to build on or farm. The Lustrafjord is ringed with tiny villages where farmers sell cherries and giant raspberries. A few interesting attractions lie along the Lustrafjord: the village

Dale Church at Luster; the impressive Nigard Glacier (a 45-minute drive up a valley); the postcard-pretty village of Solvorn; and, across the fjord, Norway's oldest stave church at Urnes. While a bit trickier to explore by public transportation, this beautiful region is easy by car, but still feels remote. There are no ATMs between Lom and Gaupne—that's how remote this region is.

SUGGESTED ROUTE FOR DRIVERS

The Lustrafjord can be seen either coming from the north (over the Sognefjell pass from the Jotunheimen region—see next chapter) or from the south (from Balestrand or the Norway in a Nutshell route—see previous chapter). Note that public buses between Lom and Sogndal follow this same route (see "Lustrafjord Connections," later).

Here's what you'll see if you're driving from the north (if you're coming from the south, read this section backward): Descending from Sognefjell, you'll hit the fjord at the village of Skjolden (decent TI in big community center, mobile 99 23 15 00). Follow Route 55 along the west bank of the fjord. In the town of Luster, consider visiting the beautifully decorated Dale Church. Farther along, near the hamlet of Nes, you'll have views across the fjord of the towering Feigumfoss waterfall. Drops and dribbles come from miles around for this 650-foot tumble. Soon Route 55 veers along an inlet to the town of Gaupne, where you can choose to detour about an hour to the Nigard Glacier (up Route 604). After Gaupne, Route 55 enters a tunnel and cuts inland, emerging at a long, fjord-like lake at the town of Hafslo. Just beyond is the turnoff for Solvorn, a town with the ferry across to Urnes and its stave church. Route 55 continues to Sogndal, where you can choose to turn off for the Kaupanger and Mannheller ferries across the Sognefjord, or continue on Route 55 to Hella and the boat across to either Dragsvik (near Balestrand) or Vangsnes (across the Sognefjord, near Vik and Hopperstad Stave Church).

Route Timings: If you're approaching from Lom in the Gudbrandsdal Valley, figure about 1.5 hours over Sognefjell to the start of the Lustrafjord at Skjolden, then another 30 minutes to Gaupne (with the optional glacier detour: 2 hours to see it, 4 hours to hike on it). From Gaupne, figure 20 minutes to Solvorn or 30 minutes to Sogndal. Solvorn to Sogndal is about 25 minutes. Sogndal to Hella, and its boat to Balestrand, takes about one hour. These estimated times are conservative, but they don't include photo stops.

Sights on the Lustrafjord

These attractions are listed as you'll reach them driving from north to south along the fjordside Route 55. If you're sleeping in this area, you could visit all four sights in a single day (but it'd be a busy, somewhat rushed day). If you're just passing through, Dale Church and Solvorn are easy, but the other two involve major detours—choose one or skip them both.

▲Dale Church (Dale Kyrkje) in Luster

The namesake town of Luster, on the west bank of the Lustrafjord, boasts a unique 13th-century Gothic church. In a land of wood-

en stave churches, this stone church, with its richly decorated interior, is worth a quick stop as you pass through town.

Cost and Hours: Free entry but donation requested, daily 10:00-20:00 but often closed for services and off-season, good posted English info inside, 5-NOK English brochure, just off the main road—look for red steeple, WC in graveyard, fresh goodies at bakery across the street.

Visiting the Church: The soapstone core of the church dates from about 1250, but the wooden bell tower and entry porch were likely built around 1600. As you enter, on the left you'll see a tall, elevated platform with seating, surrounded by a wooden grill. Nicknamed a "birdcage" for the feathery fashions worn by the ladies of the time, this high-profile pew—three steps higher than the pulpit—was built in the late 17th century by a wealthy parishioner. The beautifully painted pulpit, decorated with faded images of the four evangelists, dates from the 13th century. In the chancel (altar area), restorers have

uncovered frescoes from three different time periods: the 14th, 16th, and 17th centuries. Most of the ones you see here were likely created around the year 1500. The crucifix high over the pews, carved around 1200, predates the church, as does the old bench (with lots of runic carvings)—making them more than eight centuries old.

▲▲Jostedal's Nigard Glacier

The Nigard Glacier (Nigardsbreen) is the most accessible branch of mainland Europe's largest glacier (the Jostedalsbreen, 185 square

miles). Hiking to or on the Nigard offers Norway's best easy opportunity for a hands-on glacier experience. It's a 45-minute detour from the Lustrafjord up Jostedal Valley. Visiting a glacier is a quintessential Norwegian experience, bringing you face-to-face with the majesty of nature. If you can spare the time, it's worth the detour (even if you don't do a guided hike). But if glaciers don't give you tingles and you're feeling pressed, skip it.

Getting There: It's straightforward for **drivers.** When the main Route 55 along the Lustrafjord reaches Gaupne, turn onto Route 604, which you'll follow for 25 miles up the Jostedal Valley to the Breheimsenteret Glacier Information Center. Access to the glacier itself is down the toll road past the information center.

From mid-June through August, a **Glacier Bus** connects the Nigard Glacier to various home-base towns around the region (leaves Sogndal at 8:35 and 13:45, arrives at the glacier around 10:00 and 15:00, morning bus passes through Solvorn en route; departs glacier at 12:35 and 17:00, arrives back in Sogndal around 14:25 and 18:35; buses or boats from other towns, including Flåm and Aurland, may coordinate to meet this bus in Sogndal—ask at TI; combo-tickets include various glacier visits and hikes; for complete timetable, see www.visitnorway.no).

Visiting the Glacier: The architecturally striking Breheimsenteret Glacier Information Center services both Breheimen and Jostedalsbreen national parks. Drop by to confirm your glacier plans; you can also book excursions here. The center features a relaxing 15-minute film with highlights of the region, along with interactive glacier-related exhibits that explain these giant, slow-moving rivers of ice. The center also has a restaurant and gift shop (daily mid-June-mid-Aug 9:00-18:00, May-mid-June and mid-Aug-Sept 10:00-17:00, closed Oct-April, tel. 57 68 32 50, www.jostedal.comjostedal.com).

The best quick visit is to walk to, but not on, the glacier. (If you want to walk *on* it, see "Hikes on the Glacier," next.) From the information center, a 40-NOK toll road continues two miles to a lake facing the actual tongue of the glacier. About 75 years ago, the glacier reached all the way to today's parking lot. (It's named for the ninth farm—*ni gard*—where it finally stopped, after crushing eight farms higher up the valley.) From the lot, you can hike all the way to the edge of today's glacier (about 45 minutes each way); or, to save about 20 minutes of walking, take a special boat to a spot that's a 20-minute hike from the glacier (40 NOK one-way, 60 NOK round-trip, 10-minute boat trip, 4/hour, mid-June-mid-Sept daily 10:00-18:00).

The walk is uneven but well-marked—follow the red *T*'s and take your time. You'll hike on stone polished smooth by the glacier, and scramble over and around boulders big and small that were deposited by it. The path takes you right up to the face of the Nigardsbreen. Respect the glacier. It's a powerful river of ice, and fatal accidents do happen. If you want to walk on the glacier, see below.

Hikes on the Glacier: Don't attempt to walk on top of the glacier by yourself. The Breheimsenteret Glacier Information Center offers guided family-friendly walks that include about one hour on the ice (300 NOK, 150 NOK for kids, cash only, minimum age 6, I'd rate the walks PG-13 myself, about 4/day, generally between 11:30 and 15:00, no need to reserve—just call glacier center to find out time and show up). Leave the information

center one hour before your tour, then meet the group on the ice, where you'll pay and receive your clamp-on crampons. One hour roped up with your group gives you the essential experience. You'll find yourself marveling at how well your crampons work on the 5,000-year-old-ice. Even if it's hot, wear long pants, a jacket, and your sturdiest shoes. (Think ahead. It's awkward to empty your bladder after you're roped up.)

Longer, more challenging, and much more expensive hikes get you higher views, more exercise, and real crampons (starting at 660 NOK, includes boots; mid-May-mid-Sept daily at 10:15 and 11:45, 4 hours including 2.5 hours on the ice; 2-hour hike offered at 13:00; book by phone the day before—tel. 57 68 32 50, arrive at the information center 45 minutes early to pay for tickets and pick up your gear). If you're adventurous, ask about even longer hikes and glacier kayaking. While it's legal to go on the glacier on your own, it's dangerous and crazy to do so without crampons.

▲▲Solvorn

On the west bank of the Lustrafjord, 10 miles northeast of Sogndal, idyllic Solvorn is a sleepy little Victorian town with colorful wood-

en sheds lining its waterfront. My favorite town on the Lustrafjord is tidy and quaint, well away from the bustle of the Nutshell action. Its tiny ferry crosses the fjord regularly to Urnes and its famous stave church. While not worth going far out of your way for, Solvorn

is a mellow and surprisingly appealing place to kill some time waiting for the ferry...or just munching a picnic while looking across the fjord. A pensive stroll or photo shoot through the village's back lanes is a joy (look for plaques that explain historic buildings in English). Best of all, Solvorn also has a pair of excellent accommodations: a splurge (Walaker Hotel) and a budget place (Eplet Bed & Apple), described later under "Sleeping on the Lustrafjord."

Getting There: Solvorn is a steep five-minute **drive** down a switchback road from the main Route 55. The main road into town leads right to the Urnes ferry (see next page) and dead-ends into a handy parking lot (free, 2-hour posted—but unmonitored—limit). It's a 30-minute drive or bus trip into Sogndal, where you can transfer to other **buses** (2-4 buses/day between Solvorn and Sogndal, including the Glacier Bus to the Nigard Glacier—described earlier).

▲▲Urnes Stave Church

The hamlet of Urnes (sometimes spelled "Ornes") has Norway's oldest surviving stave church, dating from 1129. While not easy

to reach (it's across the Lustrafjord from other attractions), it's worth the scenic ferry ride. The exterior is smaller and simpler than most stave churches, but its interior—modified in fits and starts over the centuries—is uniquely eclectic. For more on stave churches, see page 9. If you want to pack along a bike (rentable in Solvorn), see "Bring a Bike?" at the end of this listing.

Cost and Hours: 90 NOK, includes 20-minute English tour (generally departs at :40 past the hour to coincide with ferry arrival); May-Sept daily 10:30-17:45, closed off-season, tel. 57 68 39 56, www.stavechurch.com.

MORE SOGNEFJORD

Getting There: Urnes is perched on the east bank of the Lustrafjord (across the fjord from Route 55 and Solvorn). Ferries generally depart Solvorn at the top of the hour and Urnes at 30 minutes past the hour (40 NOK one-way passenger fare, 110 NOK one-way for car and driver, no round-trip discount, 15-minute ride, mobile 91 72 17 19, www.lustrabaatane.no). You can either drive or walk onto the boat—but, since you can't drive all the way up to the church, you might as well leave your car in Solvorn. Once across, it's about a five-minute uphill walk to the main road and parking lot (where drivers must leave their cars; parking lot at the church only for disabled visitors). From here, it's a steep 15-minute walk up a switchback road to the church (follow signs for *Urnes*).

Planning Your Time: Don't dawdle on your way up to the church, as the tour is scheduled to depart at :40 past most hours, about 25 minutes after the ferry arrives (giving most visitors just enough time to make it up the hill to the church; last tour at 16:40). The first boat of the day departs Solvorn at 10:00 and the last boat at 16:50; the last boat back to Solvorn departs Urnes at 18:00. Confirm these times locally, especially the "last boat" times, and keep an eye on your watch to avoid getting stranded in Urnes.

Eating: A little café/restaurant is at the farm called Urnes Gard, across from the church (same hours as church, homemade apple cakes, tel. 57 68 39 44).

Visiting the Church: Most visitors to the church take the included 20-minute tour (scheduled to begin soon after the ferry arrives—described earlier). Here are some highlights:

Buy your ticket in the white house across from the church. Visit the little museum here after you see the church, so you don't miss the tour.

Many changes were made to the exterior to modernize the church after the Reformation (the colonnaded gallery was replaced,

the bell tower was added, and modern square windows were cut into the walls). Go around the left side of the church, toward the cemetery. This is the third church on this spot, but the carved doorway embedded in the wall here was inherited from the second church. Notice the two mysterious beasts—a warm-blooded predator (standing) and a cold-blooded dragon—weaving and twisting around each other, one entwining the other. Yet, as they bite each other on the neck, it's impossible to tell which one is "winning"...

perhaps symbolizing the everlasting struggle of human existence. The door you see in the middle, however, has a very different message: the harmony of symmetrical figure-eights, an appropriately calming theme for those entering the church.

Now go around to the real entry door (with a wrought-iron lock and handle probably dating from the first church) and head inside. While it feels ancient and creaky, a lot of what you see in here is actually "new" compared to the 12th-century core of the church. The exquisitely carved, voluptuous, column-topping capitals are remarkably well-preserved originals. The interior was initially stark (no pews) and dark—lit not by windows (which were added much later), but by candles laid on the floor in the shape of a cross. Looking straight ahead, you see a cross with Mary on the left (where the women stood) and John the Baptist on the right (with the men). When they finally added seating, they kept things segregated: Notice the pews carved with hearts for women, crowns for men.

When a 17th-century wealthy family wanted to build a special pew for themselves, they simply sawed off some of the pinecone-topped columns to make way for it. When the church began to lean, it was reinforced with the clumsy, off-center X-shaped supports. Churchgoers learned their lesson, and never cut anything again.

The ceiling, added in the late 17th century, prevents visitors from enjoying the Viking-ship roof beams. But all of these additions have stories to tell. Experts can read various cultural influences into the church decorations, including Irish (some of the carvings) and Romanesque (the rounded arches).

Bring a Bike? To give your Lustrafjord excursion an added dimension, take a bike on the ferry to Urnes (free passage, rentable for 300 NOK/day with helmets from Eplet Bed & Apple hostel in Solvorn, where you can park your car for free). From the stave church, bike the super-scenic fjordside road nine miles—with almost no traffic—to the big Feigumfossen waterfall, and back.

Sleeping on the Lustrafjord

These accommodations are along the Lustrafjord, listed from north to south.

IN NES

$$ Nes Gard Farmhouse B&B rents 15 homey rooms, offering lots of comfort in a grand 19th-century farmhouse (includes breakfast, three-course dinner extra, discount for staying multiple days, rooms in main building more traditional, family apartment, bike rental, mobile 95 23 26 94, www.nesgard.no, post@nesgard.no, Månum family—Mari and Asbjørn).

¢ **Viki Fjord Camping** has great fjordside huts—many directly on the water, with views and balconies—located directly across from the Feigumfossen waterfall (no breakfast, sheets extra, tel. 57 68 64 20, mobile 99 53 97 30, www.vikicamping.no, post@vikicamping.no, Berit and Svein).

IN SOLVORN

For more on this delightful little fjordside town—my favorite home base on the Lustrafjord—see the description earlier in this chapter. While it lacks the handy boat connections of Flåm, Aurland, or Balestrand, that's part of Solvorn's charm.

$$$$ Walaker Hotel, a former inn and coach station, has been run by the Walaker family since 1690 (that's a lot of pressure on ninth-generation owner Ole Henrik). The hotel, set right on the Lustrafjord (with a garden perfect for relaxing and, if necessary, even convalescing), is open May through September. In the main house, the halls and living rooms are filled with tradition. Notice the patriotic hymns on the piano. The 22 rooms are divided into two types: nicely appointed standard rooms in the modern annex; or recently renovated "historic" rooms with all the modern conveniences in two different old buildings: rooms with Old World elegance in the main house, and brightly painted rooms with countryside charm in the Tingstova house next door (sea kayak rentals, tel. 57 68 20 80, www.walaker.com, hotel@walaker.com). They serve excellent four-course dinners (625 NOK plus drinks, nightly at 19:30, savor your dessert with fjordside setting on the balcony). Their impressive gallery of Norwegian art is in a restored, historic farmhouse out back (free for guests; Ole Henrik leads one-hour tours of the collection, peppered with some family history, nightly after dinner).

¢ **Eplet Bed & Apple** is my kind of hostel: innovative and friendly. It's creatively run by Trond and Agnethe, whose entrepreneurial spirit and positive attitude attract enjoyable guests. With welcoming public spaces and 22 beds in seven rooms (all with views, some with decks), this place is worth considering even if you don't normally sleep at hostels (open mid-April-Sept only, private rooms, no breakfast, no elevator, pay laundry, kitchen, tel. 41 64 94 69, www.eplet.net, post@eplet.net). It's about 300 yards uphill from the boat dock—look for the white house with a giant red apple painted on it. It's surrounded by a raspberry-and-apple farm (they make and sell tasty juices from both). The hostel provides free loaner bikes for guests and rents them to nonguests for 300 NOK/day (helmets available).

Eating in Solvorn: The **$$$ Linahagen Kafé,** next door to Walaker Hotel, serves good meals (June-Aug Mon-Fri 12:00-

18:00, Sat until 16:00, Sun 13:00-18:00, closed Sept-May, run by Tordis and her family).

IN SOGNDAL

Sogndal is the only sizeable town in this region. While it lacks the charm of Solvorn and Balestrand, it's big enough to have a busy shopping street and a helpful **TI** (daily 9:30-23:00, inside the MIX minimart at Parkvegen 5, mobile 41 78 13 00).

¢ **Sogndal Youth Hostel** rents good, cheap beds (private rooms, June-mid-Aug only, closed 10:00-17:00, at fork in the road as you enter town, tel. 57 62 75 75, www.hihostels.no/sogndal, sogndal@hihostels.no).

Lustrafjord Connections

Sogndal is the transit hub for the Lustrafjord region.

FROM SOGNDAL BY BUS

Buses go to **Lom** over the Sognefjell pass (2/day late June-Aug only, road closed off-season, 3.5 hours, 1/day off-season, goes around the pass, 5 hours, change in Skei), **Solvorn** (3/day, fewer Sat-Sun, 30 minutes), **Balestrand** (5/day Mon-Fri, 3/day Sat-Sun, 1.5 hours, includes ride on Hella-Dragsvik ferry), **Nigard Glacier** (Glacier Bus runs 2/day mid-June-Aug only, see listing earlier for times). Most buses run less (or not at all) on weekends—check the latest at www.kringom.no.

BY BOAT

Car ferry reservations are generally not necessary except for the boat to Gudvangen, and on many short rides, aren't even possible (confirm schedules at www.kringom.no). From near Sogndal, various boats fan out to towns around the Sognefjord. Most leave from two towns at the southern end of the Lustrafjord: **Kaupanger** (a 15-minute drive from Sogndal) and **Mannheller** (a 5-minute drive beyond Kaupanger, 20 minutes from Sogndal).

From Kaupanger: While Kaupanger is little more than a ferry landing, the small stave-type church at the edge of town merits a look. Boats go from Kaupanger all the way down the gorgeous Nærøyfjord to **Gudvangen,** which is on the Norway in a Nutshell route (where you catch the bus to Voss). Taking this leisurely boat allows you to see the best part of the Nutshell fjord scenery (the Nærøyfjord), but misses the other half of that cruise (Aurlandsfjord). From June through August, boats leave Kaupanger daily at 9:00 and 15:00 (July-mid-Aug also at 12:00 and 18:00) for the nearly 3-hour trip; check in 15 minutes before departure (car and driver-750 NOK, adult passenger-350 NOK; reserve at least one day in advance—or longer in July-Aug; tel. 57 62 74 00, www. fjord2.com). Prices are high because this route is mainly taken by tourists, not locals. Verify schedules and prices online. Boats also connect Kaupanger to **Lærdal,** but the crossing from Mannheller to Fodnes is easier (described next).

From Mannheller: Ferries frequently make the speedy 15-minute crossing to **Fodnes** (74 NOK for a car and driver, 3/hour, no reservations possible). From Fodnes, drive through the five-mile-long tunnel to Lærdal and the main E-16 highway (near Borgund Stave Church, the long tunnel to Aurland, and the scenic overland road to the Stegastein fjord viewpoint—all described in the previous chapter).

To Balestrand: To reach Balestrand from the Lustrafjord, you'll take a short ferry trip (Hella-Dragsvik). For information on the car ferries to and from Balestrand, see "Balestrand Connections," earlier.

Scenic Drives from the Sognefjord

If you'll be doing a lot of driving, buy a good local map. The 1:335,000-scale *Sør-Norge nord* map by Cappelens Kart is excellent (available at local TIs and bookstores).

▲▲From the Lustrafjord to Aurland

The drive to the pleasant fjordside town of Aurland (see previous chapter) takes you either through the world's longest car tunnel,

or over an incredible mountain pass. If you aren't going as far as Lom and Jotunheimen, consider taking the pass, as the scenery here rivals the famous Sognefjell pass drive.

From Sogndal, drive 20 minutes to the Mannheller-Fodnes ferry (described earlier, under "Lustrafjord Connections"), float across the Sognefjord, then drive from Fodnes to Lærdal. From Lærdal, you have two options to Aurland: The speedy route is on E-16 through the 15-mile-long **tunnel** from Lærdal, or the Aurlandsvegen **"Snow Road"** over the pass.

The tunnel is free, and impressively nonchalant—it's signed as if it were just another of Norway's countless tunnels. But driving it is a bizarre experience: A few miles in, as you find yourself trying not to be hypnotized by the monotony, it suddenly dawns on you what it means to be driving under a mountain for 15 miles. To keep people awake, three rest chambers, each illuminated by a differently colored light, break up the drive visually. Stop and get out—if no cars are coming, test the acoustics from the center.

The second, immeasurably more scenic route is a breathtaking one-hour, 30-mile drive that winds over a pass into Aurland, cresting at over 4,000 feet and offering classic aerial fjord views (it's worth the messy pants). From the Mannheller-Fodnes ferry, take the first road to the right (to Erdal), then leave E-68 at Erdal (just west of Lærdal) for the Aurlandsvegen. This road, while well-maintained, is open only in summer, and narrow and dangerous during snowstorms (which can hit with a moment's notice, even in warm weather). Even in good weather, parts of the road can be a white-knuckle adventure, especially when meeting oncoming vehicles on the tiny, exposed hairpin turns. You'll enjoy vast and terrifying views of lakes, snowfields, and remote mountain huts and farmsteads on what feels like the top of Norway. As you begin the 12-hairpin zigzag descent to Aurland, you'll reach the "7"-shaped **Stegastein viewpoint**—well worth a stop. The "Snow Road" and viewpoint are both described on page 118.

▲From the Lustrafjord to Bergen, via Nærøyfjord and Gudvangen

Car ferries take tourists between Kaupanger and the Nutshell town of Gudvangen through an arm and elbow of the Sognefjord, including the staggering Nærøyfjord (for details on the ferry, see "Lustrafjord Connections," earlier). From Gudvangen, it's a 90-mile drive to Bergen via Voss (figure about one hour to Voss, then about an hour and a half into Bergen). This follows essentially the same route as the Norway in a Nutshell (Gudvangen-Voss bus, Voss-Bergen train) route. For additional commentary on the journey, see page 112.

Get off the ferry in Gudvangen and drive up the Nærøy valley past a river. You'll see the two giant falls and then go uphill through a tunnel. After the tunnel, look for a sign marked *Stalheim* and turn right. Stop for a break at the touristy Stalheim Hotel. Then follow signs marked *Stalheimskleiva*. This incredible road doggedly worms its way downhill back into the depths of the valley. My brakes started overheating in a few minutes. Take it easy. As you wind down, you can view the falls from several turnouts.

The road rejoins E-16. You retrace your route through the tunnel and then continue into a mellower beauty, past lakes and farms, toward Voss. Just before you reach Voss itself, watch the right side of the road for Tvindefossen, a waterfall with a handy campground/

WC/kiosk picnic area that's worth a stop. Highway E-16 takes you through Voss and into Bergen. If you plan to visit Edvard Grieg's Home and the nearby Fantoft Stave Church, now is the ideal time, since you'll be driving near them—and they're a headache to reach from downtown. Both are worth a detour if you're not rushed (see the Bergen chapter).

▲▲From Balestrand to Bergen, via Vik

If you're based in Balestrand and driving to Bergen, you have two options: Take the Dragsvik-Hella ferry, drive an hour to Kaupanger (via Sogndal), and drive the route just described; or, take the following slower, twistier, more remote, and more scenic route, with a stop at the beautiful Hopperstad Stave Church. This route is slightly longer, with more time on mountain roads and less time on the boat. Figure 15 minutes from Vangsnes to Vik, then about 1.5 hours to Voss, then another 1.5 hours into Bergen.

From Vangsnes, head into Vik on the main Route 13. In Vik, follow signs from the main road to Hopperstad Stave Church (described earlier in this chapter). Then backtrack to Route 13 and follow it south, to Voss. You'll soon begin a se-  ries of switchbacks that wind you up and out of the valley. The best views are from the Storesvingen Fjellstove restaurant (on the left). Soon after, you'll crest the ridge, go through a tunnel, and find yourself on top of the world, in a desolate and harshly scenic landscape of scrubby mountaintops, snow banks, lakes, and no trees, scattered with vacation cabins. After cruising atop the plateau for a while, the road twists its way down (next to a waterfall) into a very steep valley, which it meanders through the rest of the way to Voss. This is an hour-long, middle-of-nowhere journey, with few road signs—you might feel lost, but keep driving toward Voss. When Route 13 dead-ends into E-16, turn right (toward Voss and Bergen) and re-enter civilization. From here, the route follows the same roads as in the Lustrafjord-Bergen drive described earlier (including the Tvindefossen waterfall).

GUDBRANDSDAL VALLEY & JOTUNHEIMEN MOUNTAINS

Norway in a Nutshell is a great day trip, but with more time and a car, consider a scenic meander from Oslo to Bergen. You'll arc up the Gudbrandsdal Valley and over the Jotunheimen Mountains, then travel along the Lustrafjord.

After an introductory stop in Lillehammer, with its fine folk museum, you might spend the night in a log-and-sod farmstead-turned-hotel, tucked in a quiet valley under Norway's highest peaks. Next, Norway's highest pass takes you on an exhilarating roller-coaster ride through the heart of the myth-inspiring Jotunheimen, bristling with Norway's biggest mountains. Then the road hairpins down into fjord country (see previous chapter).

PLANNING YOUR TIME

While you could spend five or six days in this area on a three-week Scandinavian rampage, this slice of the region is worth three days.

By car, I'd spend them like this:

Day 1: Leave Oslo early, and spend midday at Lillehammer's Maihaugen Open-Air Folk Museum for a tour and picnic. Drive up the Gudbrandsdal Valley, stopping at the stave church in Lom. Stay overnight in the Jotunheimen countryside.

Day 2: Drive the Sognefjell road over the mountains, then down along the Lustrafjord, stopping to visit the Dale Church and the Nigard Glacier. Sleep in your choice

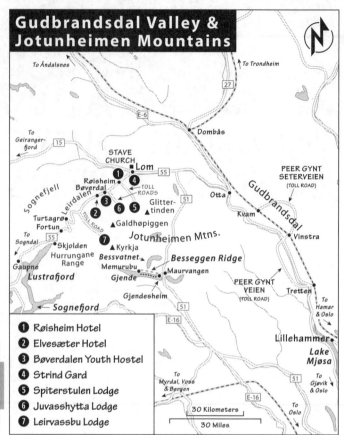

Gudbrandsdal Valley & Jotunheimen Mountains

1 Røisheim Hotel
2 Elvesæter Hotel
3 Bøverdalen Youth Hostel
4 Strind Gard
5 Spiterstulen Lodge
6 Juvasshytta Lodge
7 Leirvassbu Lodge

of fjord towns, such as Solvorn, Balestrand, or Aurland (all described in previous chapters).

Day 3: Cruise the Aurland and/or Nærøy fjords and try to
visit another stave church or two (such as Urnes, Hopperstad, or
Borgund—all described in previous chapters) before carrying on
to Bergen.

This plan can be condensed into two days if you skip the
Nigard Glacier side-trip.

Lillehammer and the Gudbrandsdal Valley

The Gudbrandsdal Valley is the tradition-steeped country of Peer Gynt, the Norwegian Huck Finn. This romantic valley of time-worn hills, log cabins, and velvet farms has connected northern and southern Norway since ancient times. While not as striking as other parts of the Norwegian countryside, Gudbrandsdal offers a suitable first taste of the natural wonders that crescendo farther north and west (in Jotunheimen and the Sognefjord). Throughout this region, the government subsidizes small farms to keep the countryside populated and healthy. (These subsidies would not be permitted if Norway were a member of the European Union.)

Orientation to Lillehammer

The de facto capital of Gudbrandsdal, Lillehammer, is a pleasant winter and summer resort town of 27,000. While famous for its brush with Olympic greatness (as host of the 1994 Winter Olympiad), Lillehammer is a bit disappointing—worthwhile only for its excellent Maihaugen Open-Air Folk Museum, or to break up the long drive between Oslo and the Jotunheimen region. If you do wind up here, Lillehammer has happy, old, woody pedestrian zones (Gågata and Storgata).

Tourist Information: Lillehammer's TI is inside the train station (Mon-Fri 8:00-18:00, Sat-Sun 10:00-16:00; shorter hours and closed Sun in off-season; Jernbanetorget 2, tel. 61 28 98 00, www.lillehammer.com).

Sights in Lillehammer

Lillehammer's two most worthwhile sights are up the hill behind the center of town. It's a fairly steep 15-minute walk from the train station to either sight and a 10-minute, mostly level walk between the two (follow the busy main road that connects them). Because the walk from the station is uphill (and not very well-signed), consider catching the bus from in front of the train station (bus #003 or #002 to Olympics Museum, 2/hour; bus #006 to Maihaugen, 1/hour; 37 NOK one-way for either bus).

▲▲Maihaugen Open-Air Folk Museum
(Maihaugen Friluftsmuseet)
This idyllic park, full of old farmhouses and pickled slices of folk culture, provides a good introduction to what you'll see as you drive

through the Gudbrandsdal Valley. Anders Sandvig, a "visionary dentist," started the collection in 1887. You'll divide your time between the fine indoor museum at the entrance and the sprawling exterior exhibits.

Upon arrival, ask about special events, crafts, or musical performances. A TV monitor shows what's going on in the park. Summer is busy with crafts in action and people re-enacting life in the past, à la Colonial Williamsburg. There are no tours, so it's up to you to initiate conversations with the "residents." Off-season it's pretty dead, with no live crafts and most buildings locked up.

Cost and Hours: 170 NOK in summer, 130 NOK off-season; 25 percent off when combined with Olympics Museum; June-Aug daily 10:00-17:00; Sept-May Tue-Sun 11:00-16:00, closed Mon; paid parking, scant English descriptions—consider purchasing the English guidebook; tel. 61 28 89 00, www.maihaugen.no.

Visiting the Museum: The outdoor section, with 200 buildings from the Gudbrandsdal region, is divided into three areas:

the "Rural Collection," with old sod-roof log houses and a stave church; the "Town Collection," with reconstructed bits of old-time Lillehammer; and the "Residential Area," with 20th-century houses that look like most homes in today's Norway. The time trip can be jarring: In the 1980s house, a bubble-gum-chewing girl enthuses about her new, "wireless" TV remote and plays ABBA tunes from a cassette-tape player.

The museum's excellent "We Won the Land" exhibit (at the entry) sweeps you through Norwegian history from the Ice Age to the Space Age. The Gudbrandsdal art section shows village life at its best. And you can walk through Dr. Sandvig's old dental office and the original shops of various crafts- and tradespeople.

Though the museum welcomes picnickers and has a simple cafeteria, Lillehammer's town center (a 15-minute walk below the museum), with lots of fun eateries, is better for lunch (see the next page).

Norwegian Olympics Museum
(Norges Olympiske Museum)

This cute museum is housed in the huge Olympic ice-hockey arena, Håkon Hall. With brief English explanations, an emphasis on Norwegians and Swedes, and an endearingly gung-ho Olympic spirit, it's worth a visit on a rainy day or for sports fans. The ground-floor exhibit traces the ancient history of the Olympics, then devotes one wall panel to each of the summer and winter Olympiads of the modern era (with special treatment for the 1952 Oslo games). Upstairs, walk the entire concourse, circling the arena seating while reviewing the highlights (and lowlights) of the 1994 games (remember Tonya Harding?). While you're up there, check out the gallery of great Norwegian athletes and the giant egg used in the Lillehammer opening ceremony.

Cost and Hours: 130 NOK, 25 percent off when combined with Maihaugen Museum; June-Aug daily 10:00-17:00; Sept-May Tue-Sun 11:00-16:00, closed Mon; tel. 61 25 21 00, https://eng.ol.museum.no.

Nearby: On the hillside above Håkon Hall (a 30-minute hike or quick drive) are two ski jumps that host more Olympics sights, including a ski lift, the ski jump tower, and a bobsled ride (www.olympiaparken.no). In the summer, ski jumpers practice on the jumps, which are sprayed with water.

Sleeping and Eating in the Gudbrandsdal Valley

I prefer sleeping in the more scenic and Norwegian-feeling Jotunheimen area (described later). But if you're sleeping here, Lillehammer and the surrounding valley offer several good options. My choices for Lillehammer are near the train station; the accommodations in Kvam provide a convenient stopping point in the valley.

IN LILLEHAMMER

Sleeping: True to its name, **$$ Mølla Hotell** is situated in an old mill along the little stream running through Lillehammer. The 58 rooms blend Old World charm with modern touches. It's more cutesy-cozy and less businesslike than other Lillehammer hotels in this price range (elevator, a block below Gågata at Elvegata 12, tel. 61 05 70 80, www.mollahotell.no, post@mollahotell.no).

$$ First Hotel Breiseth is a business-class hotel with 89 rooms in a handy location directly across from the train station (free parking, Jernbanegaten 1, tel. 61 24 77 77, www.firsthotels.no/breiseth, breiseth@firsthotels.no).

¢ Vandrerhjem Stasjonen, Lillehammer's youth hostel, is upstairs inside the train station. With 100 beds in 33 institutional but new-feeling rooms—including 21 almost hotel-like doubles—it's a winner (elevator, Jernbanetorget 2, tel. 61 26 00 24, www.stasjonen.no, lillehammer@hihostels.no).

Eating: Good restaurants are scattered around the city center, but for the widest selection, head to where the main pedestrian drag (Gågata) crosses the little stream running downhill through town. Poke a block or two up and down **Elvegata,** which stretches along the river and hosts a wide range of tempting eateries—from pubs (both rowdy and upscale) to pizza and cheap sandwich stands.

IN KVAM

This is a popular vacation valley for Norwegians, and you'll find loads of reasonable small hotels and campgrounds with huts for those who aren't quite campers (*hytter* means "cottages" or "cabins," *rom* is "private room," and *ledig* means "vacancy"). These huts normally cost about 400-600 NOK, depending on size and amenities, and can hold from four to six people. Although they are simple, you'll have a kitchenette and access to a good WC and shower. When available, sheets rent for around 60 NOK per person. Here are a couple of listings in the town of Kvam, located midway between Lillehammer and Lom.

$$ Vertshuset Sinclair has a quirky Scottish-Norwegian ambience. The 15 fine rooms are in old-fashioned motel wings. The motel was named after a Scotsman who led a band of adventurers into this valley, attempting to set up their own Scottish kingdom. They failed. All were kilt (family deals, tel. 61 29 54 50, www.vertshuset-sinclair.no, post@vertshuset-sinclair.no). The motel's **$$ cafeteria,** in the main building, is handy for a quick and filling bite on the road between Lillehammer and Lom (long hours daily).

¢ Kirketeigen Ungdomssenter ("Church Youth Center"), behind the town church, welcomes travelers year-round. They have camping spots, small cabins without water, cabins with kitchen and bath, plus simple four-bed rooms in the main building (sheets and blankets extra, tel. 61 21 60 90, www.kirketeigen.no, post@kirketeigen.no).

Jotunheimen Mountains

Norway's Jotunheimen ("Giants' Home") Mountains feature the country's highest peaks and some of its best hikes and drives. This national park stretches from the fjords to the glaciers. You can play roller-coaster with mountain passes, take rugged hikes, wind up scenic toll roads, get up close to a giant stave church...and sleep in a time-passed rural valley. The gateway to the mountains is the unassuming town of Lom.

Lom

Pleasant Lom—the main town between Lillehammer and Sogndal—feels like a modern ski resort village. It's home to one of Norway's most impressive stave churches. While Lom has little else to offer, the church causes the closest thing to a tour-bus traffic jam this neck of the Norwegian woods will ever see.

Orientation to Lom

Park by the stave church—you'll see its dark spire just over the bridge. The church shares a parking lot with a gift shop/church museum and some public WCs. Across the street is the TI, in the sod-roofed building that also houses the Norwegian Mountain Museum. If you're heading over the mountains, Lom's bank (at the Kommune building) has the last ATM until Gaupne.

Tourist Information: Lom's TI, a good source of information for hikes and drives in the Jotunheimen Mountains, is just across the river in Lom's Co-op Mega grocery store (Mon-Sat 9:00-21:00, Sun 10:00-18:00; office closed Sept-mid-June but info available by phone or email; tel. 61 21 29 90, http://visitjotunheimen.no, info@visitjotunheimen.no).

Sights in Lom

▲▲Lom Stave Church (Lom Stavkyrkje)

Despite extensive renovations, Lom's church (from 1158) remains a striking example of a Nordic stave church. For more on these distinctive medieval churches, see page 9.

Cost and Hours: Church-60 NOK, daily mid-June-mid-Aug 9:00-19:00 (until 17:00 last half of Aug), mid-May-mid-June and Sept 10:00-16:00, closed in winter and during funerals; museum-10 NOK, same hours as church in summer, shorter hours in off-season, closed Sun in winter; tel. 40 43 84 86, www.lomstavechurch.no.

Tours: Try to tag along with a guided tour of the church—or, if it's not too busy, a docent can give

GUDBRANDSDAL

you a quick private tour (included in ticket). Even outside of open-ing times—including winter—small groups can arrange a tour (60 NOK/person, 600-NOK minimum, call 97 07 53 97 in summer or 61 21 73 00 in winter).

Visiting the Church: Buy your ticket and go inside to take in the humble **interior** (still used by locals for services—notice the posted hymnal numbers). Men sat on the right, women on the left, and prisoners sat with the sheriff in the caged area in the rear. Standing in the middle of the nave, look overhead to see the earli-est surviving parts of the church, such as the circle of X-shaped St. Andrew crosses and the Romanesque arches above them. High above the door (impossible to see without a flashlight—ask a do-cent to show you) is an old painting of a dragon- or lion-like crea-ture—likely an old Viking symbol, possibly drawn here to smooth the forced conversion local pagans made to Christianity. When King Olav II (later to become St. Olav) swept through this valley in 1021, he gave locals an option: convert or be burned out of house and home.

On the white town flag, notice the spoon—a symbol of Lom. Because of its position nestled in the mountains, Lom gets less rainfall than other towns, so large spoons were traditionally used to spread water over the fields. The apse (behind the altar) was added in 1240, when trendy new Gothic cathedrals made an apse a must-have accessory for churches across Europe. Lepers came to the grilled window in the apse for a blessing. When the Reformation hit in 1536, the old paintings were whitewashed over. The church has changed over the years: Transepts, pews, and windows were added in the 17th century. And the circa-1720 paintings were done by a local priest's son.

Drop into the **gift shop/church museum** in the big black building in the parking lot. Its one-room exhibit celebrates 1,000 years of the stave church—interesting if you follow the loaner English descriptions. Inside you'll find a pair of beautiful model churches, headstones and other artifacts, and the only surviving stave-church dragon-head "steeple." In the display case near the early-1900s organ, find the little pencil-size stick carved with runes, dating from around 1350. It's actually a love letter from a would-be suitor. The woman rejected him, but she saved them both from embarrassment by hiding the stick under the church floor-boards beneath a pew...where it was found in 1973. (Docents inside the church like to show off a replica of this stick.)

Before or after your church visit, explore the tidy, thought-provoking **graveyard** surrounding the church. Also, check out the precarious-looking little footbridge over the waterfall (the best view is from the modern road bridge into town).

Norwegian Mountain Museum
(Norsk Fjellmuseum)

This worthwhile museum traces the history of the people who have lived off the land in the Jotunheimen Mountains from the Stone Age to today (and also serves as a national park office). It is one of the better museums in fjord country, with well-presented displays and plenty of actual artifacts. The exhibit, "Over the Ice: Discoveries from the Ice Show the Way," explores prehistoric human and animal migrations in the surrounding mountains based on recent archaeological finds, including a 1,300-year-old ski.

Cost and Hours: 80 NOK; daily 9:00-16:00, July-mid-Aug until 19:00, generally closed in off-season; in the sod-roofed building across the road from the Lom Stave Church parking lot, tel. 61 21 16 00, http://fjell.museum.no.

Sleeping near Lom

Lom itself has a handful of hotels, but the most appealing way to overnight in this area is at a rural rest stop in the countryside. All of these are on Route 55 south of Lom, toward Sognefjord—first is Strind Gard, then Bøverdalen, Røisheim, and finally Elvesæter (all within 20 minutes of Lom).

$$$$ Røisheim, in a marvelously remote mountain setting, is an extremely expensive storybook hotel composed of a cluster of centuries-old, sod-roofed log farmhouses. Its posh and generous living rooms are filled with antiques. Each of the 20 rooms (in 14 different buildings) is rustic but elegant, with fun "barrel bathtubs" and four-poster or canopy beds. Some rooms are in old, wooden farm buildings—*stabburs*—with low ceilings and heavy beams. The deluxe rooms are larger, with king beds and fireplaces. Call ahead so they'll be prepared for your arrival (open May-Sept; packed lunch, and an over-the-top four-course traditional dinner served at 19:30; 10 miles south of Lom on Route 55, tel. 61 21 20 31, www.roisheim.no, booking@roisheim.no).

$$ Elvesæter Hotel has its own share of Old World romance, but is bigger, cheaper, and more modest. Delightful public spaces bunny-hop through its traditional shell, while its 200 beds sprawl through nine buildings. The Elvesæter family has done a great job of retaining the historic character of their medieval farm, even though the place is big enough to handle large tour groups. The renovated "superior" rooms are new-feeling, but have sterile modern furniture; the older, cheaper "standard" rooms are well-worn but more characteristic (open May-Sept, family rooms, good three-course dinners, swimming pool, farther up Route 55, just past Bøverdal, tel. 61 21 12 10, www.topofnorway.no, elveseter@topofnorway.no). Even if you're not staying here, stop by to wander through the public spaces and pick up a flier explaining the towering Sagasøyla (Saga Column). It was started in 1926 to celebrate the Norwegian constitution, and was to stand in front of Oslo's Parliament Building—but the project stalled after World War II (thanks to the artist's affinity for things German and membership in Norway's fascist party). It was eventually finished and erected here in 1992.

¢ **Bøverdalen Youth Hostel** offers cheap-but-comfortable beds and a far more rugged clientele—real hikers rather than car hikers. While a bit institutional, it's well-priced and well-run (open late May-Sept, sheets extra, breakfast extra, hot meals, self-serve café, tel. 61 21 20 64, www.hihostels.no, boverdalen@hihostels.no, Anna Berit). It's in the center of the little community of Bøverdal (store, campground, and toll road up to Galdhøpiggen area).

¢ **Strind Gard** is your very rustic option if you can't spring for Røisheim or Elvesæter, but still want the countryside-farm experience. This 150-year-old farmhouse, situated by a soothing waterfall, rents two rooms and one apartment, plus four sod-roofed log huts. The catch: Many of the buildings have no running water, so you'll use the shared facilities at the main building. While not everyone's cup of tea, this place will appeal to romantics who always wanted to sleep in a humble log cabin in the Norwegian mountains—it's downright idyllic for those who like to rough it (sheets and towels extra, no breakfast, low ceilings, farm smells, valley views, 2 miles south of Lom on Route 55, tel. 61 21 12 37, www.strind-gard.no, post@strind-gard.no, Anne Jorunn and Trond Dalsegg).

Drives and Hikes in the Jotunheimen Mountains

Route 55, which runs between Lom and the Sognefjord to the south, is the sightseeing spine of this region. From this main (and already scenic) drag, other roads spin upward into the mountains—offering even better views and exciting drives and hikes. Many of these get you up close to Norway's highest mountain, Galdhøpiggen (8,100 feet). I've listed these attractions from north to south, as you'll reach them driving from Lom to the Sognefjord; except for the first, they all branch off from Route 55. Another great high-mountain experience nearby—the hike to the Nigard Glacier near Lustrafjord—is covered in the previous chapter.

Remember that the Norwegian Mountain Museum in Lom acts as a national park office, offering excellent maps and advice for drivers and hikers—a stop here is obligatory if you're planning a jaunt into the mountains.

Besseggen

This trail offers an incredible opportunity to walk between two lakes separated by a narrow ridge and a 1,000-foot cliff. It's one of Norway's most beloved hikes, which can make it crowded in the summer. To get to the trailhead, drivers detour down Route 51 after Otta south to Maurvangen. Turn right to Gjendesheim to park your car. From Gjendesheim, catch the boat to Memurubu, where the path starts at the boat dock. Hike along the ridge—with a blue lake (Bessvatnet) on one side and a green lake (Gjende) on the other—and keep your balance. The six-hour trail loops back to Gjendesheim. Because the boat runs sporadically, time your visit to catch one (150 NOK for 20-minute ride, 3 morning departures daily, check schedules at www.gjende.no, mobile 91 30 67 44). This is a thrilling but potentially hazardous hike, and it's a major detour: Gjendesheim is about 1.5 hours and 50 miles from Lom.

Spiterstulen

From Røisheim, this 11-mile toll road (80 NOK) takes you from Route 55 to the Spiterstulen mountain hotel/lodge in about 30 minutes (3,600 feet). This is the best destination for serious all-day hikes to Norway's two mightiest mountains, Glittertinden and Galdhøpiggen (a 5-hour hike up and a 3-hour hike down, doable without a guide). Or consider a guided, two-hour glacier walk (tel. 61 21 94 00, www.spiterstulen.no).

Juvasshytta

This toll road takes you (in about 40 minutes) to the highest you can drive and the closest you can get to Galdhøpiggen (6,050 feet) by car. The road starts in Bøverdal, and costs 85 NOK; at the end of it, daily, guided, six-hour hikes go across the glacier to the summit and back (200 NOK, late June-late Sept daily at 10:00, July-mid-Aug also daily at 11:30, check in 30 minutes before, strict age limit—no kids under age 7, 4 miles each way, easy ascent but can be dangerous without a guide, hiking boots required—possible to rent from nearby ski resort). You can sleep in the recently updated **$$ Juvasshytta lodge** (includes breakfast, dinner optional, open June-Sept, tel. 61 21 15 50, www.juvasshytta.no).

Leirvassbu

This 11-mile, 50-NOK toll road (about 30 minutes one-way from Bøverkinnhalsen, south of Elvesæter) is most scenic for car hikers. It takes you to a lodge at 4,600 feet with great views and easy walks. A serious (5-hour round-trip) hike goes to the lone peak, Kyrkja—"The Cathedral," which looms like a sanded-down mini-Matterhorn on the horizon (6,660 feet).

▲▲Sognefjell Drive to the Sognefjord

Norway's highest pass (at 4,600 feet, the highest road in northern Europe) is a thrilling drive through a cancan line of mountains, from Jotunheimen's Bøverdal Valley to the Lustrafjord (an arm of the Sognefjord). Centuries ago, the farmers of Gudbrandsdal took their horse caravans over this difficult mountain pass on treks to Bergen. Today, the road (Route 55) is still narrow, windy, and otherworldly (and usually closed mid-Oct-May).

As you begin to ascend just beyond Elvesæter, notice the viewpoint on the left for the Leirdalen Valley—capped at the end with the Kyrkja peak (described earlier). Next you'll twist up into a lake-filled valley, then through a mild canyon with grand waterfalls. Before long, as you corkscrew up more switchbacks, you're above the tree line, enjoying a "top of the world" feeling. The best views (to the south) are of the cut-glass range called Hurrungane ("Noisy Children"). The 10 hairpin turns between Turtagrø and Fortun are exciting. Be sure to stop, get out, look around, and enjoy the lavish views. Treat each turn as if it were your last.

Just before you descend to the fjord, the terrain changes, and you reach a pullout on the right, next to a hilltop viewpoint—offering your first glimpse of the fjord. The Lustrafjord village of Skjolden is just around the bend (and down several more switchbacks). Entering Skjolden, continue following Route 55, which now traces the west bank of the Lustrafjord. For more on the sights from here on out, turn to page 142.

Gudbrandsdal and Jotunheimen Connections

BY TRAIN AND BUS

Cars are better, but if you're without wheels, here are your options: Trains run from **Oslo to Lillehammer** (almost hourly, 2.5 hours, just 2 hours from Oslo airport) and **Lillehammer to Otta** (6/day, 1.5 hours). Buses meet some trains (confirm schedule at the train station in Oslo) for travelers heading from **Otta to Lom** (2/day, 1 hour) and onward from **Lom to Sogndal** (2/day late June-Aug only, road closed off-season, 3.5 hours).

ROUTE TIPS FOR DRIVERS

Use low gears and lots of patience both up (to keep the engine cool) and down (to save your brakes). Uphill traffic gets the right-of-way, but drivers, up or down, dive for the nearest fat part of the road whenever they meet. Ask backseat drivers not to scream until you've actually been hit or have left the road.

It's 2.5 hours from Oslo to Lillehammer and 3 hours after that to Lom.

From Oslo to Lillehammer: Wind out of Oslo following signs for *E-6* (not to *Drammen*, but for *Stockholm* and then to *Trondheim*). In a few minutes, you're in the wide-open pastoral countryside of eastern Norway. Norway's Constitution Hall—Eidsvoll Manor—is a five-minute detour off E-6, several miles south of Eidsvoll in Eidsvoll Verk (described on page 76; follow the signs to *Eidsvoll Bygningen*). Then E-6 takes you along Norway's largest lake (Mjøsa), through the town of Hamar, and past more lake scenery into Lillehammer. Signs direct you uphill from downtown Lillehammer to the Maihaugen Open-Air Folk Museum.

From Lillehammer to Jotunheimen: From Lillehammer, signs to *E-6/Trondheim* take you north, up the bucolic valley of

Gudbrandsdal (en route to Otta and Lom), with fine but unremarkable scenery. Along the way, a pair of toll-road side-trips (Gynt Veien and Peer Gynt Seterveien) loop off the E-6 road. While they sound romantic, they're basically windy, curvy dirt roads over high, desolate heath and scrub-brush plateaus with fine mountain views. They're scenic, but pale in comparison with the Sognefjell road between Lom and the Lustrafjord (described earlier). At Otta, exit for Lom. Halfway to Lom, on the left, look for the long suspension bridge spanning the milky-blue river—a good opportunity to stretch your legs, and a scenic spot to enjoy a picnic.

GUDBRANDSDAL

BERGEN

Bergen is permanently salted with robust cobbles and a rich sea-trading heritage. Norway's capital in the 13th century, Bergen's wealth and importance came thanks to its membership in the heavyweight medieval trading club of merchant cities called the Hanseatic League. Bergen still wears her rich maritime heritage proudly—nowhere more scenically than the colorful wooden warehouses that make up the picture-perfect Bryggen district along the harbor.

Protected from the open sea by a lone sheltering island, Bergen is a place of refuge from heavy winds for the giant working boats that serve the North Sea oil rigs. (Much of Norway's current affluence is funded by the oil it drills just offshore.) Bergen is also one of the most popular cruise-ship ports in northern Europe, hosting about 300 ships a year and up to five ships a day in peak season. Each morning is rush hour, as cruisers hike past the fortress and into town.

Bergen gets an average of 80 inches of rain annually (compared to 30 inches in Oslo). A good year has 60 days of sunshine. The natives aren't apologetic about their famously lousy weather. In fact, they seem to wear it as a badge of pride. "Well, that's Bergen," they'll say matter-of-factly as they wring out their raincoats. When I complained about an all-day downpour, one resident cheerfully informed me, "There's no such thing as bad weather—just inappropriate clothing"...a local mantra that rhymes in Norwegian.

With about 275,000 people, Bergen has big-city parking problems and high prices, but visitors sticking to the old center find it charming. Enjoy Bergen's salty market, then stroll the easy-on-foot old quarter, with cute lanes of delicate old wooden houses.

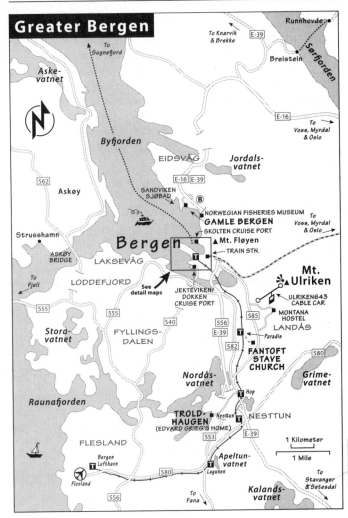

Greater Bergen

From downtown Bergen, a funicular zips you up a little mountain for a bird's-eye view of this sailors' town. A short foray into the countryside takes you to a variety of nearby experiences: a dramatic cable-car ride to a mountaintop perch (Ulriken643); an evocative stave church (Fantoft); and the home of Norway's most beloved composer, Edvard Grieg, at Troldhaugen.

PLANNING YOUR TIME

Bergen can be enjoyed even on the tail end of a day's scenic train ride from Oslo before returning on the overnight train. But that teasing taste will make you wish you had more time. On a three-week tour of Scandinavia, Bergen is worth at least one full day.

While Bergen's sights are visually underwhelming and pricey, nearly all offer thoughtful tours in English. If you take advantage of these tours, otherwise barren attractions (such as Håkon's Hall and Rosenkrantz Tower, the Bryggen quarter, the Leprosy Museum, and Gamle Bergen) become surprisingly interesting. Off-season, some sights have shorter hours (Håkon's Hall and Rosenkrantz Tower) or are closed altogether (Leprosy Museum).

Bergen in One Day

For a busy day, you could do this:

9:00 Stroll through the Fish Market and Bryggen shops.

11:00 Take the Bryggen Walking Tour (June-Aug only), then grab a quick lunch.

14:00 Visit Håkon's Hall and Rosenkrantz Tower (joining a guided tour).

15:00 Stroll through Torgallmenningen square to the KODE Art Museums to see works by famous Norwegian landscape artists and Edvard Munch.

17:00 Enjoy some free time in town (consider returning to the Bryggens Museum using your tour ticket), or catch the bus out to Gamle Bergen.

18:00 Ride up the Fløibanen funicular.

More Bergen Planning Tips

Although Bergen has plenty of charms of its own, it's most famous as the "Gateway to the Fjords." If you plan to use Bergen as a springboard for fjord country, you have three options: Pick up a rental car here (fjord wonder is a 3-hour drive away); take the express boat down the Sognefjord (about 4 hours to Balestrand and Flåm/Aurland); or do the "Norway in a Nutshell" as a scenic loop from Bergen. The "Nutshell" option also works well as a detour midway between Bergen and Oslo (hop the train from either city to Voss or Myrdal, then take a bus or spur train into the best of the Sognefjord; scenic ferry rides depart from there). While there are a million ways to enjoy the fjords, first-timers should start with this region (covered thoroughly in the Norway in a Nutshell and More on the Sognefjord chapters).

Also note that Bergen, a geographic dead-end, is actually an efficient place to begin or end your Scandinavian tour. Consider flying into Bergen and out of another city, such as Helsinki (or vice versa).

Orientation to Bergen

Bergen clusters around its harbor—nearly everything listed in this chapter is within a few minutes' walk. The busy Torget (the square with the Fish Market) is at the head

of the harbor. As you face the sea from here, Bergen's TI is at the left end of the Fish Market. The town's historic Hanseatic Quarter, Bryggen (BRUHY-gun), lines the harbor on the right. Express boats to the Sognefjord (Balestrand and Flåm) dock at the harbor on the left.

Charming cobbled streets surround the harbor and climb the encircling hills. Bergen's popular Fløibanen funicular climbs high above the city to the top of Mount Fløyen for the best view of the town. Surveying the surrounding islands and inlets, it's clear why this city is known as the "Gateway to the Fjords."

TOURIST INFORMATION

The centrally located TI is upstairs in the long, skinny, modern, Torghallen market building, next to the Fish Market (daily June-Aug 8:30-22:00, May and Sept 9:00-20:00; Oct-April Mon-Sat 9:00-16:00, closed Sun; free Wi-Fi, handy budget eateries downstairs and in Fish Market; tel. 55 55 20 00, www.visitbergen.com).

The TI covers Bergen and western Norway, provides information and tickets for tours, has a fjord information desk, books rooms, will exchange currency, and maintains a very handy events board listing today's and tomorrow's slate of tours, concerts, and other events. Pick up this year's edition of the free *Bergen Guide* (also likely at your hotel), which has a fine map and lists sights, hours, and special events. This booklet can answer most of your questions.

Bergen Card: You have to work hard to make this greedy little card pay off (240 NOK/24 hours, 310 NOK/48 hours, 380 NOK/72 hours, sold at TI and Montana Family & Youth Hostel). It gives you free use of the city's tram and buses, half off the Fløibanen funicular, free admission to most museums (but not the Hanseatic Museum; aquarium included only in winter), and discounts on some events and sights such as Edvard Grieg's Home.

ARRIVAL IN BERGEN

By Train or Bus: Bergen's train and bus stations are on Strømgaten, facing a park-rimmed lake. The small, manageable train station has an office open long hours for booking all your travel in Norway—you can get your Nutshell reservations here (Mon-Fri 6:45-19:15, Sat-Sun 7:30-16:00). There are pay baggage lockers (daily 6:00-23:30), pay toilets, a newsstand, a sandwich shop, and a coffee shop. (To get to the bus station, follow the covered walkway behind the Narvesen newsstand via the Storsenter shopping mall.) Taxis wait to the right (with the tracks at your back); a tram stop is to your left, just around the corner. From the train station, it's a 10-minute walk to the TI: Cross the street (Strømgaten) in front of the station and take Marken, a cobbled street that eventually turns into a modern retail street. Continue walking in the same direction until you reach the water.

By Plane: Bergen's sleek and modern Flesland Airport is 12 miles south of the city center (airport code: BGO, tel. 67 03 15 55, www.avinor.no/bergen). The airport **bus** runs between the airport and downtown Bergen, stopping at the Radisson Blu Royal Hotel in Bryggen, the harborfront area near the TI (if you ask), the Radisson Blu Hotel Norge (in the modern part of town at Ole Bulls Plass), and the bus station (about 120 NOK, pay driver, 6/hour at peak times, fewer in slow times, 30-minute ride). **Taxis** take up to four people and cost about 400 NOK for the 20-minute ride (depending on time of day).

The cheapest option is to take the Bybanen **tram** (departs every 5-10 minutes, 45-minute trip, schedule at www.skyss.no) to the end of the line at Byparken. But keep in mind that this stop—on Kaigaten, between Bergen's little lake and Ole Bulls Plass—is several blocks from most of my recommended hotels. For tram ticket details, see "Getting Around Bergen," later.

By Car: Driving is a headache in Bergen; avoid it if you can. Approaching town on E-16 (from Voss and the Sognefjord area), follow signs for *Sentrum*, which spits you out near the big, modern bus station and parking garage. Parking is difficult and costly—ask your hotelier for tips. Note that all drivers entering Bergen must pay a 19-NOK toll (45-NOK during rush hour). There are no toll-collection gates, since the system is automated. Assuming they bill you, it'll just show up on your credit card (which they access through your rental-car company). For details, ask your rental company or see www.bomringenbergen.no.

By Cruise Ship: Bergen is easy for cruise passengers, regardless of which of the city's two ports your ship uses. A taxi into downtown from either port costs about 150-170 NOK.

The **Skolten** cruise port is just past the fortress on the main harborfront road. Arriving here, simply walk into town (stroll with the harbor on your right, figure about 10 minutes to Bryggen, plus five more minutes to the Fish Market and TI). After about five minutes, you'll pass the fortress—the starting point for my self-guided walk. Hop-on, hop-off buses also pick up passengers at the port (though in this compact town, I'd just walk).

The **Jekteviken/Dokken** cruise port is in an industrial zone to the south, a bit farther out (about a 20-minute walk). To discourage passengers from walking through all the containers, the port operates a convenient and free **shuttle bus** that zips you into town. It drops you off along Rasmus Meyers Allé in front of the KODE Art Museums, facing the cute man-made lake called Lille Lungegårds-vannet. From here, it's an easy 10-minute walk to the TI and Fish Market: Walk with the lake on your right, pass through the park (with the pavilion) and head up the pedestrian mall called Ole Bulls Plass, and turn right (at the bluish slab) up the broad square called Torgallmenningen. Note that my self-guided Bergen walk conveniently ends near the shuttle-bus stop.

For more in-depth cruising information, pick up my *Rick Steves Scandinavian & Northern European Cruise Ports* guidebook.

HELPFUL HINTS

Museum Tours: Many of Bergen's sights are hard to appreciate without a guide. Fortunately, several offer wonderful and intimate guided tours. Make the most of the following sights by taking advantage of their tours: Håkon's Hall and Rosenkrantz Tower, Bryggens Museum, Hanseatic Museum, Leprosy Museum, Gamle Bergen, and Edvard Grieg's Home.

Crowd Control: In high season, cruise-ship passengers mob the waterfront between 10:00 and 15:00; to avoid the crush, consider visiting an outlying sight during this time, such as Gamle Bergen or Edvard Grieg's Home.

Laundry: Drop your laundry off at **Hygienisk Vask & Rens,** and pick it up clean the next day (no self-service, Mon-Fri 8:30-16:30, closed Sat-Sun, Halfdan Kjerulfgate 8, tel. 55 31 77 41).

GETTING AROUND BERGEN

Most in-town sights can easily be reached by foot; only the aquarium, the Norwegian Fisheries Museum, and Gamle Bergen (and farther-flung sights such as the Fantoft Stave Church, Edvard Grieg's Home at Troldhaugen, and the Ulriken643 cable car) are more than a 10-minute walk from the TI.

By Bus: City buses cost 60 NOK per ride (pay driver in cash), or 37 NOK per ride if you buy a single-ride ticket from a machine or convenience stores such as Narvesen, 7-Eleven, Rimi, and Deli de Luca. The best buses for a Bergen joyride are #6 (north along the coast) and #11 (into the hills).

By Tram: Bergen's light-rail line (Bybanen) is a convenient way to visit Edvard Grieg's Home and the Fantoft Stave Church, or to get to Flesland Airport. The tram begins next to Byparken (on Kaigaten, between Bergen's little lake and Ole Bulls Plass), then heads to the train station and continues south, ending at the airport. Buy your 37-NOK ticket from the machine before boarding (to use a US credit card, you'll need your PIN, also accepts coins). You can also buy single-ride tickets at Narvesen, 7-Eleven, Rimi, and Deli de Luca stores—you'll get a gray *minikort* pass. Validate the pass when you board by holding it next to the card reader (watch how other passengers do it). Ride it about 20 minutes to the Paradis stop for **Fantoft** Stave Church (don't get off at the "Fantoft" stop, which is farther from the church); or continue to the next stop, Hop, to hike to **Troldhaugen.**

By Ferry: The *Beffen,* a little orange ferry, chugs across the harbor (Vågen) every half-hour, from the dock a block south of the Bryggens Museum to the dock—directly opposite the fortress—a block from the Nykirken church (25 NOK, Mon-Fri 7:30-16:00, plus Sat May-Aug 11:00-16:00, fewer on Sun, 4-minute ride). Another *Beffen* ferry runs from the right side of the Fish Market (as you face the water) to the Norwegian Fisheries Museum (for details, see the Hanseatic Museum listing under "Sights in Bergen"). The *Vågen* "Akvariet" ferry runs from the left side of the Fish Market every half-hour to a dock near the aquarium (see the Aquarium listing under "Sights in Bergen"). All of these "poor man's cruises" offer good harbor views.

By Taxi: For a taxi, which can be pricey, call 07000 or 08000.

Tours in Bergen

▲▲▲Bryggen Walking Tour

This tour of the historic Hanseatic district is one of Bergen's best activities. Local guides take visitors on an excellent 1.5-hour walk

in English through 900 years of Bergen history via the old Hanseatic town (20 minutes in Bryggens Museum, 20-minute visit to the medieval Hanseatic Assembly Rooms (Schøtstuene), 20-minute walk through Bryggen, and 20 minutes in Hanseatic Museum). Tours leave from the Bryggens Museum (next to the Radisson Blu Royal Hotel). When you consider that the price includes entry tickets to all three sights, the tour more than pays for itself (150 NOK, June-Aug daily at 11:00 and 12:00, maximum 30 in group, no tours Sept-May, tel. 55

30 80 30, post@bymuseet.no). While the museum visits are a bit rushed, your tour ticket allows you to re-enter the museums for the rest of the day. The 11:00 tour can sell out, especially in July; to be safe, you can call, email, or drop by ahead of time to reserve a spot.

Local Guide
Sue Lindelid is a British expat who has spent more than 25 years showing visitors around Bergen (1,200 NOK/2-hour tour, 1,600 NOK/3-hour tour; mobile 90 78 59 52, suelin@hotmail.no).

▲Bus Tours
The TI sells tickets for various bus tours, including a 2.5-hour Grieg Lunch Concert tour that goes to Edvard Grieg's Home at Troldhaugen—a handy way to reach that distant sight (250 NOK, 50-NOK discount with Bergen Card, includes 30-minute concert but not lunch, May-Sept daily at 11:30, departs from TI). Buses are comfy, with big views and a fine recorded commentary. There are also several full-day tour options from Bergen, including bus/boat tours to nearby Hardanger and Sogne fjords. The TI is packed with brochures describing all the excursions.

Hop-On, Hop-Off Buses
City Sightseeing links most of Bergen's major sights and also stops at the Skolten cruise port, but doesn't go to the Fantoft Stave Church, Troldhaugen, or Ulriken643 cable car. If your sightseeing plans don't extend beyond the walkable core of Bergen, skip this (275 NOK/24 hours, early May-late Sept 9:00-16:00, every 30 minutes, also stops in front of Fish Market, mobile 97 78 18 88, www.citysightseeing.no/bergen).

Inflatable Boat Tour
After a scenic cruise along the Bergen harborfront, you'll zip out into the open fjord past islands and rocky skerries aboard a fast and breezy Fjord Tours rigid inflatable boat (RIB). Before heading out you'll don a survival suit and goggles for the thrilling high-speed part of the journey. Tours last 50 minutes and depart from near the round Narvesen kiosk on the Bryggen side of the Fish Market. Get tickets at the TI (595 NOK, meet at dock at 13:10, 1 tour/day, www.fjordtours.com).

Tourist Train
The tacky little "Bergen Express" train departs from in front of the Hanseatic Museum for a 55-minute loop around town (200 NOK, 1/hour daily June-Aug 10:00-18:00, less frequent off-season, headphone English commentary).

BERGEN

Bergen

To Norwegian Fisheries Museum

SKOLTEN CRUISE TERMINAL

SKOLTEGRUNNS-KAIEN

INTERNATIONAL FERRIES

SKUTEVIKSTORGET

B

585

❶ BERGENHUS FORTRESS

❷ HÅKON'S HALL

FESTNINGS-KAIEN

Harbor

NORDNES

TOTEM POLE

● AQUARIUM

⓯

STRANDGATEN

C. SUNDTS GATE

POOL

SWIMMING BEACH

HAUGEVEIEN

Nordnesparken

STRANDSIDEN

NORDNESVEIEN

ROSEN-KRANTZ TOWER

HARBOR FERRIES

NYKIRKEN

C. SUNDTS GATE

STRANDGATEN

Puddefjorden

HAUGEVEIEN

HOLBERGSALLM.

KLOSTERGATEN

SKOTTEGATEN

NØSTEGATEN

ENGEN

NØSTEGATTEN

HURTIGRUTEN TERMINAL (COASTAL CRUISES)

555

TORBORG NEDREAASGATE

JEKTEVIKEN/DOKKEN CRUISE PORT

Walk
❶ Bergenhus Fortress
❷ Bergenhus Rampart Perch
❸ St. Mary's Church
❹ Bryggens Museum
❺ Hanseatic Quarter & Hanseatic Museum
❻ Fish Market
❼ Seafarers' Monument
❽ Torgallmenningen (Main Square)
❾ Ole Bulls Plass

Additional Sights
⓾ Theta Museum
⑪ Fløibanen Funicular
⑫ Cathedral
⑬ Leprosy Museum
⑭ KODE Art Museums
⑮ Aquarium
⑯ To Gamle Bergen
⑰ Bus to Ulriken643 Cable Car
⑱ Bybanen Tram to Troldhaugen, Fantoft Stave Church & Airport
⑲ Bus to Jekteviken/Dokken Cruise Port

BERGEN

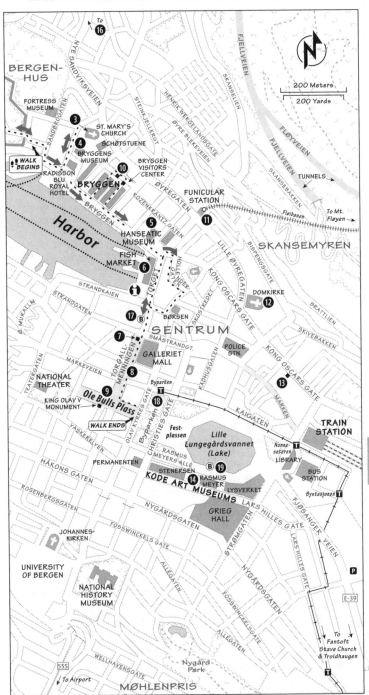

BERGEN

Bergen at a Glance

▲▲▲**Bryggen Walking Tour** Wonderful 1.5-hour tour of the historic Hanseatic district that covers 900 years of history and includes short visits to the Bryggens Museum, Hanseatic Assembly Rooms, and Hanseatic Museum, plus a walk through Bryggen. **Hours:** June-Aug daily at 11:00 and 12:00. See page 172.

▲▲**Bryggens Museum** Featuring early bits of Bergen (1050-1500), found in an archaeological dig. **Hours:** Daily 10:00-16:00; Sept-mid-May Mon-Fri 11:00-15:00, Sat-Sun 12:00-16:00. See page 188.

▲▲**Hanseatic Museum and Schøtstuene** Museum highlighting Bryggen's glory days, featuring an old merchant house furnished with artifacts from the time German merchants were tops in trading and a separate building housing assembly rooms—most interesting with included tour. **Hours:** Daily 9:00-17:00, June-Aug until 18:00, Oct-April 11:00-15:00 except Schøtstuene closed Sun. See page 189.

▲▲**Fløibanen Funicular** Zippy lift to top of Mount Fløyen for super views of Bergen, islands, and fjords, with picnic ops, an eatery, playground, and hiking trails. **Hours:** Mon-Fri 7:30-23:00, Sat-Sun from 8:00. See page 191.

▲**Fish Market** Lively market with cheap seafood eateries and free samples. **Hours:** May-Oct daily 8:00-23:00; Nov-Dec Mon-Sat 9:00-21:00, Sun from 11:00-21:00; Jan-April Sat only 9:00-15:00. See page 182.

▲**Bergenhus Fortress: Håkon's Hall and Rosenkrantz Tower** Fortress with a 13th-century medieval banquet hall, a climbable tower offering a history exhibit and views, and a worthwhile guided tour. **Hours:** Hall open daily 10:00-16:00, tower from 9:00; mid-Sept-mid-May hall daily 12:00-15:00, tower Sun only. See page 186.

BERGEN

Bergen Walk

For a quick self-guided orientation stroll through Bergen, follow this walk from the city's fortress, through its old wooden Hanseatic Quarter and Fish Market, to the modern center of town. This walk is also a handy sightseeing spine, passing most of Bergen's best museums; ideally, you'll get sidetracked and take advantage of their excellent tours along the way. I've pointed out the museums you'll pass en route—all are described in greater detail later, under "Sights in Bergen."

▲**KODE Art Museums** Collection spread among four neighboring lakeside buildings: KODE 4 (international and Norwegian artists), KODE 3 (Norwegian artists, including Munch), KODE 2 (contemporary art), and KODE 1 (decorative arts). **Hours:** Daily 11:00-17:00 (KODE 3 10:00-18:00), closed Mon mid-Sept-mid-May. See page 193.

▲**St. Mary's Church** Bergen's oldest church, dating to the 12th century. **Hours:** Mon-Fri 9:00-16:00, closed mid-Sept-May. See page 191.

▲**Aquarium** Well-presented sea life, with a walk-through "shark tunnel" and feeding times at the top of most hours in summer. **Hours:** Daily May-Aug 9:00-18:00, shorter hours off-season. See page 194.

▲**Gamle Bergen (Old Bergen)** Quaint gathering of 50 homes and shops dating from 18th-20th century, with guided tours of museum interiors at the top of the hour. **Hours:** Daily 9:00-16:00, closed Sept-mid-May. See page 194.

Near Bergen
▲▲**Edvard Grieg's Home, Troldhaugen** Home of Norway's greatest composer, with artifacts, tours, and concerts. **Hours:** Daily 9:00-18:00, Oct-April 10:00-16:00. See page 197.

▲**Ulriken643 Cable Car** A quick ride up to the summit of Ulriken, Bergen's tallest mountain, with nonstop views, a restaurant, and hiking trails. **Hours:** Daily 9:00-21:00, off-season until 17:00. See page 196.

BERGEN

• *Begin where Bergen did, at its historic fortress. From the harborfront road, 50 yards before the stone tower with the water on your left, veer up the ramp behind the low stone wall on the right, through a gate, and into the fortress complex. Stand before the stony skyscraper.*

❶ Bergenhus Fortress
In the 13th century, Bergen became the Kingdom of Norway's first real capital. (Until then, kings would circulate, staying on royal farms.) This fortress—built in the 1240s and worth ▲—was a garrison, with a tower for the king's residence (Rosenkrantz Tower) and a large hall for his banquets (Håkon's Hall).

Rosenkrantz Tower, the keep of the 13th-century castle, was expanded in the 16th century by the Danish-Norwegian king, who wanted to exercise a little control over the German merchants who dominated his town. He was tired of the Germans making all the money without paying taxes. This tower—with its cannon trained not on external threats but toward Bryggen—while expensive, paid for itself many times over as Germans got the message and paid their taxes.

• *Step through the gate (20 yards to the right of the tower) marked 1728 and into the courtyard of the Bergenhus Fortress. In front of you stands Håkon's Hall with its stepped gable. Tours for both the hall and the tower leave from the building to the right of Håkon's Hall.*

Pop into the museum lobby to enjoy a free exhibit about the massive 1944 explosion of the German ammunition ship in the harbor. For the best view of Håkon's Hall, walk through the gate and around the building to the left. Stand on the rampart between the hall and the harbor.

Håkon's Hall is the largest secular medieval building in Norway. When the pope sent a cardinal to perform Håkon's coronation there was no suitable building in Norway for such a VIP. King Håkon fixed that by having this impressive banqueting hall built in the mid-1200s. When Norway's capital moved to Oslo in 1299, the hall was abandoned and eventually used for grain storage. For a century it had no roof. In the Romantic 19th century, it was appreciated and restored. It's essentially a giant, grand reception hall used today as it was eight centuries ago: for banquets.

• *Continue walking along the rampart (climbing some steps and going about 100 yards past Håkon's Hall) to the far end of Bergenhus Fortress where you find a statue of a king and a fine harbor view.*

❼ Bergenhus Rampart Perch and Statue of King Håkon VII

The cannon on the ramparts here illustrates how the fort protected this strategic harbor. The port is busy with both cruise ships and supply ships for the nearby North Sea oil rigs. Long before this modern commerce, this is where the cod fishermen of the north met the traders of Europe. Travelers in the 12th century described how there were so many trading vessels here "you could cross the harbor without getting your feet wet." Beyond the ships is an island protecting Bergen from the open sea.

Look left and right at the dangerous edge with no railing. If someone were to fall and get hurt here and then try to sue, the Norwegian judge's verdict would be: stupidity—case dismissed. Around you are Bergen's "seven mountains." One day each summer locals race to climb each of these in rapid succession, accomplishing the feat in less than 12 hours.

The statue is of the beloved King Håkon VII (1872-1957),

grandfather of today's king. While exiled in London during World War II, King Håkon kept up Norwegian spirits through radio broadcasts. The first king of modern Norway (after the country won its independence from Sweden in 1905), he was a Danish prince married to Queen Victoria's granddaughter—a savvy monarch who knew how to play the royalty game.

A few steps behind the statue (just right of tree-lined lane) is the site of Bergen's first cathedral, built in 1070. A hedge grows where its walls once stood. The statue of Mary marks the place of the altar, its pedestal etched with a list of 13th-century kings of Norway crowned and buried here.

These castle grounds (notice the natural amphitheater on the left) host cultural events and music festivals; Elton John, Paul McCartney, and Kygo have all packed this outdoor venue in recent years.

Continuing around Håkon's Hall, follow the linden tree-lined lane. On the left, a massive concrete structure disguised by ivy looms as if evil. It was a German bunker built during the Nazi occupation—easier now to ignore than dismantle.

Twenty yards ahead on the right is a rare set of free public toilets. Notice they come with blue lights to discourage heroin junkies from using these WCs as a place to shoot up. The blue lights make it hard to see veins.

• *You've now returned to the tower and circled the castle grounds. Before leaving, consider taking a guided tour of the hall and tower. Head back down the ramp, out to the main road, and continue with the harbor on your right. (After a block, history buffs could follow* Bergenhus *signs, up the street to the left, to the free and fascinating* **Fortress Museum***—with its collection of Norwegian military history and Nazi occupation exhibits.) Proceed one more block along the harbor until you reach the open, parklike space on your left. Walk 100 yards (just past the handy Rema 1000 supermarket) to the top of this park where you'll see…*

❸ St. Mary's Church (Mariakirken)

Dating from the 12th century, this is Bergen's oldest preserved building. This stately church of the Hanseatic merchants has a dour stone interior, but it's enlivened by a colorful, highly decorated pulpit.

In the park below the church, find the statue of Snorri Sturlason. In the 1200s, this Icelandic scribe and scholar wrote down the Viking sagas. Thanks to him, we have a better understanding of this Nordic era. A few steps to the right, look through the window of the big modern building at an archaeological site showing the oldest remains of Bergen—stubs of the 12th-century trading town's streets tumbling to the harbor before land reclamation pushed the harbor farther out.

• *The window is just a sneak peek at the excellent* ❹ *Bryggens Museum, which provides helpful historical context for the Hanseatic Quarter we're about to visit. The museum's outstanding Bryggen Walking Tour is your best bet for seeing this area (June–Aug daily at 11:00 and 12:00; see "Tours in Bergen," earlier). Continue down to the busy harborfront. On the left is the most photographed sight in town, the Bryggen quarter. To get your bearings, first read the "Bryggen's History" sidebar; if it's nice out, cross the street to the wharf and look back for a fine overview of this area. (Or, in the rain, huddle under an awning.)*

❺ Bergen's Hanseatic Quarter (Bryggen)

Bergen's fragile wooden old town is its iconic front door. The long "tenements" (rows of warehouses) hide atmospheric lanes that creak and groan with history.

Remember that while we think of Bergen as "Norwegian," Bryggen was German—the territory of *Deutsch*-speaking merchants and traders. (The most popular surname in Bergen is the German name Hanson—"son of Hans.") From the front of Bryggen, look back at the Rosenkrantz Tower. The little red holes at its top mark where cannons once pointed at the German quarter, installed by Norwegian royalty who wanted a slice of all that taxable trade revenue. Their threat was countered by German grain—without which the Norwegians would've starved.

Notice that the first six houses are perfectly straight; they were built in the 1980s to block the view of a modern hotel behind. The more ramshackle stretch of 11 houses beyond date from the early 1700s. Each front hides a long line of five to ten businesses.

• *To wander into the heart of this woody medieval quarter, head down Bredsgården, the lane a couple of doors before the shop sign featuring the anatomically correct unicorn. We'll make a loop to the right: down this lane nearly all the way, under a passage into a square (with a well, a vibrant outdoor restaurant, and a big wooden cod), and then back to the harbor down a parallel lane. Read the information below, then explore, stopping at the big wooden cod.*

Bit by bit, Bryggen is being restored using medieval techniques and materials. As you explore, you may stumble upon a rebuilding project in action.

Strolling through Bryggen, you feel swallowed up by history. Long rows of planky buildings (medieval-style double tenements)

lean haphazardly across narrow alleys. The last Hanseatic merchant moved out centuries ago, but this is still a place of (touristy) commerce. You'll find artists' galleries, T-shirt boutiques, leather workshops, atmospheric restaurants, fishing tackle shops, sweaters, sweaters, sweaters...and trolls.

Look up at the winch-and-pulley systems on the buildings. These connected ground-floor workrooms with top-floor storerooms. Notice that the overhanging storerooms upstairs were supported by timbers with an elbow created by a tree trunk and its root—considered the strongest way to make a right angle in construction back then. Turning right at the top of the lane, you enter a lively cobbled square. On the far side is that big wooden fish.

The wooden cod (next to a well) is a reminder that the economic foundation of Bergen—the biggest city in Scandinavia until 1650 and the biggest city in Norway until 1830—was this fish. The stone building behind the carved cod was one of the fireproof cookhouses serving a line of buildings that stretched to the harbor. Today it's the Hetland Gallery, filled with the entertaining work of a popular local artist famous for fun caricatures of the city. Facing the same square is the Bryggen visitors center, worth peeking into.

• *Enjoy the center and the shops. Then return downhill to the harborfront, turn left, and continue the walk.*

Half of Bryggen (the brick-and-stone stretch to your left between the old wooden facades and the head of the bay) was torn down around 1900. Today the stately buildings that replaced it—far less atmospheric than Bryggen's original wooden core—are filled with tacky trinket shops and touristy splurge restaurants. They do make a nice architectural cancan of pointy gables, each with its date of construction indicated near the top.

Head to the lone wooden red house at the end of the row, which houses the **Hanseatic Museum.** The man who owned this building recognized the value of the city's heritage and kept its 18th-century interior intact. Once considered a nutcase, today he's celebrated as a visionary, as his decision has left visitors with a fine example of an old merchant house that they can tour. This highly recommended museum is your best chance to get a peek inside one of those old wooden tenements.

• *The Fish Market is just across the street. Before enjoying that, we'll circle a few blocks inland and around to the right.*

The red-brick building (with frilly white trim, stepped gable, and a Starbucks) is the old meat market. It was built in 1877, after the importance of hygiene was recognized and the meat was moved inside from today's Fish Market. At the intersection just beyond, look left (uphill past the meat market) to see the Fløibanen station. Ahead, on the right, is an unusually classy McDonald's in a 1710 building that was originally a bakery.

Across the street, Anne Madam Restaurant is a celebration of white and fishy cuisine—very Norwegian, with a few Norwegian meat dishes thrown in. Notice the Los Tacos restaurant next door; Norwegians love Tex-Mex food, and "Taco Friday" has become a tradition for many. A few steps uphill, the tiny red shack flying the Norwegian flags is the popular, recommended 3-Kroneren hot-dog stand. Review the many sausage options.

At the McDonald's, wander the length of the cute lane of 200-year-old buildings. Called Hollendergaten, its name comes from a time when the king organized foreign communities of traders into various neighborhoods; this was where the Dutch lived. The curving street marks the former harborfront—these buildings were originally right on the water.

Hooking left, you reach the end of Hollendergaten. Turn right back toward the harborfront. Ahead is the grand stone Børsen building (now Matbørsen, a collection of trendy restaurants), once the stock exchange. Step inside to enjoy its 1920s Art Deco-style murals celebrating Bergen's fishing heritage.

• *Now, cross the street and immerse yourself in Bergen's beloved Fish Market.*

❻ Fish Market (Fisketorget)

A fish market has thrived here since the 1500s, when fishermen rowed in with their catch and haggled with hungry residents.

While it's now become a food circus of eateries selling fishy treats to tourists—no local would come here to actually buy fish—this famous market is still worth ▲, offering lots of smelly photo fun and free morsels to taste (May-Oct daily 8:00-23:00, but vendors may close earlier if they're not busy;

Nov-Dec Mon-Sat 9:00-21:00, Sun from 11:00; Jan-April Sat only 9:00-15:00).

Many stands sell premade smoked-salmon *(laks)* sandwiches, fish soup, and other snacks ideal for a light lunch (confirm prices before ordering). To try Norwegian jerky, pick up a bag of dried cod snacks *(tørrfisk)*. The red meat is minke (pronounced mink-ee) whale, caught off the coast of northern Norway. Norwegians, notorious for their whaling, defend it as a traditional livelihood for many of their people. They remind us that they only harvest the minke whale, which is not on an endangered list. In recent years, Norway has assigned itself a quota of nearly 1,000 minke whales a year, with the actual catch coming to a bit over half of that.

• *Watch your wallet: If you're going to get pickpocketed in Bergen, it'll likely be here. When done exploring, with your back to the market, hike a block to the right (note the pointy church spire in the distance and the big blocky stone monument dead ahead) into the modern part of town and a huge wide square. Pause at the intersection just before crossing into the square, about 20 yards before the blocky monument. Look left to see Mount Ulriken with its TV tower. A cable car called Ulriken643 takes you to its 2,110-foot summit. (Shuttle buses leave from this corner, at the top and bottom of the hour, to its station; for summit details, see page 196.) Now, walk up to that big square monument and meet some Vikings.*

❼ Seafarers' Monument

Nicknamed "the cube of goat cheese" for its shape, this 1950 monument celebrates Bergen's contact with the sea and remembers

those who worked on it and died in it. Study the faces: All social classes are represented. The statues relate to the scenes depicted in the reliefs above. Each side represents a century (start with the Vikings and work clockwise): 10th century—Vikings, with a totem pole in the panel above recalling the pre-Columbian Norwegian discovery of America; 18th century—equipping Europe's ships; 19th century—whaling; 20th century—shipping and war. For the 21st century, see the real people—a cross-section of today's Norway—sitting at the statue's base. Major department stores (Galleriet, Xhibition, and Telegrafen) are all nearby.

• *The monument marks the start of Bergen's main square...*

❽ Torgallmenningen

Allmenningen means "for all the people." Torg means "square."

BERGEN

Bryggen's History

Pretty as Bryggen is today, it has a rough-and-tumble history. A horrific plague decimated the population and economy of Norway in 1350, killing about half of its people. A decade later, German merchants arrived and established a Hanseatic trading post, bringing order to that rustic society. For the next four centuries, the port of Bergen was essentially German territory.

Bergen's old German trading center was called "the German wharf" until World War II (and is now just called "the wharf," or "Bryggen"). From 1370 to 1754, German merchants controlled Bergen's trade. In 1550, it was a Germanic city of 1,000 workaholic merchants—surrounded and supported by some 5,000 Norwegians.

The German merchants were very strict and lived in a harsh, all-male world (except for Norwegian prostitutes). This wasn't a military occupation, but a mutually beneficial economic partnership. The Norwegian cod fishermen of the far north shipped their dried cod to Bergen, where the Hanseatic merchants marketed it to Europe. Norwegian cod provided much of Europe with food (a source of easy-to-preserve protein) and cod oil (which lit the lamps until about 1850).

While the city dates from 1070, little survives from before the last big fire in 1702. In its earlier heyday, Bergen was one of the largest wooden cities in Europe. Congested wooden buildings, combined with lots of small fires (to provide heat and light in this cold and dark corner of Europe), spelled disaster for Bergen. Over the centuries, the city suffered countless fires, including 10 devastating ones. Back then, it wasn't a question of *if* there would be a fire, but *when* there would be a fire—with major blazes every 20 or so years. Each time the warehouses burned, the merchants would toss the refuse into the bay and rebuild. Gradually,

And, while this is the city's main gathering place, it was actually created as a firebreak. The residents of this wood-built city knew fires were inevitable. The street plan was designed with breaks, or open spaces like this square, to help contain the destruction. In 1916, it succeeded in stopping a fire, which is why it has a more modern feel today.

Walk the length of the square to the angled slab of blue stone (quarried in Brazil) at the far end. This is a monument to King Olav V, who died in 1991, and a popular meeting point: Locals like to say, "Meet you at the Blue Stone." It marks the center of a parklike swath known as...

the land crept out, and so did the buildings. (Looking at the Hanseatic Quarter from the harborfront, you can see how the buildings have settled. The foundations, composed of debris from the many fires, settle as they rot.)

After 1702, the city rebuilt using more stone and brick, and suffered fewer fires. But this one small wooden quarter was built after the fire, in the early 1700s. To prevent future blazes, the Germans forbade all fires and candles for light or warmth except in isolated and carefully guarded communal houses behind each tenement. It was in these communal houses that apprentices studied, people dried out their soggy clothes, hot food was cooked, and the men drank and partied. When there was a big banquet, one man always stayed sober—a kind of designated fire watchman.

Flash forward to the 20th century. One of the biggest explosions of World War II occurred in Bergen's harbor on April 20, 1944. An ammunition ship loaded with 120 tons of dynamite blew up just in front of the fortress. The blast leveled entire neighborhoods on either side of the harbor (notice the ugly 1950s construction opposite the fortress) and did serious damage to Håkon's Hall and Rosenkrantz Tower. How big was the blast? There's a hut called "the anchor cabin" a couple of miles away in the mountains. That's where the ship's anchor landed. The blast is considered to be accidental, despite the fact that April 20 happened to be Hitler's 55th birthday and the ship blew up about 100 yards away from the Nazi commander's headquarters (in the fortress).

After World War II, Bryggen was again slated for destruction. Most of the locals wanted it gone—it reminded them of the Germans who had occupied Norway for the miserable war years. Then excavators discovered rune stones indicating that the area predated the Germans. This boosted Bryggen's approval rating, and the quarter was saved. Today this picturesque and historic zone is the undisputed tourist highlight of Bergen.

BERGEN

❾ Ole Bulls Plass

This drag leads from the National Theater (above on right) to a little lake (below on left).

Detour a few steps up for a better look at the **National Theater,** built in Art Nouveau style in 1909. Founded by violinist Ole Bull in 1850, this was the first theater to host plays in the Norwegian language. After 450 years of Danish and Swedish rule, 19th-century Norway enjoyed a cultural awakening, and Bergen became an artistic power. Ole Bull collaborated with the playwright Henrik Ibsen. Ibsen commissioned Edvard Grieg to compose the music for his play *Peer Gynt*. These three lions of Norwegian culture all lived and worked right here in Bergen.

Head downhill on the square to a delightful fountain featuring a **statue of Ole Bull** in the shadow of trees. Ole Bull was an 1800s version of Elvis. A pop idol and heartthrob in his day, Ole Bull's bath water was bottled and sold by hotels, and women fainted when they heard him play violin. Living up to his name, he fathered over 40 children. Speaking of children, I love to hang out here watching families frolic in the pond, oblivious to the waterfall troll (see the statue with the harp below Ole Bull). According to legend, the troll bestows musical talent on anyone—like old Ole—who gives him a gift (he likes meat).

From here, the park spills farther downhill to a cast-iron pavilion given to the city by Germans in 1889, and on to the little man-made lake (Lille Lungegårdsvannet), which is circled by an enjoyable path. This green zone is considered a park and is cared for by the local parks department.

• *If you're up for a lakeside stroll, now's your chance. Also notice that alongside the lake (to the right as you face it from here) is a row of buildings housing the enjoyable* **KODE Art Museums.** *And to the left of the lake are some fine residential streets (including the picturesque, cobbled Marken); within a few minutes' walk is the* **Leprosy Museum** *and the* **cathedral.**

Sights in Bergen

Several museums listed here—including the Bryggens Museum, Håkon's Hall, Rosenkrantz Tower, Leprosy Museum, and Gamle Bergen—are part of the Bergen City Museum (Bymuseet) organization. If you buy a ticket to any of them, you'll pay half-price at any of the others simply by showing your ticket.

▲Bergenhus Fortress: Håkon's Hall and Rosenkrantz Tower

The tower and hall, sitting boldly out of place on the harbor just beyond Bryggen, are reminders of Bergen's importance as the first permanent capital of Norway. Both sights feel vacant and don't really speak for themselves; the guided tours, which provide a serious introduction to Bergen's history, are essential for grasping their significance.

Cost and Hours: Hall and tower-120 NOK for both (or 80 NOK each), half-price with ticket to another Bergen City Museum; hall open daily 10:00-16:00, tower from 9:00; mid-Sept-mid-

May hall open daily 12:00-15:00, tower open Sun only; tel. 55 30 80 30, free WC.

Tours: 20 NOK extra for guided tour that includes both buildings (mid-June-Aug tours leave daily at 11:00, 14:00, and 15:00 from the building to the right of Håkon's Hall).

Håkon's Hall, dating from the 13th century, was built as a banqueting hall, and that's essentially what it still is today. It was

restored in the early 20th century, but was heavily damaged in World War II when a munitions ship exploded in the harbor, leaving nothing but the walls standing. In the 1950s it was restored again, with the grand wooden ceiling and roof modeled after the medieval roof on a church in northern Norway. Beneath the hall is a whitewashed cellar that is thought to have been used mainly for storage.

Rosenkrantz Tower, the keep of a 13th-century castle, is today a stack of barren rooms connected by tight spiral staircases,

with a good history exhibit on the top two floors and a commanding view from its rooftop. In the 16th century, the ruling Danish-Norwegian king enlarged the tower and trained its cannon on the German-merchant district, Bryggen, to remind the merchants of the importance of paying their taxes.

Fortress Museum (Bergenhus Festningmuseum)

This humble museum (which functioned as a prison during the Nazi occupation), set back a couple of blocks from the fortress, will interest historians with its thoughtful exhibits about military history, especially Bergen's WWII experience (look for the Norwegian Nazi flag). You'll learn about the resistance movement in Bergen (including its underground newspapers), the role of women in the Norwegian military, and Norwegian troops who have served with UN forces in overseas conflicts.

Cost and Hours: Free, Tue-Sun 11:00-17:00, ask to borrow a translation of the descriptions, just behind Thon Hotel Orion at Koengen, tel. 55 54 63 87.

The Hanseatic League, Blessed by Cod

Middlemen in trade, the clever German merchants of the Hanseatic League ruled the waves of northern Europe for 500 years (c. 1250-1750). These sea-traders first banded together in a Hanse, or merchant guild, to defend themselves against pirates. As they spread out from Germany, they established trading posts in foreign lands, cut deals with local leaders for trading rights, built boats and wharves, and organized armies to protect ships and ports.

By the 15th century, these merchants had organized more than a hundred cities into the Hanseatic League, a free-trade zone that stretched from London to Russia. The League ran a profitable triangle of trade: Fish from Scandinavia was exchanged for grain from the eastern Baltic and luxury goods from England and Flanders. Everyone benefited, and the German merchants—the middlemen—reaped the profits.

At its peak in the 15th century, the Hanseatic League was the dominant force—economic, military, and political—in northern Europe. This was an age when much of Europe was fragmented into petty kingdoms and dukedoms. Revenue-hungry kings and robber-baron lords levied chaotic and extortionist tolls and duties. Pirates plagued shipments. It was the Hanseatic League, rather than national governments, that brought the stability that allowed trade to flourish.

▲▲Bryggens Museum

This modern museum explains the 1950s archaeological dig to uncover the earliest bits of Bergen (1050-1500). Brief English explanations are posted. From September through May, when there is no tour, consider buying the good museum guidebook (25 NOK).

Cost and Hours: 80 NOK; in summer, entry included with Bryggen Walking Tour described earlier; daily 10:00-16:00; Sept-mid-May Mon-Fri 11:00-15:00, Sat-Sun 12:00-16:00; inexpensive cafeteria; in big, modern building just beyond the end of Bryggen and the Radisson Blu Royal Hotel, tel. 55 30 80 30, www.bymuseet.no.

Visiting the Museum: The manageable, well-presented permanent exhibit occupies the ground floor. First up are the foundations from original wooden tenements dating back to the 12th century (displayed right where they were excavated) and a giant chunk of the hull of a 100-foot-long, 13th-century ship that was found here. Next, an exhibit (roughly shaped like the long, wooden

Bergen's place in this Baltic economy was all about cod—a form of protein that could be dried, preserved, and shipped anywhere. Though cursed by a lack of natural resources, the city was blessed with a good harbor conveniently located between the rich fishing spots of northern Norway and the markets of Europe. Bergen's port shipped dried cod and fish oil southward and imported grain, cloth, beer, wine, and ceramics.

Bryggen was one of four principal Hanseatic trading posts (Kontors), along with London, Bruges, and Novgorod. It was the last Kontor opened (c. 1360), the least profitable, and the final one to close. Bryggen had warehouses, offices, and living quarters. Ships docked here were unloaded by counterpoise cranes. At its peak, as many as a thousand merchants, journeymen, and apprentices lived and worked here.

Bryggen was a self-contained German enclave within the city. The merchants came from Germany, worked a few years here, and retired back in the home country. They spoke German, wore German clothes, and attended their own churches. By law, they were forbidden to intermarry or fraternize with the Bergeners, except on business.

The Hanseatic League peaked around 1500, then slowly declined. Rising nation-states were jealous of the Germans merchants' power and wealth. The Reformation tore apart old alliances. Dutch and English traders broke the Hanseatic monopoly. Cities withdrew from the League and Kontors closed. In 1754, Bergen's Kontor was taken over by the Norwegians. When it closed its doors on December 31, 1899, a sea-trading era was over, but the city of Bergen had become rich...by the grace of cod.

double-tenements outside) shows off artifacts and explains lifestyles from medieval Bryggen. Behind that is a display of items you might have bought at the medieval market. You'll finish with exhibits about the church in Bergen, the town's role as a royal capital, and its status as a cultural capital. Upstairs are two floors of temporary exhibits.

▲▲Hanseatic Museum and Schøtstuene (Det Hanseatiske Museum og Schøtstuene)

The **Hanseatic Museum** offers the best possible look inside the wooden houses that are Bergen's trademark. Its creaky old rooms—with hundred-year-old cod hanging from the ceiling—offer a time-tunnel experience back to Bryggen's glory days. It's located in an atmospheric old merchant house furnished with dried fish, antique ropes, an old oxtail (used for wringing spilled cod-liver oil back into the bucket), sagging steps, and cupboard beds from the early 1700s—one sporting what some claim is a medieval pinup girl. You'll explore two upstairs levels, fully furnished and with funhouse floors. The place still feels eerily lived-in; neatly sorted desks with tidy ledgers seem to be waiting for the next workday to begin.

Included with your admission are visits to the **Schøtstu-ene** (Hanseatic Assembly Rooms) and the Norwegian Fisheries Museum (described below). The

Schøtstuene assembly rooms are in a building near St. Mary's Church that's accessed behind Bryggen from Øvregaten. Here, Hanseatic merchants would cook hot meals and gather to feast, hold court, conduct ceremonies, be schooled, and get warm—fires were allowed in this building only because it was separate from the other (highly flammable) Bryggen offices.

Cost: 160 NOK ticket (sold May-mid-Sept) includes all three sights and shuttle bus to Fisheries Museum, 100 NOK Oct-April; 100 NOK after 15:45 for Hanseatic Museum only. (Bryggen Walking Tour entry does not include Fisheries Museum.)

Hours: Daily 9:00-18:00, May and Sept until 17:00, Oct-April 11:00-15:00 except Schøtstuene closed Sun; Finnegården 1a, tel. 55 54 46 90, www.museumvest.no.

Tours: The Hanseatic Museum has scant English explanations—it's much better if you take the good, included 30-minute guided tour (3/day in English—call to confirm, June-mid-Sept only, times displayed on a monitor). Even if you tour the museum with the Bryggen Walking Tour, you're welcome to revisit (using the same ticket) and take this tour.

Norwegian Fisheries Museum: Just up the coast (along the water just north of Bryggen) is the Norwegian Fisheries Museum, an authentic wharfside warehouse with exhibits about life along and on the sea. Catch the free shuttle bus from the Hanseatic Museum (5-minute ride) or cruise 20 minutes aboard the *Beffen* ferry to the museum (130 NOK round-trip, June-Aug hourly 11:00-17:00, departs from the Bryggen side of the Fish Market).

Theta Museum

This small museum highlights Norway's resistance movement. You'll peek into the hidden world of a 10-person cell of courageous students, whose group—called Theta—housed other fighters and communicated with London during the Nazi occupation in World

War II. It's housed in Theta's former headquarters—a small upstairs room in a wooden Bryggen building.

Cost and Hours: 50 NOK, June-Aug Tue, Sat, and Sun 14:00-16:00, closed Mon, Wed-Fri, and Sept-May, Enhjørningsgården.

▲▲Fløibanen Funicular

Bergen's popular funicular climbs 1,000 feet in seven minutes to the top of Mount Fløyen for the best view of the town, surrounding islands, and fjords all the way to the west coast. The top is a popular picnic spot, perfect for enjoying the sunset. The **$$** Fløien Folkerestaurant, the white building at the top of the funicular, offers affordable self-service food all day in season. Behind the station, you'll find a playground and a fun giant troll photo op. The top is also the starting point for many peaceful hikes.

You'll buy your funicular ticket at the base of the Fløibanen (notice the photos in the entry hall of the construction of the funicular and its 1918 grand opening).

If you'll want to hike down from the top, ask for the *Fløyen Hiking Map* when you buy your ticket; you'll save 50 percent by

purchasing only a one-way ticket up. From the top, walk behind the station and follow the signs to the city center. The top half of the 30-minute hike is a gravelly lane through a forest with fine views. The bottom is a paved lane passing charming old wooden homes. It's a steep descent. To save your knees, you could ride the lift most of the way down and get off at the Promsgate stop to wander through the delightful cobbled and shiplap lanes (note that only the :00 and :30 departures stop at Promsgate).

Cost and Hours: 90 NOK round-trip, 45 NOK one-way, lines can be long if cruise ships are in town—buy tickets online to skip the line; Mon-Fri 7:30-23:00, Sat-Sun from 8:00, departures 4/hour—on the quarter-hour most of the day, runs continuously if busy; tel. 55 33 68 00, www.floyen.no.

▲St. Mary's Church (Mariakirken)

The oldest parish church and preserved building in Bergen dates to between 1130 and 1170, and is said to be one of the best-decorated

BERGEN

medieval churches in Norway. For many years, St. Mary's Church was known as the "German Church," as it was used by the German merchants of the Hanseatic League from 1408 to 1766. The last service in German was held in 1906. The stony interior is accented with a golden altarpiece, a Baroque pulpit of Dutch origin partly made from exotic materials (such as turtle skin), and artworks from various time periods.

Cost and Hours: 50 NOK, Mon-Fri 9:00-16:00, closed mid-Sept-May; 25-minute English guided tour (75 NOK, including church entry) runs June-Aug Mon-Fri at 15:30; http://bergendomkirke.no, tel. 55 59 71 75.

Cathedral (Domkirke)

Bergen's main church, dedicated to St. Olav (the patron saint of Norway), dates from 1301. The cathedral may be closed for renovation during your visit, but if it's open, drop in to enjoy its stoic, plain interior with stuccoed stone walls and a giant wooden pulpit. Sit in a hard, straight-backed pew and just try to doze off. Like so many old Norwegian structures, its roof makes you feel like you're huddled under an overturned Viking ship. The church is oddly lopsided, with just one side aisle. Before leaving, look up to see the gorgeous wood-carved organ over the main entrance. In the entryway, you'll see portraits of each bishop dating all the way back to the Reformation.

Cost and Hours: Free; Mon-Fri 10:00-16:00, Sun 9:30-13:00, closed Sat; shorter hours mid-Aug-mid-June.

Leprosy Museum (Lepramuseet)

Leprosy is also known as "Hansen's Disease" because in the 1870s a Bergen man named Armauer Hansen did groundbreaking work

in understanding the ailment. This unique museum is in St. Jørgens Hospital, a leprosarium that dates back to about 1700. Up until the 19th century, as much as 3 percent of Norway's population had leprosy. This hospital—once called "a graveyard for the living" (its last patient died in 1946)—has a meager exhibit in a thought-provoking dorm for the dying. It's most worthwhile if you read the translation of the exhibit (borrow a copy at the entry) or take the free tour (at the top of each hour). As you leave, if you're interested, ask if you can see the medicinal herb garden out back.

Cost and Hours: 80 NOK, half-price with ticket to another Bergen City Museum, daily 11:00-15:00, closed Sept-mid-May, between train station and Bryggen at Kong Oscars Gate 59, tel. 55 30 80 30, www.bymuseet.no.

▲KODE Art Museums

If you need to get out of the rain (and you enjoyed the National Gallery in Oslo), check out this collection, filling four neighboring buildings facing the lake along Rasmus Meyers Allé. The KODE 4 building, on the far left, has an eclectic cross-section of both international and Norwegian artists. The KODE 3 branch specializes in Norwegian artists and has an especially good Munch exhibit. The KODE 2 building has installations of contemporary art and a big bookstore on the first floor, while the KODE 1 building has decorative arts and silver crafts from Bergen. Small description sheets in English are in each room.

Cost and Hours: 100 NOK, daily 11:00-17:00 except KODE 3 10:00-18:00, closed Mon mid-Sept-mid-May, Rasmus Meyers Allé 3, tel. 53 00 97 04, www.kodebergen.no.

Visiting the Museums: Many visitors focus on **KODE 4** (from outside, enter through Door 4), featuring an easily digestible

collection. Here are some of its highlights: The ground floor includes an extensive display of works by Nikolai Astrup (1880-1928), who depicts Norway's fjords with bright colors and Expressionistic flair. One flight up is a great collection titled *Bergen and the World, 1400-1900*, which depicts fascinating stories from Europe and Norway. Another section has paintings by J. C. Dahl and his students, who captured the majesty of Norway's natural wonders (look for Adelsteen Normann's impressive, photorealistic view of Romsdalsfjord). "Norwegian Art 1840-1900" includes works by Christian Krohg, as well as some portraits by Harriet Backer and realistic scenes of everyday life by Frits Thaulow.

Up on the third floor, things get modern. The Tower Hall (Tårnsalen) features Norwegian modernism and a large exhibit of Bergen's avant-garde art (1966-1985), kicked off by "Group 66." The International Modernism section has four stars: Pablo Picasso (sketches, etchings, collages, and a few Cubist paintings), Paul Klee (the Swiss childlike painter), and the dynamic Norwegian duo of Edvard Munch and Ludvig Karisten. Rounding it out are a smattering of Surrealist, Abstract Expressionist, and Op Art pieces.

KODE 3 presents one of the finest collections of work by Edvard Munch, including such masterpieces as *Jealousy, Melancholy, Woman in Three Stages,* and *Evening on Karl Johan.* Also on hand is a fine collection from Norway's Golden Age (1880-1905), including highlights from the careers of romantic landscape painters Hans Gude and J. C. Dahl. And don't miss the iconic troll and folktale drawings and watercolors by Theodor Kittelsen.

KODE 2 focuses on contemporary art from 1980 to the present. **KODE 1** hosts temporary exhibitions and a permanent exhibition showcasing the rich legacy and craftsmanship of Bergen silversmiths.

▲Aquarium (Akvariet)

Small but fun, this aquarium claims to be the second-most-visited sight in Bergen. It's wonderfully laid out and explained in English. Check out the view from inside the "shark tunnel" in the tropical shark exhibit.

Cost and Hours: 270 NOK, kids-185 NOK, daily May-Aug 9:00-18:00, shorter hours off-season, feeding times at the top of most hours in summer, cheery cafeteria with light sandwiches, Nordnesbakken 4, tel. 55 55 71 71, www.akvariet.no.

Getting There: It's at the tip of the peninsula on the south end of the harbor—about a 20-minute walk or short ride on bus #11 from the city center. Or hop on the handy little *Vågen* "Akvariet" ferry that sails from the Fish Market to near the aquarium (50 NOK one-way, 80 NOK round-trip, show ferry ticket for 20 percent off aquarium admission, 2/hour, 10-minute ride, June-Aug 10:00-17:30, off-season until 16:00).

Nearby: The lovely park behind the aquarium has views of the sea and a popular swimming beach (described later, under "Activities in Bergen"). The totem pole erected here was a gift from Bergen's sister city in the US—Seattle.

▲Gamle Bergen (Old Bergen)

This Disney-cute gathering of 50-some 18th- through 20th-century homes and shops was founded in 1934 to save old buildings from destruction as Bergen modernized. Each of the buildings was moved from elsewhere in Bergen and reconstructed here. Together, they create a virtual town that offers a cobbled look at the old life. It's free to wander through the town and park to enjoy the facades of the historic buildings, but to get into the 20 or so museum buildings, you'll have to join a tour (departing on the hour 10:00-16:00).

Cost and Hours: 100 NOK, half-price with ticket to another Bergen City Museum, daily 9:00-16:00, closed Sept-mid-May, tel. 55 39 43 04, www.bymuseet.no.

Getting There: Take any bus heading west from Bryggen (such as #4, #5, or #6, direction: Lønborglien) to Gamle Bergen (stop: Gamle Bergen). You'll get off after the tunnel at a freeway pullout and walk 200 yards, following signs to the museum. Any bus heading back into town takes you to the center (buses come by

every few minutes). With the easy bus connection, there
to taxi.

ACTIVITIES IN BERGEN
▲Strolling
Bergen is a great town for wandering. Enjoy a little Norwegian
paseo. On a balmy Norwegian summer evening, I'd stroll from
the castle, along the harborfront, up the main square to Ole Bulls
Plass, and around the lake.

For a slightly more strenuous yet rewarding walk, head up the
zig-zagging road behind the Fløibanen funicular station to a city
viewpoint in front of a white building with a lookout tower. The
building was once a fire station (which explains the tower). The lake
next to it used to be a reservoir. And the white houses past the lake
were built by firemen on land given to them so that they could live
close to the station. After enjoying the city views, you can either
return to town the way you came, or follow Øvre Blekeveien down
past the lake and white houses; then take any road to the left off
Blekeveien back down to the harbor.

Shopping
Most shops are open Monday through Friday 9:00-17:00, Thursday until 19:00, Saturday 9:00-15:00, and closed Sunday. Many of
the tourist shops at the harborfront strip along Bryggen are open
daily—even during holidays—until 20:00 or 21:00. You'll see the
same products offered at different prices, so shopping around can
be a good idea.

Ting (Things) offers a fun alternative to troll shopping, with
contemporary housewares and quirky gift ideas (daily 9:00-22:30,
at Bryggen 13, a block past the Hanseatic Museum, tel. 55 21 54
80).

Nilssen på Bryggen, next to the Hanseatic Museum, is one of
the oldest shops in Bergen. You'll find Norwegian yarn for knitting
and modern-style Sandnes wool sweaters, along with souvenirs and
hand-embroidered Christmas items (Mon-Sat 10:00-18:00, closed
Sun, Bryggen 3, tel. 55 31 67 90).

Husfliden is a shop popular for its handmade goodies and re-
liably Norwegian sweaters (fine variety and quality but expensive,
just off Torget, the market square, at Vågsallmenninge 3, tel. 55
54 47 40).

The Galleriet Mall, a shopping center on Torgallmenningen,
holds six floors of shops, cafés, and restaurants. You'll find a pharmacy, photo shops, clothing, sporting goods, bookstores, mobile-
phone shops, and a basement grocery store (Mon-Fri 9:00-21:00,
Sat 9:00-18:00, closed Sun).

e public swimming
um and the other in
is a great local scene
ordnes Sjøbad, near
the aqua... wimmers an outdoor
heated pool and a protected area of the
sea (80 NOK, kids-35 NOK, mid-May-
Aug Mon-Fri 7:00-19:00, Sat 9:00-14:00,
Sun 10:00-14:00, Sat-Sun until 19:00 in
good weather, closed off-season, Nordnesparken 30, tel. 53 03 91 90). **Sandviken
Sjøbad,** at Gamle Bergen, is free and
open all summer. It comes with changing
rooms, a roped-off bit of the bay (no pool),
a high dive, and lots of sunbathing space.

SIGHTS NEAR BERGEN
▲Ulriken643 Cable Car

It's amazingly easy and quick to zip up six minutes to the
643-meter-high (that's 2,110 feet) summit of Ulriken, the tallest

mountain near Bergen. Stepping out of the cable car, you
enter a different world, with
views stretching to the ocean.
A chart clearly shows the many
well-marked and easy hikes
that fan out over the vast,
rocky, grassy plateau above the
tree line (circular walks of vari-
ous lengths, a 40-minute hike down, and a 4-hour hike to the top
of the Fløibanen funicular). For less exercise, you can simply sun-
bathe, crack open a picnic, or enjoy the Ulriken restaurant.

Cost and Hours: 110 NOK one-way, 170 NOK round-trip,
8/hour, daily 9:00-21:00, off-season until 17:00, tel. 53 64 36 43,
www.ulriken643.no.

Getting There: It's about three miles southeast of Bergen.
From the Fish Market, you can take a blue double-decker shuttle
bus that includes the cost of the cable-car ride (270 NOK, ticket
valid 24 hours, May-Sept daily 9:00-18:00, hourly, departs from
the corner of Torgallmenningen and Strandgaten, buy ticket as
you board or at TI). Alternatively, public buses #2 and #3 run
from Småstrandgaten in the city center and stop 200 yards from
the lift station.

BERGEN

▲▲Edvard Grieg's Home, Troldhaugen

Norway's greatest composer spent his last 22 summers here (1885-1907), soaking up inspirational fjord beauty and composing many

of his greatest works. Grieg fused simple Norwegian folk tunes with the bombast of Europe's Romantic style. In a dreamy Victorian setting, Grieg's "Hill of the Trolls" is pleasant for anyone and essential for diehard fans. You can visit his house on your own, but it's more enjoyable if you take the included 20-minute tour. The house and adjacent museum are full of memories and artifacts, including the composer's Steinway. The walls are festooned with photos of the musical and literary superstars of his generation. When the hugely popular Grieg died in 1907, 40,000 mourners attended his funeral. His little studio hut near the water makes you want to sit down and modulate.

Cost and Hours: 100 NOK, includes guided tour in English, daily 9:00-18:00, Oct-April 10:00-16:00, café, tel. 55 92 29 92, www.griegmuseum.no.

Grieg Lunch Concert: Troldhaugen offers a great guided tour/concert package that includes a shuttle bus from the Bergen TI to the doorstep of Grieg's home on the fjord (departs 11:00), an hour-long tour of the home, a half-hour concert (Grieg's greatest piano hits, at 13:00), and the ride back into town (you're back in the center by 14:25). Your guide will narrate the ride out of town as well as take you around Grieg's house (250 NOK, daily May-Sept). Lunch isn't included, but there is a café on site, or you could bring a sandwich along. You can skip the return bus ride and spend more time in Troldhaugen. While the tour rarely sells out, it's wise to drop by the TI earlier that day to reserve your spot.

Evening Concerts: Ask at the TI about piano performances in the concert hall at Grieg's home—a gorgeous venue with the fjord stretching out behind the big black grand piano (350 NOK, 300 NOK with Bergen Card, concerts roughly mid-June-Sept Sun at 18:00, free round-trip shuttle

bus leaves TI at 16:30, show your concert ticket).

Getting to Troldhaugen: It's six miles south of Bergen. The Bybanen tram drops you a long 20-minute walk away from Troldhaugen. Catch the tram in the city center at its terminus near Byparken (between the lake and Ole Bulls Plass), ride it for about 25 minutes, and get off at the stop called Hop. Walk in the direction of Bergen (about 25 yards), cross at the crosswalk, and follow signs to Troldhaugen. Part of the way is on a pedestrian/bike path; you're halfway there when the path crosses over a busy highway. If you want to make the 13:00 lunchtime concert, leave Bergen at 12:00.

To avoid the long walk from the tram stop, consider the Grieg Lunch Concert package (described earlier). If you're driving into Bergen from the east (such as from the Sognefjord), you'll drive right by Troldhaugen on your way into town.

Fantoft Stave Church

This huge, preserved-in-tar stave church burned down in 1992. It was rebuilt and reopened in 1997, but it will never be the same (for more on stave churches, see page 9). Situated in a quiet forest next to a mysterious stone cross, this replica of a 12th-century wooden church is bigger, though no better, than others covered in this book. But it's worth a look if you're in the neighborhood, even after-hours, for its atmospheric setting.

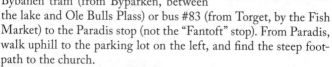

Cost and Hours: 60 NOK, mid-May-mid-Sept daily 10:30-18:00, interior closed off-season, no English information, tel. 55 28 07 10, www.fantoftstavkirke.com.

Getting There: It's three miles south of Bergen on E-39 in Paradis. Take the Bybanen tram (from Byparken, between the lake and Ole Bulls Plass) or bus #83 (from Torget, by the Fish Market) to the Paradis stop (not the "Fantoft" stop). From Paradis, walk uphill to the parking lot on the left, and find the steep foot-path to the church.

BERGEN NIGHTSPOTS

With the high latitude, Bergen stays light until 23:00 in the summer. On warm evenings, people are out enjoying the soft light and the mellow scene.

For a selection of cool nightspots, visit the **Pingvinen** and **Café Opera** (both described in "Eating in Bergen," later) and explore the neighboring streets.

For something a little funkier, **Skostredet** ("Shoe Street," recalling the days when cobblers set up shop here) is emerging as the hip, bohemian-chic area. You'll sort through cafés, pubs, and retro shops. There's an American-style Rock and Roll '59er Diner. And

Folk og Røvere ("People and Robbers") is an unpretentious bar with cheap beer (nightly until late, Skostredet 12).

For candlelit elegance, enjoy a drink at the historic **Dyvekes Wine Cellar.** Named for the mistress of King Christian II of Denmark (her portrait is on the signboard hanging above the door), the atmosphere of the ground-floor bar and the cellar downstairs is hard to beat (daily from 15:00, 80-90 NOK for wine by glass, beer on tap, Hollendergaten 7).

For live music, try **Madam Felle Nightclub** (on the Bryggen strip), which usually has musicians on the weekends (sometimes without a cover). And if you're really drunk at 3:00 in the morning and need a spicy hotdog, the **3-Kroneren** *pølse* stand is open.

Sleeping in Bergen

Busy with business travelers and popular with tourists, Bergen can be jammed any time of year. Even with this crush, proud and pricey hotels may be willing to make deals. You might save a bundle by checking the websites of the bigger hotels for their best prices. Otherwise, Bergen has some fine budget alternatives to normal hotels that can save you money.

HOTELS

$$$$ Hotel Havnekontoret, with 116 rooms and the best location in town, fills a grand old shipping headquarters dating from the 1920s. It's an especially fine value on weekends and in the summer, for those who eat the included dinner. While part of a chain, it has a friendly spirit. Guests are welcome to climb its historic tower (with a magnificent view) or enjoy its free sauna and exercise room downstairs. If you aren't interested in fancy dining, the room price includes virtually all your food—a fine breakfast, self-service waffles in the afternoon, fruit and coffee all day, and a light dinner buffet each evening. If you take advantage of them, these edible extras are easily worth 600 NOK per day per couple, making the cost of this fancy hotel little more than a hostel (facing the harbor across the street from the Radisson Blu Royal Hotel at Slottsgaten 1, tel. 55 60 11 00, www.choicehotels.no, cc.havnekontoret@choice.no).

$$$$ Hotel Park Bergen is classy, comfortable, and in a fine residential neighborhood a 15-minute uphill walk from the town center (10 minutes from the train station). It's tinseled in Old World, lived-in charm, yet comes with all of today's amenities. The 35 rooms are split between two buildings, with 22 in the classy old-fashioned hotel and 13 in the modern annex across the street. They also offer eight fully furnished apartments (Harald Hårfagres Gate 35, tel. 55 54 44 00, www.hotelpark.no, booking@hotelpark.no).

$$$$ Thon Hotel Rosenkrantz, with 129 rooms and an

BERGEN

Bergen Hotels & Restaurants

To Norwegian Fisheries Museum

SKOLTEN CRUISE TERMINAL

Ⓑ SKUTEVIKSTORGET

585

BERGENHUS FORTRESS

HÅKON'S HALL

SKOLTEGRUNNS-KAIEN

INTERNATIONAL FERRIES

NORDNES

Harbor

FESTNINGS-KAIEN

ROSEN-KRANTZ TOWER

TOTEM POLE

AQUARIUM

STRANDGATEN

C. SUNDTS GATE

HARBOR FERRIES

POOL

HAUGEVEIEN

SWIMMING BEACH

Nordnesparken

STRANDSIDEN

NORDNESVEIEN

NYKIRKEN

C. SUNDTS GATE

Puddefjorden

STRANDGATEN

HAUGEVEIEN

HOLBERGSALM

KLOSTERGATEN

SKOTTEGATEN

NØSTEGATEN

ENGEN

HURTIGRUTEN TERMINAL (COASTAL CRUISES)

NØSTEGATTEN

555

TORBORG NEDREAASGATE

JEKTEVIKEN/DOKKEN CRUISE PORT

Accommodations

1. Hotel Havnekontoret
2. Hotel Park Bergen
3. Thon Hotel Rosenkrantz
4. Thon Hotel Orion
5. P-Hotel
6. Best Western Plus Hotel Hordaheimen
7. Citybox
8. Guest House Skiven
9. Marken Gjestehus
10. Bergen YMCA Hostel & Pygmalion Restaurant
11. To Montana Family & Youth Hostel

Eateries & Other

12. Enhjørningen, Restaurant To Kokker, Baker Brun & Madam Felle Nightclub
13. Bryggeloftet & Stuene
14. Anne Madam Restaurant
15. Pingvinen
16. Café Opera
17. Dickens
18. To Fløien Folkerestaurant Cafeteria
19. Peppes Pizza
20. Deli de Luca (3)
21. Zupperia (2)
22. Fish Market
23. 3-Kroneren Hot-Dogs
24. Lido Restaurant
25. Söstrene Hagelin Fast Fish Joint
26. Krohnhagen Café
27. Rema 1000 Supermarket
28. Bunnpris
29. Folk og Røvere Bar
30. Dyvekes Wine Cellar
31. Laundry

BERGEN

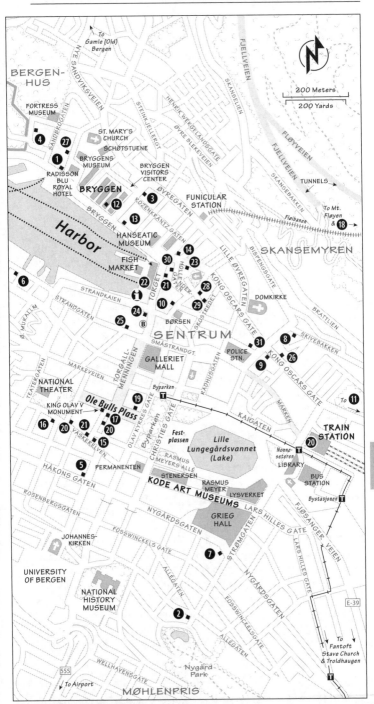

included light dinner, is one block behind Bryggen, between the Bryggens Museum and the Fløibanen funicular station—right in the heart of Bergen's appealing old quarter. Ask for a double even if you're traveling alone—they go for the same price as a single, and you'll get a bigger bed (elevator, Rosenkrantzgaten 7, tel. 55 30 14 00, www.thonhotels.comno/rosenkrantz, rosenkrantz@thonhotels.no).

$$$$ Thon Hotel Orion, beyond Bryggen near Håkon's Hall, has 219 rooms with a light dinner included. But be aware that many rooms face the fortress grounds, which sometimes host summer evening concerts. If you love music ask for a room on the concert side and enjoy the show; otherwise ask for a room on the quiet side and bring earplugs—or stay somewhere else (elevator, Bradbenken 3, tel. 55 30 87 00, www.thonhotels.com, orion@olafthon.no).

$$$ P-Hotel has 114 basic rooms just up from Ole Bulls Plass. While it's not particularly charming and some rooms come with noise from the street and a ground-floor disco, it's in a prime location. Ask for a room facing the courtyard in the renovated wing (credit card only, box breakfast in your room, elevator, Vestre Torggate 9, tel. 80 04 68 35, www.p-hotels.no, bergen@p-hotels.no).

$$$ Best Western Plus Hotel Hordaheimen is Bergen's oldest hotel, dating back to 1918. It has 88 well-priced rooms with hardwood floors and a welcoming decor. The charming breakfast room is decorated with vintage Kinsarvik wood furniture, giving it a traditional feel (elevator, tel. 55 33 50 00, www.hordaheimen.no, booking@hordaheimen.no).

$$ Citybox is a unique, no-nonsense hotel concept: plain, white, clean, and practical. It rents 122 rooms online or by phone, and provides you with a confirmation number. Check-in is automated—just punch in your number and get your ticket. The call-in reception is staffed 24 hours daily (family room, no breakfast, elevator, rooftop terrace, self-service laundry, just away from the bustle in a mostly residential part of town at Nygårdsgaten 31, tel. 55 31 25 00, www.citybox.no, post@citybox.no).

$ Guest House Skiven is a humble little place beautifully situated on a steep, traffic-free cobbled lane called "the most painted street in Bergen." Alf and Elizabeth Heskja (who live upstairs) rent four bright, nonsmoking doubles. Rooms have their own sinks, but share a shower, two WCs, and a kitchen (no breakfast, 4 blocks from train station, at Skivebakken 17, mobile 90 05 30 30, www.skiven.no, rs@skiven.no). From the train station, go down Kong Oscars Gate, uphill on D. Krohns Gate, and up the stairs at the end of the block on the left.

DORMS AND HOSTELS

¢-$$ Marken Gjestehus is a quiet, tidy, and conveniently positioned 100-bed place between the station and the harborfront. Its rooms, while spartan, are modern and cheery. Prices can rise with demand, especially in summer (private rooms available, breakfast extra, elevator, open all year but with limited reception hours, fourth floor at Kong Oscars Gate 45, tel. 55 31 44 04, http://marken.publish.visbook.com, post@marken-gjestehus.com).

¢-$$ Bergen YMCA Hostel, located two blocks from the Fish Market, is the best location for the price, and its rooms are nicely maintained (private rooms available, family room with private bathroom and kitchen, breakfast extra, roof terrace, fully open June-Aug, Nedre Korskirkeallmenningen 4, tel. 55 60 60 55, www.bergenhostel.com, booking@bergenhostel.com).

Away from the Center: ¢-$ Montana Family & Youth Hostel (IYHF), while one of Europe's best, is high-priced for a hostel and way out of town. Still, the bus connections (#12, 20 minutes from the center) and the facilities—modern rooms, classy living room, no curfew, huge free parking lot, and members' kitchen—are excellent (private rooms available, 30 Johan Blytts Vei, tel. 55 20 80 70, www.montana.no, bergen.montana@hihostels.no).

Eating in Bergen

Bergen has numerous choices: restaurants with rustic, woody atmosphere, candlelight, and steep prices; trendy pubs and cafés that offer good-value meals; cafeterias, chain restaurants, and ethnic eateries with less ambience where you can get quality food at lower prices; and takeaway sandwich shops, bakeries, and cafés for a light bite.

You can always get a glass or pitcher of water at no charge, and fancy places give you free seconds on potatoes—just ask. Remember, if you get your food to go, it's taxed at a lower rate and you'll save 12 percent.

SPLURGES AT BRYGGEN

You'll pay a premium to eat at these restaurants, but you'll have a memorable meal in a pleasant setting. If they appear to be beyond your budget, remember that you can fill up on potatoes and drink tap water to dine for exactly the price of the dinner plate.

$$$$ Enhjørningen Restaurant ("The Unicorn") is *the* place in Bergen for fish. With thickly painted walls and no right angles, this dressy-yet-old-time wooden interior wins my "Bryggen Atmosphere" award. The dishes, while not hearty, are close to gourmet and beautifully presented (main dishes, multicourse meals, nightly 16:00-23:00, reservations smart, #29 on Bryggen harborfront—look for anatomically correct unicorn on the old wharf facade and dip into the alley and up the stairs, tel. 55 30 69 50, www.enhjorningen.no).

$$$$ Restaurant To Kokker, down the alley from Enhjørningen (and with the same owners), serves more meat and game. The prices and quality are equivalent, but even though it's also in an elegant old wooden building, I like The Unicorn's atmosphere much better (main dishes, multicourse meals, Mon-Sat 18:00-23:00, closed Sun, tel. 55 30 69 55).

$$$ Bryggeloftet & Stuene Restaurant, in a brick building just before the wooden stretch of Bryggen, is a vast eatery serving seafood, vegetarian, and traditional meals. To dine memorably yet affordably, this is your best Bryggen bet. Upstairs feels more elegant and less touristy than the main floor—if there's a line downstairs, just head on up (lunches, dinners, Mon-Sat 11:00-23:30, Sun from 13:00, try reserving a view window upstairs—no reservations for outside seating, #11 on Bryggen harborfront, tel. 55 30 20 70).

NEAR THE FISH MARKET

$$ Pygmalion Restaurant has a happy salsa vibe, with local art on the walls and a fun, healthy international menu. It's run with creativity and passion by Sissel. Her burgers are a hit, and there are always good vegetarian options, hearty salads, and pancakes (wraps, burgers, main plates, Mon-Sat 11:00-22:00, Sun 12:00-23:00, two blocks inland from the Fish Market at Nedre Korskirkealmenning 4, tel. 55 31 32 60).

$$ Anne Madam Restaurant serves up well-priced Norwegian-inspired dishes in a laid-back atmosphere. It's close to the Fish Market and a good choice if you are up for some seafood, though they also serve traditional Norwegian meat dishes (sandwiches, burgers, main dishes, Sun-Thu 11:00-23:00, Fri-Sat until late, Kong Oscars Gate 2a, tel. 46 52 06 62).

CHARACTERISTIC PLACES NEAR OLE BULLS PLASS

Bergen's "in" cafés are stylish, cozy, small, and open very late. Around the cinema on Neumannsgate, there are numerous ethnic restaurants, including Italian, Middle Eastern, and Chinese.

$$$ Pingvinen ("The Penguin") is a homey place in a charming neighborhood, serving traditional Norwegian home cooking to an enthusiastic local clientele. The pub has only indoor seating, with a long row of stools at the bar and five charming, living-room-cozy tables—a great setup for solo diners. After the kitchen closes, the place stays open very late as a pub. For Norwegian fare in an untouristy atmosphere, this is a good, affordable option. Their seasonal menu (reindeer in the fall, whale in the spring) is listed on the board (nightly until 22:00, Vaskerelven 14 near the National Theater, tel. 55 60 46 46).

$$$ Café Opera, with a playful-slacker vibe and chessboards for the regulars, is the hip budget choice for its loyal, youthful following. With two floors of seating and tables out front across from the theater, it's a winner (light sandwiches until 16:00, daily 10:00-23:30, Engen 18, tel. 55 23 03 15).

$$$ Dickens is a lively, checkerboard-tiled, turn-of-the-century-feeling place. The window tables in the atrium are great for people-watching, as is the fine outdoor terrace, but you'll pay higher prices for the view (lunch and dinner, daily 11:00-23:00, Kong Olav V's Plass 4, tel. 55 36 31 30).

ATOP MOUNT FLØYEN,
AT THE TOP OF THE FUNICULAR

$$ Fløien Folkerestaurant Cafeteria offers meals indoors and out with a panoramic view. It's self-service, with 60-NOK sandwiches and a 139-NOK soup buffet (daily 10:00-22:00, Sept-April Sat-Sun only 12:00-17:00, tel. 55 33 69 99).

GOOD CHAIN RESTAURANTS

You'll find these chain restaurant in Bergen and throughout Norway. All are open long hours daily. In good weather, enjoy a takeout meal with sun-worshipping locals in Bergen's parks.

$$$ Peppes Pizza on Ole Bulls Plass has cold beer and good pizzas—consider the Thai Chicken, with satay-marinated chicken, pineapple, peanuts, and coriander (Mon-Wed 11:00-23:00, Thu-Sat until 24:00, Sun 12:00-23:00, seating inside or takeaway, Olav Kyrres Gate 11, tel. 22 22 55 55).

$ Baker Brun makes 75-100-NOK sandwiches, including wonderful shrimp baguettes, and pastries such as *skillingsboller*—cinnamon rolls—warm out of the oven for 29 NOK. Their shop at Bryggen is a prime spot for a simple, inexpensive bite (open from 7:00, a little later Sat-Sun, seating inside or takeaway).

$ Deli de Luca is a cut above other takeaway joints, adding sushi, noodle dishes, and calzones to the normal lineup of sandwiches. While a bit more expensive than the others, the variety and quality are appealing (open daily 24 hours, branches in train station and near Ole Bulls Plass at Torggaten 5, branch with indoor seating on corner of Engen and Vaskerelven, tel. 55 23 11 47).

$$$ Zupperia is a lively, popular chain that offers burgers, salads, Norwegian fare, and Asian dishes; their Thai soup is a local favorite. For a lighter (and cheaper) meal, order off the lunch menu any time of day (Sun-Wed 12:00-22:00, Thu-Sat until 23:30). Branches are across from the Fish Market at Torget 13 and near the National Theater at Vaskerelven 12.

BUDGET BETS NEAR THE FISH MARKET

The Fish Market has lots of stalls bursting with salmon sandwiches, fresh shrimp, fish-and-chips, and fish cakes. For a tasty, memorable, and inexpensive Bergen meal, assemble a seafood picnic here (ask for prices first; May-Oct daily 8:00-23:00, vendors may close early if they're not busy; Nov-Dec Mon-Sat 9:00-21:00, Sun from 11:00; Jan-April Sat only 9:00-15:00). Also be sure to peruse the places next door on the ground floor of the TI building, Torghallen.

$ 3-Kroneren, your classic hot-dog stand, sells a wide variety of sausages (including reindeer). The well-described English menu makes it easy to order your choice of artery-clogging guilty pleasures (tiny, medium, and jumbo weenies; open daily from 11:00 until 5:00 in the morning—you'll see the little hot-dog shack a block up Kong Oscars Gate from the harbor, Kenneth is the boss). Each dog comes with a free little glass of fruit punch.

$$$ Lido Restaurant offers a varied menu with great harbor and market views and a museum's worth of old-town photos on the walls. Lunch, served until 17:00, includes open-face sandwiches and small plates (Mon-Sat 11:00-22:00, Sun until 23:00; second floor at Torgallmenningen 1a, tel. 55 32 59 12).

$ Söstrene Hagelin Fast Fish Joint is an easygoing eatery that's cheerier than its offerings—a pale extravaganza of Norway's white cuisine. It's all fish here: fish soup, fish burgers, fish balls, fish cakes, fish wraps, and even fish pudding (Mon-Fri 9:00-19:00, Sat 10:00-17:00, closed Sun, Strandgaten 3, tel. 55 90 20 13).

$ Krohnhagen Café, a humble community center next to a retirement home, is run by the church and partly staffed by volunteers. While it's designed to give Bergen's poor (and the retired) an inviting place to enjoy, everyone's welcome (it's a favorite of local guides). The dining area is bright and spacious, the staff friendly, and the menu is simple yet tasty (salad and dinner buffets, soup, waffles, cheap sandwiches, Mon-Fri 11:00-16:00, closed Sat-Sun, Wi-Fi, Kong Oscars Gate 54, tel. 45 22 07 95).

PICNICS AND GROCERIES

While you'll be tempted to drop into 7-Eleven-type stores, you'll pay for the convenience. Pick up your groceries for half the price at a real supermarket. The **Rema 1000 supermarket,** just across from the Bryggens Museum and St. Mary's Church, is particularly handy (Mon-Fri 7:00-23:00, Sat 8:00-21:00, closed Sun). For groceries on a Sunday, check out **Bunnpris**—just a short walk inland from the Fish Market, across the street from Korskirken church (Mon-Fri 8:00-22:00, Sat from 9:00, Sun from 10:00, Nedre Korskirkeallmenningen 3a).

Bergen Connections

Bergen is conveniently connected to **Oslo** by plane and train (trains depart Bergen daily at 7:57, 11:59, 15:50, and 22:59—but no night train on Sat, arrive at Oslo seven scenic hours later, additional departures in summer and fall, confirm times at station, 50-NOK seat reservation with second-class rail pass required—but free with first-class rail pass, book well in advance if traveling mid-July-Aug and look for cheaper "minipris" tickets at www.nsb.no). From Bergen, you can take the Norway in a Nutshell train/bus/ferry route; for information, see the Norway in a Nutshell chapter. Train info: Tel. 61 05 19 10, and then 9 for English.

To get to **Stockholm** or **Copenhagen,** you'll go via Oslo (see "Oslo Connections" on page 96). Before buying a ticket for a long train trip from Bergen, look into cheap flights.

By Express Boat to Balestrand and Flåm (on Sognefjord): A handy express boat links Bergen with Balestrand (4 hours) and Flåm (5.5 hours). For details, see page 140.

By Bus to Kristiansand: If you're heading to Denmark on the ferry from Kristiansand, catch the Nor-Way express bus (departing Bergen daily at 9:00, www.nor-way.no). After a one-hour layover in Stavanger, take the bus at 14:45, arriving at 18:35 in Kristiansand in time for the evening ferry to Denmark (for boat details, see page 223).

By Boat to Denmark: Fjordline runs a boat from Bergen to Hirtshals, Denmark (18 hours; departs daily at 13:30; boat from Hirtshals departs daily at 20:00; seat in reclining chair around 1,750 NOK, tel. 81 53 35 00, www.fjordline.com).

By Boat to the Arctic: Hurtigruten coastal cruises depart nearly daily (June-Oct at 20:00, Nov-May at 22:30) for the seven-day trip north up the scenic west coast to Kirkenes on the Russian border.

This route was started in 1893 as a postal and cargo delivery service along the west coast of Norway. Although no longer delivering mail, their ships still fly the Norwegian postal flag by special permission and deliver people, cars, and cargo from Bergen to Kirkenes. A lifeline for remote areas, the ships call at 34 fishing villages and cities.

For the seven-day trip to Kirkenes, allow from $1,600 and up per person based on double occupancy (includes three meals per day, taxes, and port charges). Prices vary greatly depending on the season (highest June-July), cabin, and type of ship. Their fleet includes those with a bit of brass built in the 1960s, but most of the ships in service were built in the mid-1990s and later. Shorter voyages are possible (including even just a day trip to one of the villages along the route). Cabins should be booked well in advance. Ship services include a 24-hour cafeteria, a launderette on newer boats, and optional port excursions. Check online for senior and off-season (Oct-March) specials at www.hurtigruten.us.

Call Hurtigruten in New York (US tel. 866-552-0371) or in Norway (tel. 81 00 30 30). For most travelers, the ride makes a great one-way trip, but a flight back south is a logical last leg (rather than returning to Bergen by boat—a 12-day round-trip).

Route Tips for Drivers: For tips on connecting Bergen to Denmark via the Setesdal Valley and the Kristiansand ferry, see the South Norway chapter.

SOUTH NORWAY

Stavanger • Setesdal Valley • Kristiansand

South Norway is not about must-see sights or jaw-dropping scenery—it's simply pleasant and pretty. Spend a day in the harborside town of Stavanger. Delve into the oil industry at the surprisingly interesting Norwegian Petroleum Museum. Peruse the Stavanger Cathedral, window-shop in the old town, cruise the harbor, or hoof it up Pulpit Rock for a fine view. A series of time-forgotten towns stretch across the Setesdal Valley, with sod-roofed cottages and locals who practice fiddles and harmonicas, rose painting, whittling, and gold- and silver-work.

PLANNING YOUR TIME

The main draw in this part of Norway is the famous Pulpit Rock hike; poking around Stavanger, a pleasant port city and the springboard for reaching Pulpit Rock, helps round out your time here. The hike takes the better part of a day, requiring at least one overnight. Several cruises also call at Stavanger.

The Setesdal Valley—covered at the end of this chapter—is for people with ample time, a car, and a desire to explore a scenic corner of Norway. Since it's not "on the way" to much of anything (except dreary Kristiansand and the ferry to Denmark), it only makes the cut for Norway completists.

Stavanger

This burg of about 125,000 is a mildly charming (if unspectacular) waterfront city with streets that are lined with unpretentious shiplap cottages that echo its perennial ties to the sea. Stavanger feels more cosmopolitan than most small Norwegian cities, thanks in part to its oil industry—which brings multinational workers (and their money) into the city. Known as Norway's festival city, Stavanger hosts several lively events, including jazz in May (www.maijazz. no), Scandinavia's biggest food festival in July (www.gladmat.no), and chamber music in August (www.icmf.no).

From a sightseeing perspective, Stavanger barely has enough to fill a day: The Norwegian Petroleum Museum is the only bigtime sight in town, Gamle Stavanger (the "old town") offers pleasant wandering on cobbled lanes, and the city's fine cathedral is worth a peek. For most visitors, the main reason to come to Stavanger is to use it as a launch pad for side-tripping to the famous, iconic Pulpit Rock: an eerily flat-topped rock thrust-ing 2,000 feet above the fjord, offering an eagle's-eye view deep into the Lysefjord.

Orientation to Stavanger

Stavanger is most interesting around its harbor, where you'll find the Maritime Museum, lots of shops and restaurants (particularly around the market plaza and along Kirkegata, which connects the cathedral to the Petroleum Museum), the indoor fish market, and a produce market (closed Sun). The artificial Lake Breiavatnet—bordered by Kongsgaten on the east and Olav V's Gate on the west—separates the train and bus stations from the harbor.

TOURIST INFORMATION

The centrally located TI can help with day trips, including logistics for reaching Pulpit Rock and other scenic hikes (June-Aug daily 8:00-18:00; Sept-May Mon-Fri 9:00-16:00, Sat until 14:00, closed Sun; free Wi-Fi, Strandkaien 61, tel. 51 85 92 00, www. regionstavanger.com).

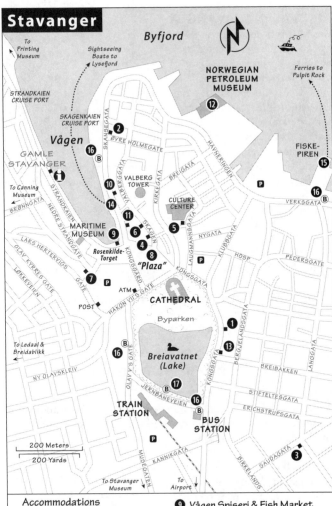

Stavanger

Byfjord

To Printing Museum

Sightseeing Boats to Lysefjord

STRANDKAIEN CRUISE PORT

SKAGENKAIEN CRUISE PORT

Vågen

GAMLE STAVANGER

To Canning Museum

BRØNNGATA

ØVRE HOLMEGATE

SKANSEGATA

VALBERG TOWER

KIRKEGATA

BREIGATA

HAVNERINGEN

NORWEGIAN PETROLEUM MUSEUM

Ferries to Pulpit Rock

FISKE-PIREN

VERKSGATA

MARITIME MUSEUM

STRANDKAIEN

NEDRE STRANDGATE

LARS HERTERVIGS GATE

OLAV KYRRES GATE

LØKKEVEIEN

VALBERGGATA

SKAGEN

Rosenkilde-Torget

KONGSGARD

"Plaza"

CULTURE CENTER

NYGATA

LAUGMANNSGATA

KLUBBGATA

HOSP

PEDERSGATE

ATM

HÅKON VII'S GATE

POST

KONGSGATA

CATHEDRAL

Byparken

BERGJELANDSGATA

LANGGATA

To Ledaal & Breidablikk

NY OLAVSKLEIV

OLAV V'S GATE

Breiavatnet (Lake)

KONGSGATA

BREIBAKKEN

STIFTELTESGATA

JERNBANEVEIEN

ERICHSTRUPSGATA

TRAIN STATION

BUS STATION

200 Meters

200 Yards

MUSÉGATEN

KANNIKGATA

BIRKELANDS

GAUDAGATA

To Stavanger Museum

To Airport

Accommodations
1. Thon Hotel Maritim
2. Hotel Victoria
3. Stavanger B&B

Eateries & Other
4. XO Mat & Vinhus
5. Renaa Xpress
6. Skagen Bageri
7. Supermarket
8. Market Plaza Eateries
9. Vågen Spiseri & Fish Market
10. N. B. Sørensen's Dampskibsexpedition
11. Sjøhuset Skagen
12. Bølgen og Moi
13. Launderette
14. Sightseeing Boats to Lysefjord
15. Ferry to Pulpit Rock
16. Flybussen Stops (4)
17. Bus to Fjordline Terminal (Ferries to Hirtshals, Denmark)

ARRIVAL IN STAVANGER

Cruise liners dock right at the Vågen harbor in the very center of town. Some tie up on the west side of the harbor (called Strandkaien) next to the TI, and others put in along the east side (called Skagenkaien)—but both are an easy walk to the central market plaza. Stavanger's **train and bus stations** are a five-minute walk

around Lake Breiavatnet to the inner harbor and cathedral.

Stavanger's **Sola Airport** is about nine miles outside the city (airport code: SVG, tel. 67 03 10 00, www.avinor.no). The airport bus, called Flybussen, connects to the train and bus stations, city center, and ferry terminal (see www.flybussen.no).

HELPFUL HINTS

Money: ATMs are on buildings facing the harbor, opposite the cathedral.

Laundry: Renseriet offers expensive drop-off service and afford-able self-service (Mon-Fri 8:30-16:30, Thu until 19:00, Sat 9:00-15:00, closed Sun, Kongsgata 40, tel. 51 89 56 53, www. renseriet.as).

Sights in Stavanger

▲Stavanger Cathedral (Domkirke)

While it's hardly the most impressive cathedral in Scandinavia, Stavanger's top church—which overlooks the town center on a small ridge—has a harmonious interior and a few intriguing de-tails worth lingering over. Good English information throughout the church brings meaning to the place.

Cost and Hours: 30 NOK, open daily 11:00-16:00, tel. 51 84 04 00, www.stavangerdomkirke.no.

Visiting the Church: St. Swithun's Cathedral (its official name) was originally built in 1125 in a Norman style, with basket-handle Romanesque arches. After a fire badly damaged the church in the 13th century, a new chancel was added in the pointy-arched Gothic style. You can't miss where the archi-tecture changes about three-quarters of the way up the aisle. On the left, behind the baptismal font, notice the ivy-lined railing on the stone stair-case; this pattern is part of the city's coat of arms. And nearby, ap-

preciate the colorful, richly detailed "gristle Baroque"-style pulpit (from 1658). Notice that the whole thing is resting on Samson's stoic shoulders—even as he faces down a lion.

Stroll the church, perusing its several fine "epitaphs" (tomb markers), which are paintings in ornately decorated frames. Go on a scavenger hunt for two unique features; both are on the second columns from the back of the church. On the right, at the top facing away from the nave, notice the stone carvings of Norse mythological figures: Odin on the left, and a wolf-like beast on the right. Although the medieval Norwegians were Christians, they weren't ready to entirely abandon all of their pagan traditions. On the opposite column, circle around the base and look at ankle level, facing away from the altar. Here you see a grotesque sculpture that looks like a fish head with human hands. Notice that its head has been worn down. One interpretation is that early worshippers would ritualistically put their foot on top of it, as if to push the evil back to the underworld. Mysteriously, both of these features are one-offs—you won't find anything like them on any other column in the church.

▲▲Norwegian Petroleum Museum (Norsk Oljemuseum)

This entertaining, informative museum—dedicated to the discovery of oil in Norway's North Sea in 1969 and the industry built up around it—offers an unapologetic look at the country's biggest moneymaker. With half of Western Europe's oil reserves, the formerly poor agricultural nation of Norway is the Arabia of the North, and a world-class player. It's ranked third among the world's top oil exporters, producing 1.6 million barrels a day.

Cost and Hours: 120 NOK; daily 10:00-19:00; Sept-May Mon-Sat 10:00- 16:00, Sun until 18:00; tel. 51 93 93 00, www. norskolje.museum.no. The small museum shop sells various petroleum-based products. The museum's Bølgen og Moi restaurant, which has an inviting terrace over the water, serves lunch and dinner; see "Eating in Stavanger," later.

Visiting the Museum: The exhibit describes how oil was formed, how it's found and produced, and what it's used for. You'll see models of oil rigs, actual drill bits, see-through cylinders that you can rotate to investigate different types of crude, and lots of explanations (in English) about various aspects of oil. Interactive exhibits cover everything from the "History of the Earth" (4.5 billion years displayed on a large overhead globe, showing how our planet has changed—stay for the blast that killed the dinosaurs), to day-to-day life on an offshore platform, to petroleum products in our lives (though the peanut-butter-and-petroleum-jelly sandwich is a bit much). Kids enjoy climbing on the model drilling platform, trying out the emergency escape chute at the platform outside, and playing with many other hands-on exhibits.

Several included movies delve into specific aspects of oil: The main movie, *Oljeunge (Oil Kid)*, stars a fictional character who was born in 1969—the year Norway discovered oil—and shows how that discovery changed Norwegian society over the last 50 years. Other movies (in the cylindrical structures outside) highlight intrepid North Sea divers and the construction of an oil platform. Each film runs in English at least twice hourly.

Even the museum's architecture was designed to echo the foundations of the oil industry—bedrock (the stone building), slate and chalk deposits in the sea (slate floor of the main hall), and the rigs (cylindrical platforms). While the museum has its fair share of propaganda, it also has several good exhibits on the environmental toll of drilling and consuming oil.

Gamle Stavanger

Stavanger's "old town" centers on Øvre Strandgate, on the west side of the harbor. Wander the narrow, winding, cobbled back lanes, with tidy wooden houses, oasis gardens, and flower-bedecked entranceways. Peek into a workshop or gallery to find ceramics, glass, jewelry, and more. Many shops are open roughly daily 10:00-17:00, coinciding with the arrival of cruise ships (which loom ominously right next to this otherwise tranquil zone).

Museum Stavanger (M.U.S.T.)

This "museum" is actually 10 different museums scattered around town (covered by individual tickets or a single combo-ticket, most closed Mon off-season, for details see www.museumstavanger.no). The various branches include the **Stavanger Museum,** featuring the history of the city and a zoological exhibit (Muségate 16); the **Maritime Museum** (Sjøfartsmuseum), near the bottom end of Vågen harbor (Nedre Strandgate 17-19); the **Norwegian Canning Museum** (Norsk Hermetikkmuseum—the *brisling,* or herring, is smoked the first Sunday of every month—Øvre Strandgate 88A); **Ledaal,** a royal residence and manor house (Eiganesveien 45); and **Breidablikk,** a wooden villa from the late 1800s (Eiganesveien 40A).

DAY TRIPS TO LYSEFJORD AND PULPIT ROCK

The nearby Lysefjord is an easy day trip. Those with more time (and strong legs) can hike to the top of 2,000-foot-high Pulpit Rock (Preikestolen). Its dramatic 270-square-foot natural platform gives you a fantastic view of the fjord and surrounding mountains. The TI has brochures for several boat tour companies and sells tickets.

Boat Tour of Lysefjord

Rødne Clipper Fjord Sightseeing offers three-hour round-trip excursions from Stavanger to Lysefjord (including a view of Pulpit Rock—but no stops). Conveniently, their boats depart from the main Vågen harbor in the heart of town (east side of the harbor, in front of Skansegata, along Skagenkaien; 490 NOK; May-Sept daily at 10:00 and 14:00, also at 12:00 July-Aug; April and Oct daily at 11:00; Jan-Feb and Nov-Dec Wed-Sun at 11:00; tel. 51 89 52 70, www.rodne.no). A different company, **Norled**, also runs similar trips, as well as slower journeys up the Lysefjord on a "tourist car ferry" (www.norled.no).

Ferry and Bus to Pulpit Rock (Preikestolen)

Hiking up to the top of Pulpit Rock is a popular outing that will take the better part of a day; plan on at least four hours of hiking (two hours up, two hours down), plus time to linger at the top for photos, plus round-trip travel from Stavanger (about an hour each way by a ferry-and-bus combination)—eight hours minimum should do it. The trailhead is easily reached in summer by public transit or tour package.

Two different companies sell ferry-and-bus packages to the trailhead from Stavanger. Ferries leave from the Fiskepiren boat terminal to Tau; buses (labeled *Preikestolen*) meet the incoming ferries and head to the Preikestolen Fjellstue lodge and Preikestolhytta hostel, both near the trailhead. Be sure to time your hike so that you don't miss the last bus leaving the trailhead for the ferry (confirm time when booking your ticket). These trips generally go daily from mid-May through mid-September; weekends-only in April, early May, and late September; and not at all from October to March (when the ferry stops running). Confirm schedules with the TI or the individual companies: **Tide Reiser** (320 NOK, best options for an all-day round-trip are weekdays at 8:40 or 9:20 or Sat-Sun at 9:00, return bus from trailhead corresponds with ferry to Stavanger, tel. 55 23 88 87, www.tidereiser.com) and **Boreal** (190 NOK for the bus plus 112 NOK for the ferry round-trip—you'll buy the ferry ticket separately, best options depart at 8:40 or 9:20, last bus from trailhead to ferry leaves at 21:15, tel. 51 74 02 40, www.pulpitrock.no).

Rødne Clipper Fjord Sightseeing (listed earlier) runs a handy trip that begins with a scenic Lysefjord cruise (2.5 hours), then drops you off at Oanes to catch the bus to the Pulpit Rock hut trailhead; from there you can do the four-hour round-trip trek to Pulpit Rock and back; afterwards, you catch the bus to Tau for the ferry return to Stavanger. It's similar to the options described above, but adds a scenic fjord cruise at the start (780 NOK plus 56 NOK for return ferry to Stavanger, May-Sept daily at 10:00, also July-Aug at 12:00, tel. 51 89 52 70, www.rodne.no).

Hiking to Pulpit Rock

At just over 4.5 miles round-trip, with an elevation gain of about 1,100 feet, this hike takes four hours total—longer if the trail is very crowded. The hike is fairly stren-uous and includes scrambling over sometimes tricky, rocky ter-rain. Bring food and plenty of water, pack extra clothes as the weather is changeable, and wear sturdy hiking shoes or boots. Start early or you'll be sharing the trail with dogs on long leash-es, toddlers navigating boulders,  and the unprepared Bermuda-shorts crowd in flip-flops.

The trail starts by the big sign at the entrance to the main parking lot. From there the path climbs steadily through forest at first and eventually into open, rocky terrain. Along the way, you can thank Nepalese Sherpas—who were hired to improve sections of the route—for their fine stonework on the trail.

The farther and higher you go, the more rocky and spectacular the scenery becomes. Whenever the trail disappears onto bare rock, look for the red T's painted on stones or posts marking the route. As you near Pulpit Rock, the path tiptoes along the cliff's edge with airy views out to the Lysefjord that can only be topped by those from the rock itself.

Before you head back, scramble up the mountainside behind the rock for that iconic, tourist-brochure scene of the people-speckled Pulpit Rock soaring out over the fjord 2,000 feet below.

Sleeping at the Pulpit Rock Trailhead

The Pulpit Rock trail is usually very crowded during the middle of the day, even in bad weather. I prefer to spend the night at the trailhead, and get an early start on the trail the next morning. If you don't have a car, you can still get here from Stavanger by using one of the ferry-and-bus options listed above.

$$$$ Preikestolen Fjellstue is a modern building with 27 bright, simple, functional rooms and a **$$$** restaurant with a lovely lake view (includes breakfast, free parking). Below the Fjellstue and closer to the lake, the rustic, grass-roofed **$ Preikestolhytta** hostel has rooms that sleep 2-4 and bathrooms down the hall (includes breakfast). Both are run by the Norwegian Trekking Association (tel. 51 74 20 74, www.preikestolenfjellstue.no—use Norwegian site to book rooms, post@preikestolenfjellstue.no).

Guided Hike to Pulpit Rock

Outdoorlife Norway offers guided tours for individuals or small groups. They'll pick you up at your hotel and even provide hiking poles. Check out their "Preikestolen Off the Beaten Track Hike" (1,290 NOK, April-Sept) or "Preikestolen Sunrise Hike" (1,290 NOK, April-Oct, mobile 97 65 87 04, www.outdoorlifenorway. com, booking@outdoorlifenorway.com).

Sleeping in Stavanger

$$$ Thon Hotel Maritim, with 140 rooms, is two blocks from the train station near the artificial Lake Breiavatnet. It can be a good deal for a big business-class hotel (elevator, Kongsgaten 32, tel. 51 85 05 00, www.thonhotels.no/maritim, maritim@olavthon.no).

$$$ Hotel Victoria has 107 business-class rooms over a stately, high-ceilinged lobby facing the Skagenkaien embankment right on the harbor (elevator, Skansegata 1, tel. 51 86 70 00, www. victoria-hotel.no, victoria@victoria-hotel.no).

$ Stavanger B&B is Stavanger's best budget option. This large red house among a sea of white houses has tidy, tiny rooms. The lodgings are basic, verging on institutional—not cozy or doily—but they're affordable and friendly. The shared toilet is down the hall; 14 rooms have their own showers, while eight share showers down the hall. Waffles, coffee, and friendly chatter are served up every evening at 21:00 (10-minute uphill walk behind train station in residential neighborhood, Vikedalsgate 1A, tel. 51 56 25 00, www.stavangerbedandbreakfast.no, post@sbb.no). If you let them know in advance, they may be able to pick you up or drop you off at the boat dock or train station.

Eating in Stavanger

CASUAL DINING

$$$ XO Mat & Vinhus, in an elegant setting, serves up big portions of traditional Norwegian food and pricier contemporary fare (Mon-Wed 14:30-23:30, Thu 11:00-23:00, Fri-Sat 11:30 until late, closed Sun, a block behind main drag along harbor at Skagen 10 ved Prostebakken, mobile 91 00 03 07).

$$ Renaa Xpress, popular with the locals, is inside Stavanger's library and cultural center. It's a cozy café where bakers make their own bread and pastries. In addition to a variety of sandwiches, salads, and soups, they also offer sourdough pizza after 13:00

(Mon-Thu 10:00-22:00, Fri-Sat until 24:00, Sun 12:00-22:00, Sølvberggata 2, mobile 94 00 93 48).

$ Skagen Bageri, in a lovely, leaning wooden building dating to the 1700s, serves baked goods and traditional open-face sandwiches at reasonable prices in a cozy, rustic-elegant setting (Mon-Fri 8:00-15:00, Sat until 16:00, closed Sun; in the blue-and-white building a block off the harborfront at Skagen 18; tel. 51 89 51 71).

Meny is a large supermarket with a good selection and a fine deli for super picnic shopping (Mon-Fri 7:00-20:00, Sat 9:00-18:00, closed Sun, in Straen Senteret shopping mall, Lars Hertervigs Gate 6, tel. 51 50 50 10).

Market Plaza Eateries: The busy square between the cathedral and the harbor is packed with reliable Norwegian chain restaurants. If you're a fan of **Deli de Luca, Dolly Dimple's,** or **Dickens Pub,** you'll find them within a few steps of here.

DINING ALONG THE HARBOR WITH A VIEW

The harborside street of Skansegata is lined with lively restaurants and pubs, and most serve food. Here are a few options:

$$$$ Vågen Spiseri, in the same building as the fish market, serves tasty seafood dishes based on the catch of the day (affordable lunch specials, Mon-Wed 11:00-21:00, Thu-Sat until 24:00, closed Sun, Strandkaien 37, tel. 51 52 73 50, www.fisketorget-stavanger.no).

$$$$ N. B. Sørensen's Dampskibsexpedition consists of a lively pub on the first floor (pasta, fish, meat, and vegetarian dishes; Mon-Wed 16:00-24:00, Sat 11:00-late, Sun 13:00-23:00) and a fine-dining restaurant on the second floor, with tablecloths, view tables overlooking the harbor, and a pricey menu (Mon-Sat 18:00-23:00, closed Sun, Skagenkaien 26, tel. 51 84 38 20, www. herlige-stavanger.no). The restaurant is named after an 1800s company that shipped from this building, among other things, Norwegians heading to the US. Passengers and cargo waited on the first floor, and the manager's office was upstairs. The place is filled with emigrant-era memorabilia.

$$$$ Sjøhuset Skagen, with a woodsy interior, invites diners to its historic building for lunch or dinner. The building, from the late 1700s, once housed a trading company. Today, you can choose from local seafood specialties with an ethnic flair, as well as plenty of meat options (Mon-Sat 11:30-24:00, Sun from 13:00, Skagenkaien 16, tel. 51 89 51 80, https://skagenrestaurant.no/en).

$$$$ Bølgen og Moi, the restaurant at the Petroleum Museum, has fantastic views over the harbor (good lunch specials, lunch daily 11:00-16:00; dinner Tue-Sat 18:00-20:00—reservations recommended; Kjeringholmen 748, tel. 51 93 93 53, www. bolgenogmoi.no).

Stavanger Connections

From Stavanger by Train to: Kristiansand (6/day, 3 hours), **Oslo** (5/day, 8 hours, overnight possible).

By Bus to Bergen: Kystbussen operates buses between Stavanger and Bergen (hourly, 5.5 hours, tel. 52 70 35 26, http://kystbussen.no).

By Boat to Denmark: Fjordline ferries sail overnight from Stavanger to Hirtshals, Denmark (11 hours, www.fjordline.com).

The Setesdal Valley

Welcome to the remote, and therefore very traditional, Setesdal Valley. Probably Norway's most authentic cranny, the valley is a mellow montage of sod-roofed water mills, ancient churches, derelict farmhouses, yellowed recipes, and gentle scenery. The Setesdal Valley isn't "on the way" to anything (except the ferry crossing from Kristiansand to Hirtshals, in Denmark). But that's sort of the point. Come here only if you have ample time, and really want to commune with time-passed, rural Norway.

The famous Setesdal filigree echoes the rhythmical designs of the Viking era and Middle Ages. Each town has a weekly rotating series of hikes and activities for the regular, stay-put-for-a-week visitor. The upper valley is dead in the summer but enjoys a bustling winter.

The Setesdal Valley joined the modern age with the construction of the valley highway in the 1950s. All along the valley you'll see the unique two-story storage sheds called *stabburs* (the top floor was used for storing clothes; the bottom, food) and many sod roofs. Even the bus stops have rooftops the local goats love to munch.

In the high country, just over the Sessvatn summit (3,000 feet), you'll see herds of goats and summer farms. If you see an *ekte geitost* sign, that means genuine, homemade goat cheese is for sale. (It's sold cheaper and in more manageable sizes in grocery stores.) To some, it looks like a decade's accumulation of earwax. I think it's delicious. Remember, *ekte* means all-goat—really strong. The more popular and easier-to-eat version is a mix of cow and goat cheese.

Without a car, the Setesdal Valley is not worth the trouble. There are no trains in the valley, bus schedules are as sparse as the

SOUTH NORWAY

population, and the sights are best for joyriding. But if you're in Bergen with a car, and want to get to Denmark, this route is more interesting than repeating Oslo.

For more information on the Setesdal Valley, see www. setesdal.com.

Sights in the Setesdal Valley

I've described these roadside sights from north to south, most logically connected on a 10-hour drive from Bergen to Kristiansand.

From Bergen, drive about two hours to catch the 9:00 Kvanndal-Utne ferry to give yourself plenty of time (www.norled. no). To reach **Kvanndal,** take Route E-16 toward Voss and Oslo (signs for *Nestune, Landås, Nattland*); then, after a long tunnel, leave the Voss road and take Route 7 heading for Norheimsund, and then Kvanndal. This road, treacherous for the famed beauty of the Hardanger Fjord it hugs as well as for its skinniness, is faster and safer if you beat the traffic.

The Kvanndal ferry drops you in **Utne,** where a lovely road takes you south along the Hardanger Fjord. At the fjord's end, just past the huge zinc-and-copper industrial plant, you'll hit the industrial town of **Odda** (TI on market square at Torget 2-4, tel. 53 65 40 05, www.visitodda.com). Odda brags that Kaiser Wilhelm came here a lot, but he's dead and I'd drive right through. If you want to visit the tongue of a glacier, drive to Buer and hike an hour to Buerbreen.

From Odda, drive into the land of boulders. The many mighty waterfalls that line the road seem to have hurled huge rocks (with rooted trees) into the rivers and fields. Stop at the giant **double waterfall** called Låtefossen (on the left, pullout on the right, drive slowly through it if you need a car wash).

Continue over Røldalsfjellet and follow E-134 into the valley below, where the old town of **Røldal** is trying to develop some tourism (drive on by—its old church isn't worth the stop). Lakes are like frosted mirrors, making desolate huts come in pairs. Farther along on the Hardangervidda plateau is **Haukeliseter**—a group of sod-roofed buildings filled with cultural clichés and tour groups, offering light food in a lakeside setting.

At the Haukeli transportation junction, turn south on Route 9 and wind up to **Sessvatn** at 3,000 feet (toward Hovden). Enter the upper Setesdal Valley. From here, you'll follow the Otra River downhill for 140 miles south to the major port town of Kristiansand. Skip the secondary routes.

A ski resort at the top of the Setesdal Valley (2,500 feet), **Hovden** is barren in the summer and painfully in need of charm. Still, it makes a good home base if you want to explore the area (TI tel. 37 93 93 70, www.hovden.com). Hovden has boat rental (at Hegni Center, south edge of town, tel. 37 93 93 70); a swimming pool (Hovden Badeland, tel. 37 93 93 93, www.badeland.com); the free Museum of Iron Production (Jernvinnemuseum—learn about iron production from the late Iron Age with the aid of drawings, exhibits, and recorded narration in English from a "Viking," about 100 yards behind the Hegni Center); and plenty of choices for hikes and mountain biking. Good walks offer you a chance to see reindeer, moose, arctic fox, and wabbits—so they say. Berry picking is popular in late August, when small, sweet blueberries are in season. A sporadically running chairlift sometimes takes sightseers to the top of a nearby peak, with great views in clear weather; bikers can ride the trails downhill. Hunting season starts in late August for reindeer (only in higher elevations) and later in the fall for grouse and moose *(elg)*. In fact, the TI offers a 2.5-hour "moose safari"— a late-night drive through Setesdal's back roads with a stop for moose-meat soup.

For an affordable place to sleep or eat in Hovden, consider the big, old ski chalet called ¢ **Hovden Fjellstoge.** Check out the mural in the balcony overlooking the lobby—an artistic rendition of this area's history. Behind the mural is a frightening taxidermy collection (tel. 37 93 95 43, www.hovdenfjellstoge.no).

Leaving Hovden, you enter the most scenic stretch of the drive. Nine miles south of Hovden is a two-mile side-trip to a 400-foot-high rock-pile dam, called **Dammar Vatnedalsvatn,** with great view and an impressive rockery. Sit out of the wind a few rows down the rock pile and ponder the vastness of Norwegian wood.

Farther south, the most interesting folk museum and church in Setesdal are in the teeny town of **Bykle.** The 17th-century church has two balconies—one for men and one for women (www.setesdalsmuseet.no).

On the east side of the main road (at the *Grasbrokke* sign) is an old water mill (1630). A few minutes farther south, at the sign for *Sanden Såre Camping,* exit onto a little road to stretch your legs at another old water mill with a fragile, rotten-log sluice.

In Flateland, the **Setesdal Museum** (Rygnestadtunet) offers more of what you saw at Bykle; unless you're a glutton for culture, I wouldn't do both (www.setesdalsmuseet.no). Past Flateland at **Honnevje** is a nice picnic and WC stop, with a dock along the water for swimming...for hot-weather days or polar bears.

Valle is Setesdal's prettiest village (but don't tell Bykle). In the center, you'll find fine silver- and gold-work, homemade crafts next to the TI (tel. 37 93 75 29), and occasional *lefse* cooking demonstrations. The fine suspension bridge attracts kids of any age (b-b-b-b-bounce), and anyone interested in a great view over the river to strange mountains that look like polished, petrified mudslides. European rock climbers, tired of the over-climbed Alps, often entertain spectators with their sport. Is anyone climbing? To sleep in Valle, consider the basic **Valle Motell** (www.valle-motell.no).

South of Valle, the area has a lot more logging (and is less scenic). In **Nomeland,** the Sylvartun silversmith shop, whose owner Hallvard Bjørgum is also a renowned Hardanger fiddle player, sells Setesdal silver in a 17th-century, grass-roofed log cabin next to the main road.

Farther south, the road traces first the west and then the east shore of the long and scenic freshwater Byglandsfjord to **Grendi,** where the Ardal Church (1827) has a rune stone in its yard. Three hundred yards south of the church is a 900-year-old oak tree.

A huge town by Setesdal standards (3,500 people), **Evje** is famous for its gems and mines. Fancy stones fill the shops here. Rock hounds find the nearby mines fun; for a small fee, you can hunt for gems (TI tel. 37 93 14 00). The **Setesdal Mineral Park** is on the main road, two miles south of town (www.mineralparken.no).

From Evje, it's about an hour's drive to this region's transportation hub, **Kristiansand.**

NEAR THE SETESDAL VALLEY: KRISTIANSAND

The "capital of the south," Kristiansand has 85,000 inhabitants, a pleasant Renaissance grid-plan layout (Posebyen), a famous zoo with Norway's biggest amusement park, a daily bus to Bergen, lots of big boats going to Denmark, and a TI (Rådhusgata 18, tel. 38 12 13 14, www.visitkrs.no). It's the closest thing to a beach resort in Norway. Markensgate is the bustling pedestrian market street—an enjoyable place for good browsing, shopping, eating, and people-watching. Stroll along the Strand Promenaden (marina) to Christiansholm Fortress. The otherwise uninteresting harbor area has a cluster of wooden buildings called **Fiskebasaren** ("Fish Bazaar")—with an indoor fish market (only open during the day) and numerous restaurants offering a nice dinner atmosphere.

Sleeping in Kristiansand: You may need to sleep here to break up your Setesdal journey. Hotels are expensive and nondescript; consider the **$$$$ Rica Hotel Norge** (Dronningensgate 5, tel. 38 17 40 00, www.hotel-norge.no) or the **$$$$ Thon Hotel Wergeland** (ask for quiet room, Kirkegate 15, tel. 38 17 20 40, www.thonhotels.no/wergeland).

Kristiansand Connections: Trains connect to **Stavanger** (6/day, 3 hours) and **Oslo** (5/day, 4.5 hours). Kristiansand is also a hub for the three-hour **ferry to Hirtshals, Denmark,** operated by two companies: Color Line (2/day year-round, more in summer, www.colorline.com) and Fjordline (1-2/day in summer, none in winter, www.fjordline.com). You can either drive on or walk on.

PRACTICALITIES

This section covers just the basics on traveling in this region (for much more information, see *Rick Steves Scandinavia*). You'll find free advice on specific topics at www.ricksteves.com/tips.

MONEY

In Norway, credit cards are widely accepted, even for small purchases, but you can generally pay with cash if you prefer. If you need cash, Norway uses the Norwegian kroner (NOK): 1 NOK equals about $0.13. To roughly convert prices in kroner to dollars, divide by eight (e.g., 100 NOK = about $12.50). Check www. oanda.com for the latest exchange rates.

The standard way for travelers to get kroner is to withdraw money from an ATM using a debit card, ideally with a Visa or MasterCard logo. Before departing, call your bank or credit-card company: Confirm that your card(s) will work overseas, ask about international transaction fees, and alert them that you'll be making withdrawals in Europe. Also ask for the PIN number for your credit card—you may need it for Europe's "chip-and-PIN" payment machines (see below; allow time for your bank to mail your PIN to you). To keep your valuables safe while traveling, wear a money belt.

Dealing with "Chip and PIN": Most credit and debit cards now have chips that authenticate and secure transactions. European cardholders insert their chip card into the payment slot, then enter a PIN. (Until recently, most US cards required a signature.) Any American card with a chip will work at Europe's hotels, restaurants, and shops—although sometimes the clerk may ask for a signature. But some self-service payment machines—such as those at train stations, toll roads, or unattended gas pumps—may not accept your card, even if you know the PIN. If your card won't work, look for a cashier who can process the transaction manually—or pay in cash.

Dynamic Currency Conversion: If merchants or hoteliers offer to convert your purchase price into dollars (called dynamic currency conversion, or DCC), refuse this "service." You'll pay more in fees for the expensive convenience of seeing your charge in dollars. If an ATM offers to "lock in" or "guarantee" your conversion rate, choose "proceed without conversion." Other prompts might state, "You can be charged in dollars: Press YES for dollars, NO for kroner." Always choose the local currency.

STAYING CONNECTED

The simplest solution is to bring your own device—mobile phone, tablet, or laptop—and use it just as you would at home (following the tips below, such as connecting to free Wi-Fi whenever possible).

To call Norway from a US or Canadian number: Whether you're phoning from a landline, your own mobile phone, or a Skype account, you're making an international call. Dial 011-47 and then the local number. (The 011 is our international access code, and 47 is Norway's country code.) If dialing from a mobile phone, you can enter + in place of the international access code—press and hold the 0 key.

To call Norway from a European country: Dial 00-47 followed by the local number. (The 00 is Europe's international access code.)

To call within Norway: Just dial the local number.

To call from Norway to another country: Dial 00 followed by the country code (for example, 1 for the US or Canada), then the area code and number. If you're calling European countries with phone numbers that begin with 0, you'll usually have to omit that 0 when you dial.

Tips: If you bring your own mobile phone, consider signing up for an international plan; most providers offer a global calling plan that cuts the per-minute cost of phone calls and texts, and a flat-fee data plan.

Use Wi-Fi whenever possible. Most hotels and many cafés offer free Wi-Fi, and you'll likely also find it at tourist information offices (TIs), major museums, and public-transit hubs. With Wi-Fi you make free or inexpensive domestic and international calls via a calling app such as Skype, FaceTime, or Google+ Hangouts. When you can't find Wi-Fi, you can use your cellular network to connect to the Internet, send texts, or make voice calls. When you're done, avoid further charges by manually switching off "data roaming" or "cellular data."

Without a mobile device, you can make calls from your hotel and get online using public computers (there's usually one in your

Sleep Code

Hotels are classified based on the average price of a typical en suite double room with breakfast in high season.

$$$$	**Splurge:** Most rooms over 1,500 NOK
$$$	**Pricier:** 1,200-1,500 NOK
$$	**Moderate:** 900-1,200 NOK
$	**Budget:** 600-900 NOK
¢	**Hostel/Backpacker:** Under 600 NOK
RS%	**Rick Steves discount**

Unless otherwise noted, credit cards are accepted, and free Wi-Fi is available. Comparison-shop by checking prices at several hotels (on each hotel's own website, on a booking site, or by email). For the best deal, always book directly with the hotel. Ask for a discount if paying in cash; if the listing includes **RS%,** request a Rick Steves discount.

hotel lobby or at local libraries). Most hotels charge a high fee for international calls—ask for rates before you dial. For more on phoning, see www.ricksteves.com/phoning. For a one-hour talk on "Traveling with a Mobile Device," see www.ricksteves.com/travel-talks.

SLEEPING

I've categorized my recommended accommodations based on price, indicated with a dollar-sign rating (see sidebar). I recommend reserving rooms in advance, particularly during peak season. Once your dates are set, check the specific price for your preferred stay at several hotels. You can do this either by comparing prices on sites such as Hotels.com or Booking.com, or by checking the hotels' own websites. To get the best deal, contact my family-run hotels directly by phone or email. When you go direct, the owner avoids any third-party commission, giving them wiggle room to offer you a discount, a nicer room, or free breakfast. If you prefer to book online or are considering a hotel chain, it's to your advantage to use the hotel's website.

For complicated requests, send an email with the following information: number and type of rooms; number of nights; arrival date; departure date; and any special requests. Use the European style for writing dates: day/month/year. Hoteliers typically ask for your credit-card number as a deposit. In general, hotel prices can soften if you do any of the following: offer to pay cash, stay at least three nights, or travel off-season.

Even though most hotels in Norway base their prices on demand, it is possible to find lower prices during the summer and on weekends. Check hotel websites for deals. To find an apartment or room in a private home, try Airbnb or www.bbnorway.com.

Restaurant Price Code

I've assigned each eatery a price category, based on the average cost of a typical main course. Drinks, desserts, and splurge items (steak and seafood) can raise the price considerably.

$$$$ **Splurge:** Most main courses over 175 NOK
$$$ **Pricier:** 125-175 NOK
$$ **Moderate:** 75-125 NOK
$ **Budget:** Under 75 NOK

In Norway, a Deli de Luca or other takeout spot is **$**; a sit-down café is **$$**; a casual but more upscale restaurant is **$$$**; and a swanky splurge is **$$$$**.

EATING

I've categorized my recommended eateries based on price, indicated with a dollar-sign rating (see sidebar).

Restaurants are often expensive. Alternate between picnics (outside or in your hotel or hostel); cheap, forgettable, but filling cafeteria or fast-food fare ($20 per person); and atmospheric, carefully chosen restaurants popular with locals ($40 per person and up). Ethnic eateries—Indian, Turkish, Greek, Italian, and Asian—offer a good value and a break from Norwegian fare.

The *smörgåsbord* (known in Norway as the *store koldt bord*) is a revered Scandinavian culinary tradition. Seek it out at least once during your visit. Begin with the fish dishes, along with boiled potatoes and *knekkebrød* (crisp bread). Then move on to salads, egg dishes, and various cold cuts. Next it's meatball time! Pour on some gravy as well as a spoonful of lingonberry sauce. Still hungry? Make a point to sample the Nordic cheeses and the racks of traditional desserts, cakes, and custards.

Hotel breakfasts are a huge and filling buffet, generally included but occasionally a $15-or-so option. It usually features fruit, cereal, various milks, breads and crackers, cold cuts, pickled herring, caviar paste, and boiled eggs. The brown cheese with the texture of earwax and a slightly sweet taste is *geitost* ("goat cheese").

In Norway, alcohol is sold only at state-run liquor stores called Vinmonopolet (though weak beer is also sold at supermarkets). To avoid extremely high restaurant prices for alcohol, many Norwegians—and tourists—buy their wine, beer, or spirits at a store and then drink at a public square; this is illegal although often done. One local specialty is *akvavit*, a strong, vodka-like spirit distilled from potatoes and flavored with anise, caraway, or other herbs and spices—then drunk ice-cold.

Service: Good service is relaxed (slow to an American). When you want the bill, say, *"Regningen, takk."* Throughout Norway, a service charge is included in your bill, so there's no need to leave an additional tip. In fancier restaurants or any restaurant where you enjoy great service, round up the bill (about 5-10 percent of the total check).

TRANSPORTATION

By Train and Bus: Trains cover many of my recommended Norwegian destinations. To see if a rail pass could save you money, check www.ricksteves.com/rail. If you're buying tickets as you go, note that prices can fluctuate. To research train schedules and fares, visit the Norwegian train website, www.nsb.no. Nearly any long-distance train ride requires you to make a reservation before boarding (the day before is usually fine). If you're taking the Norway in a Nutshell route in summer, book well in advance—four to five weeks is best (see www.fjordtours.com).

Don't overlook long-distance buses, which are usually slower than trains but have considerably cheaper and more predictable fares. On certain routes (e.g., Oslo-Stockholm), the bus is less expensive but slower than the train. Norway's biggest bus carrier is Nor-Way Bussekspress (www.nor-way.no).

By Car: It's cheaper to arrange most car rentals from the US. For tips on your insurance options, see www.ricksteves.com/cdw, and for route planning, consult www.viamichelin.com. Bring your driver's license. Local road etiquette is similar to that in the US. Ask your car-rental company for details, or check the US State Department website (www.travel.state.gov, select "International Travel," then "Country Information," then search for your destination and click "Traffic Safety and Road Conditions"). Use your headlights day and night; it's required in most of Scandinavia. A car is a worthless headache in any big city—park it safely (get tips from your hotelier). To minimize tolls in Norway, register as a visitor at www.autopass.no and prepay a lump sum with your credit card.

By Boat: Boats are both a necessary and spectacular way to travel through Norway's fjords or along its coast (for various routes, see www.fjordtours.no, www.fjord1.no, and www.tide.no). Reserve ahead if you're planning on taking overnight boats in summer or on weekends to link Oslo and Copenhagen (www.dfdsseaways.com). It's also possible to connect Norway and northern Denmark; see www.fjordline.com and www.colorline.com.

By Plane: SAS is the region's dominant airline (www.fly-sas.com) and is affiliated with Oslo-based Widerøe Air (www.wideroe.no). Another option is Norwegian Airlines (hubs in Oslo and Bergen, www.norwegian.no). Well-known cheapo airlines EasyJet (www.easyjet.com) and Ryanair (www.ryanair.com) fly into Scandinavia.

HELPFUL HINTS

Emergency Help: To summon the **police** or an **ambulance**, call 112. For passport problems, call the **US Embassy** (in Oslo: passport services by appointment only, Mon-Fri 8:30-17:00, tel. 21 30 85 40, https://no.usembassy.gov).

If you have a minor illness, do as the locals do and go to a pharmacist for advice. Or ask at your hotel for help—they'll know of the nearest medical and emergency services. For other concerns, get advice from your hotelier.

Theft or Loss: To replace a passport, you'll need to go in person to an embassy (see above). Cancel and replace your credit and debit cards by calling these 24-hour US numbers collect: Visa— tel. 303/967-1096, MasterCard—tel. 636/722-7111, American Express—tel. 336/393-1111. In Norway, to make a collect call to the US, dial 800-190-11; press zero or stay on the line for an operator. File a police report either on the spot or within a day or two; you'll need it to submit an insurance claim for lost or stolen rail passes or travel gear, and it can help with replacing your passport or credit and debit cards. Precautionary measures can minimize the effects of loss—back up your photos and other files frequently. For more information, see www.ricksteves.com/help.

Time: Europe uses the 24-hour clock. It's the same through 12:00 noon, then keep going: 13:00, 14:00, and so on. Norway, like most of continental Europe, is six/nine hours ahead of the East/West Coasts of the US.

Holidays and Festivals: Europe celebrates many holidays, which can close sights and attract crowds (book hotel rooms ahead). For info on holidays and festivals in Norway, check the Scandinavia Tourist Board website: www.goscandinavia.com. For a simple list showing major—though not all—events, see www.ricksteves.com/festivals.

Numbers and Stumblers: What Americans call the second floor of a building is the first floor in Europe. Europeans write dates as day/month/year, so Christmas 2020 is 25/12/20. Commas are decimal points and vice versa—a dollar and a half is 1,50, and there are 5.280 feet in a mile. Europe uses the metric system: A kilogram is 2.2 pounds; a liter is about a quart; and a kilometer is six-tenths of a mile.

RESOURCES FROM RICK STEVES

This Snapshot guide is excerpted from the latest edition of *Rick Steves Scandinavia*, one of many titles in my ever-expanding series of guidebooks on European travel. I also produce a public television series, *Rick Steves' Europe*, and a public radio show, *Travel with Rick Steves*. My website, www.ricksteves.com, offers free travel information, a forum for travelers' comments, guidebook updates, my travel blog, an online travel store, and information on European rail passes and our tours of Europe. If you're bringing a mobile device on your trip, you can download my Rick Steves Audio Europe app, featuring dozens of self-guided audio tours of the top sights in Europe and travel interviews about Europe. You can get Rick Steves Audio Europe via Apple's App Store, Google Play, or the Amazon Appstore. For more information, see www.ricksteves.com/audioeurope.

ADDITIONAL RESOURCES

Tourist Information: www.goscandinavia.com
Passports and Red Tape: www.travel.state.gov
Packing List: www.ricksteves.com/packing
Travel Insurance: www.ricksteves.com/insurance
Cheap Flights: www.kayak.com or www.google.com/flights
Airplane Carry-on Restrictions: www.tsa.gov
Updates for This Book: www.ricksteves.com/update

HOW WAS YOUR TRIP?

If you'd like to share your tips, concerns, and discoveries after using this book, please fill out the survey at www.ricksteves.com/feedback. Thanks in advance—it helps a lot.

INDEX

INDEX

Start your trip at

Our website enhances this book and turns

Explore Europe

At ricksteves.com you can browse through thousands of articles, videos, photos and radio interviews, plus find a wealth of money-saving travel tips for planning your dream trip. And with our mobile-friendly website, you can easily access all this great travel information anywhere you go.

TV Shows

Preview the places you'll visit by watching entire half-hour episodes of Rick Steves' Europe (choose from all 100 shows) on-demand, for free.

your travel dreams into affordable reality

Radio Interviews

Enjoy ready access to Rick's vast library of radio interviews covering travel

tips and cultural insights that relate specifically to your Europe travel plans.

Travel Forums

Learn, ask, share! Our online community of savvy travelers is a great resource for first-time travelers to Europe, as well as seasoned pros. You'll find forums on each country, plus travel tips and restaurant/hotel reviews. You can even ask one of our well-traveled staff to chime in with an opinion.

Travel News

Subscribe to our free Travel News e-newsletter, and get monthly updates from Rick on what's happening in Europe.

Rick's Free Travel App

Get your FREE **Rick Steves Audio Europe**™ app to enjoy…

- Dozens of self-guided tours of Europe's top museums, sights and historic walks
- Hundreds of tracks filled with cultural insights and sightseeing tips from Rick's radio interviews
- All organized into handy geographic playlists
- For Apple and Android

With Rick whispering in your ear, Europe gets even better.

Find out more at ricksteves.com

Gear up for your next adventure at ricksteves.com

Light Luggage

Pack light and right with Rick Steves' affordable, custom-designed rolling carry-on bags, backpacks, day packs and shoulder bags.

Accessories

From packing cubes to moneybelts and beyond, Rick has personally selected the travel goodies that will help your trip go smoother.

Shop at ricksteves.com

Rick Steves has

Experience maximum Europe

Save time and energy

This guidebook is your independent-travel toolkit. But for all it delivers, it's still up to you to devote the time and energy it takes to manage the preparation and logistics that are essential for a happy trip. If that's a hassle, there's a solution.

Rick Steves Tours

A Rick Steves tour takes you to Europe's most interesting places with great

great tours, too!

with minimum stress

guides and small groups of 28 or less. We follow Rick's favorite itineraries, ride in comfy buses, stay in family-run hotels, and bring you intimately close to the Europe you've traveled so far to see. Most importantly, we take away the logistical headaches so you can focus on the fun.

travelers—nearly half of them repeat customers—along with us on four dozen different itineraries, from Ireland to Italy to Athens. Is a Rick Steves tour the right fit for your travel dreams? Find out at ricksteves.com, where you can also request Rick's latest tour catalog. Europe is best experienced with happy travel partners. We hope you can join us.

Join the fun

This year we'll take thousands of free-spirited

See our itineraries at ricksteves.com

A Guide for Every Trip

BEST OF GUIDES

Full color easy-to-scan format, focusing on Europe's most popular destinations and sights.

Best of England
Best of Europe
Best of France
Best of Germany
Best of Ireland
Best of Italy
Best of Spain

COMPREHENSIVE GUIDES

City, country, and regional guides with detailed coverage for a multi-week trip exploring the most iconic sights and venturing off the beaten track.

Amsterdam & the Netherlands
Barcelona
Belgium: Bruges, Brussels, Antwerp & Ghent
Berlin
Budapest
Croatia & Slovenia
Eastern Europe
England
Florence & Tuscany
France
Germany
Great Britain
Greece: Athens & the Peloponnese
Iceland
Ireland
Istanbul
Italy
London
Paris
Portugal
Prague & the Czech Republic
Provence & the French Riviera
Rome
Scandinavia
Scotland
Spain
Switzerland
Venice
Vienna, Salzburg & Tirol

E BEST OF ROME

Italy's capital, is studded with
remnants and floodlit-fountain
s. From the Vatican to the Colos-
with crazy traffic in between, Rome
rful, huge, and exhausting. The
the heat, and the weighty history

of the Eternal City where Caesars walked
can make tourists wilt. Recharge by taking siestas, gelato breaks, and after-dark
walks, strolling from one atmospheric
square to another in the refreshing evening air.

Rick Steves guidebooks are published by Avalon Travel, an imprint of Perseus Books, a Hachette Book Group company.